Popular education and socialization in the nineteenth century

Edited by Phillip McCann

METHUEN & CO LTD
11 New Fetter Lane London Ec4

First published in 1977 by
Methuen & Co Ltd
11 New Fetter Lane, London EC4P 4EE

First published as an Education Paperback in 1979

Set by Hope Services, Abingdon, Oxon
and printed in Great Britain at the
University Press, Cambridge

ISBN 0 416 81110 8 (hardback)
ISBN 0 416 81120 5 (paperback)

To Professor W.H.G. ARMYTAGE

Contents

List of Illustrations

Acknowledgements

The editor and publishers wish to thank the following for permission to reproduce the illustrations and maps appearing in this book:

Bishopsgate Institute for Plate II
Bootle Central Reference Library for Plates XIII and XV
Brynmor Jones Library, University of Hull, for Plates XVI and XVIII
Rev. R.E. Dennis for Plate XIV
Mr Ian Dewhirst for Plate IX
Greater London Council Library for Plates XVIII and XIX
Phillip McCann for Plate III
Manchester Public Libraries for Plates V, VI, VII and VIII
National Union of Teachers for Plate X
Radio Times Hulton Picture Library for Plates I, XI and XII
Trustees of the British Library for Plate IV
University of Liverpool, Cartography Section, Department of Geography, for Maps 1, 2, 4 and 5
University of Liverpool, School and Institute of Education, for Map 3

Editor's Introduction

This collection of studies explores ways in which various types of elementary education, at different periods of the nineteenth century, attempted to prepare the working-class child for life and labour in industrial capitalist society. Though not a new field of inquiry for educational historians, it is certainly a neglected one. The traditional orientation of educational history has been towards empirical and descriptive studies of institutions in isolation from the contemporary economic, social and political setting. The institutions have, moreover, been mainly those at the upper and intermediate levels — universities, public schools and secondary schools; popular education has largely been treated from the administrative standpoint — the policies and operations of the Committee of Council on Education, of the National and British Societies and of school boards are very much better known than the day-to-day working of the denominational or board schools which they administered.

As the growth of economic and social history has in recent decades modified the old political history, so new trends in the history of education have to some extent modified or displaced the traditional emphasis on institutional and administrative topics. Studies of the educational policies of the labour movement, progressive educators, the social role of the churches, the connection between literacy and the development of industry and of various forms of popular culture, have greatly modified the concept of education in its historical development and the way in which it may be defined and interpreted. To the extent that historians of education are ceasing to view education in one dimension, largely from above, and examining it as a many-faceted phenomenon concerned with the everyday life and development of millions of young people, to that extent are they beginning to ask 'sociological' questions and to attempt, more consciously, to utilize theoretical concepts. An important stage in that development was the conference called by the History of Education Society in 1970 to discuss the relationship between sociology and the history of education, the papers of which were published under the title *History, Sociology and Education* (1971). The debate then and since has centred on the ways in which each discipline can assist in extending the boundaries of the other.

This volume utilizes one particular sociological concept – socialization – in the investigation of education at the grass roots level, in schools provided 'from above' for the instruction of working-class children. The modern functionalist definition of socialization is usually on the lines of 'the transmission of culture, the process whereby men learn the rules and practices of social groups'; the family is considered as the primary agency and the school or other formal educational institution as secondary, transmitting skills, values and social norms. The claim that the concept was 'value-free' has in recent years been strongly contested, and the assumptions on which it is based – the need for society to guide, restrain or control its members (particularly the younger generation), and the readiness of the latter to 'internalize' or make part of their nature the socially accepted norms of thought and behaviour – have been characterized as fundamentally problems of value. From this standpoint the question of who guides, modifies or controls the behaviour of whom and for what purpose is as important as the more technical aspect of the procedures by which it is accomplished.

Both aspects are dealt with in the following contributions and attention is thus focused on popular education as a social process, an interaction between the aims of the ruling interests and the determination of the working class to construct a meaningful social existence. Historians have often tended to confuse the aim with its fulfilment and educational historians in particular have assumed that what schools set out to do was achieved, without taking into account the problematic nature of the response of the working-class pupil and his parents.

This perspective challenges the educational historian not only to seek out new or unsuspected sources but also to re-interpret those already known. Some useful material may be found in the autobiographies and diaries of those who attended elementary-type schools. These records are often assumed to be so rare and unrepresentative as to be of little use, but as Professor John Burnett has shown in *Useful Toil* (1974), they exist in hitherto unsuspected quantities. The literature and records of working-class and labour organizations often provide evidence of the influence of education on their members and the kind of mental universe which they inhabited. School log books,

attendance records and minute books, again only recently being collected and examined, can, if carefully interpreted, throw much light on
the attitudes of teachers, pupils and parents. The voluminous accounts
of the life and education of the poor and the working class by middle-
class educationists, investigators and observers are well known, but their
full significance may be apparent only when used in conjunction with
material from the above sources. Where data are quantifiable, socio-
metric techniques can be used with advantage to establish the incidence
and location of educational provision, trends in attendance and the
extent to which different sections of the working class made use of the
educational opportunities provided.

The contributions to this volume do not provide the basis for generalizations about popular education in the nineteenth century but several
issues are raised which deserve further discussion and research. First,
the degree to which popular education operated as an agency of political
socialization rather than as a transmitter of literacy, skills and knowledge, and the function of religion, political economy and authoritarian
ideologies in this process. Second, the role of working-class parents in
the operation of their children's schools; this involves not only the
question of attendance, for on regular and protracted attendance
depended the success of schools as socialization agencies, but also investigation of which section of the working class supported the schools,
the kind of support given and the degree to which it contributed to the
viability of the institution. Third, and perhaps most important, the
total effect of popular education on the attitudes, behaviour and subsequent life-activity of the working-class child; the difficulties inherent
in this question should not be a deterrent to attempts to assess it. Without a serious and detailed treatment of the educational experience of
the working class and its effects on their behaviour there can be no
solution to what is arguably the most important task which faces the
educational historian – an examination of the part which mass education
has played in the formation of the social consciousness of the British
people.

Chapter 1:

Popular education, socialization and social control: Spitalfields 1812-1824.

Phillip McCann

The vulgar are the subjects of phaenomena, the learned explain them.
William Wilberforce

On 28 March 1819, the Rev. Daniel Wilson, a rising star in the Evangelical party, preached a sermon on behalf of the new Spitalfields National School to a congregation of two thousand in Hawksmoor's lofty Christ Church, a few yards from the house in which he had been born. Wilson took as his theme the importance of the instruction of the children of the poor in the doctrines of the Bible; a knowledge of the Scriptures, he pointed out, not only made children 'wise unto salvation' but also equipped them, should they find in their homes 'prophaneness, irreligion, violation of the Sabbath, evil passions or discontent', to lead their parents into better ways. The religious education of the poor was thus of great social importance:

> In every country, but especially in this free state, the mass of your Poor, like the base of the cone, if it be unsteady and insecure, will quickly endanger every superincumbent part. Religious education, then, is the spring of public tranquillity. It not only cherishes the interior principle of conscience; but by infusing the higher sentiments of penitence and faith and gratitude and the love of God, communicates the elements of a cheerful and uniform subjection to all lawful authority.[1]

Wilson spoke with a frankness that would be unacceptable today, but the sentiments were a commonplace of both Anglican and Dissenting thought in the early nineteenth century; their significance lies in their application to Spitalfields, the centre of the silk weaving industry, where nearly all the social problems which accompanied the birth of popular education, and left their imprint upon it, were concentrated: a high and increasing density of population, great numbers of 'the poor', economic distress, a high incidence of juvenile delinquency, and a decline in allegiance to the Church. But in Spitalfields, in the period under review, the establishment of schools was part of a large-scale programme of the charitable provision of food, clothing and money and the distribution of Bibles and tracts, undertaken by the largely Evangelical and Dissenting upper and middle class with the aim of controlling the populace in the interests of social and economic stability. A study of Spitalfields at this date thus throws into relief one of the most important aspects of the early history of popular education – its function as a means of countering social change and as an agent of the socialization of the children of the poor for life in a stratified, exploit-ative industrial society.

Spitalfields was the name given to the densely populated and over-crowded mass of narrow streets and small houses to the north-east of the City beyond Bishopsgate, with the modern Petticoat Lane market forming more or less its south-west boundary; more precisely it consisted of the parishes of Christ Church Spitalfields and St Matthew Bethnal Green, the 'hamlet' of Mile End New Town and the 'liberties' of Norton Folgate and the Old Artillery Ground, which abutted the western border of Christ Church.[2] Spitalfields had been the centre of the silk weaving industry since the seventeenth century when the Huguenot weavers had settled there following the Revocation of the Edict of Nantes in 1685.

In the early nineteenth century it was one of the fastest growing districts in the metropolis. Between 1811 and 1831 the population soared from 59,000 to 90,000, most of the increase taking place in Bethnal Green. It was also one of the poorest. *Per capita* taxable income of the Tower Division, of which Spitalfields was a part, was only £5, compared with £16 for Westminster and £54 for the City of London.[3] Spitalfields and the poor, in fact, were almost interchange-able terms; 'we had a greater number of poor people congregating together ... than in the same given space in any part of the British Empire', declared William Hale, silk manufacturer, in 1828, looking back on over twenty years of public work in Christ Church parish.[4] In 1813, no less than 67 per cent of the population, according to Schwarz's study of East End occupations and incomes, were manual workers; of these, only 10 per cent were skilled, the remainder semi- or unskilled. Six out of ten workers earned less than 40s. per week, the lowest fifth less than 20*s*.[5] Hours were long; the chimes of Christ Church called people to work at 6 a.m., where they remained until the bells tolled the curfew at 8 p.m.[6] Houses were small and badly built, without proper foundations or sewerage, and open drains were common, making the district notorious for fevers.[7]

The periodic incidence of economic distress and unemployment, notably in 1800–1, 1811–12 and 1816–17, combined with a population increase of some 25 per cent per decade, much of it by immigration of the poor, had gradually worsened conditions. Between 1800 and 1817 the number of inmates of the workhouse in Spitalfields parish had nearly doubled and the number receiving outdoor relief quadrupled, though the population had risen by only 20 per cent. In the latter year, 3,000 people were wholly or partly maintained from the poor rate, receiving only 5*s*. per week in relief.[8] In the dreaded workhouse the inmates could expect only poor food, menial labour and sleeping four or more to a bed.[9] Life for the majority of the population was hard, brutal and often violent. Literacy among the poor stood at something like 60 per cent.[10] The public house, the skittle alley and the occasional fair formed the main diversions, and the hunting of bullocks through the streets was popular until the mid-1820s.[11] The quality of life was not improved by the presence of a criminal population, attracted to the area by the cheap accommodation, though it confined its operations largely to the wealthier districts to the west; few people in Spitalfields, it was pointed out, had anything worth stealing.[12]

In this environment the children of Spitalfields grew up. The socialization of the children of the weavers, however, was somewhat different from that of the rest of the population. In 1813 the weavers formed 26 per cent of the labouring population, a decline from the figure of 55 per cent in 1770.[13] Their earnings, except for those of the quarter engaged on fancy or figured work, were not high, averaging some 17*s*. per week.[14] But weaving was a domestic industry and most weavers owned their own means of production, the loom; they were able to work at their own pace, free from the discipline of the factory and to associate with their families throughout the day. Most of their children were brought up in the trade and received what education they had from their parents. At six or seven years of age the children would be set to quill silk, at nine or ten to pick silk and at about thirteen or so would be introduced to the loom, learning to weave plain fabrics. Children would be fairly constantly under the eye of the mother and father from birth to adolescence, learning by doing, by example rather than precept,[15] and weavers on the whole were said to be 'remarkably attached' to them, taking great 'pains and patience' in teaching them the trade.[16] Weavers' daughters were reputed to have a love of finery in dress and to know little of needlework, cooking, or other housewifely accomplishments, apparently on the presumption that skill at the loom would be more advantageous to a weaver husband.[17] William Bresson, a velvet weaver and loom broker, was exceptional in having his son taught the violin and his daughter the piano.[18] The domestic atmosphere was considered to be more favourable to morality, both for weavers' children and apprentices, than that of other trades in which there was opportunity in a common workshop for contact with 'idle and dissolute companions'.[19] Nevertheless, however benign the regimen and however superior the environment of the home might be to that of a factory, the fact remained that the early age at which they started work robbed the weavers' children of their youth and stunted their intellectual development.

The greatest difference between the upbringing of the children of workers in other trades and those of the weavers was that the children of the former did not see much of their parents. According to Samuel Wilderspin, master of Spitalfields Infant School in the early 1820s, the father in many cases had to get up before the children were awake to go to work in the City,[20] and often did not return until they were in bed at night. Among the poorer and unskilled labourers the mother had also to work to make ends meet; girl child-minders were sometimes employed, but as these often came from families poorer still and were totally uneducated, they passed on to their charges, in Wilderspin's words, 'deceit, lying, pilfering, and extreme filthiness'. This forced neglect of children — and many poor parents were unable to take care of their children, however well-disposed they might be — had serious consequences. Left in garrets three or four stories high, they often burned themselves in fires or fell out of windows and downstairs. If, as often happened, they roamed the streets or nearby fields, they were run over by coaches or fell into ponds. The possibility of such accidents to their children, Wilderspin noticed, was a 'dead weight of concern' to parents, whose work was often affected by their anxiety. In addition to these hazards, poverty, overcrowding, poor food and lack of medical services led them to succumb in large numbers to measles, whooping cough, smallpox and various kinds of fever.[21] For labourers' children, menial work outside the home was common, particularly for girls, who were sent at seven or eight years of age to service or work for a shilling per week, which probably accounted, Wilderspin thought, for the preponderance of boys in almost every London school.[22]

One of the most striking facts about children was their sheer numbers. In the Tower Division in 1821 no less than 37 per cent of the population was under fifteen years of age.[23] The pressure of numbers, the pressure of poverty, the lack of schools (before 1817) and the complete absence of recreational facilities drove many children into the sort of adventures that the respectable were only too ready to label 'vice and crime'.[24] If many children fought, lied, stole, swore and were sexually precocious, Wilderspin found that they could also be affectionate and courteous and could face the presence of death with equanimity; his pupils visited his wife on her death bed and voluntarily kept quiet in the school playground because 'governess was dying'.[25] It was this early acquaintance with the harsh facts of adult life, the forced independence and forwardness that caused middle-class moralists to view working-class children with such alarm. 'Filthy and very ragged . . . rude and unmannerly in the extreme, being under no sort of control', snapped the Rev. Joshua King when asked to describe the children of Bethnal Green.[26] How different were the children of the well-to-do, protected, dependent and accustomed to a stable environment and benevolent parental authority.[27] It is hardly surprising that the upper and middle classes of Spitalfields found the children of the poor strange and unnatural and a potential threat to order and stability.[28]

The small local bourgeoisie – no more than 6 per cent of the population[29] – had other fears beside that of wild-running youth. Islanded in a working-class sea, they were well aware of the traditional anti-authoritarian disposition of the London crowd,[30] and the constant apprehension that bad economic conditions would drive the Spitalfields poor into insurrection runs like a thread through all the evidence to Parliamentary committees in this period. It was fed by the spectre of the French Revolution, the Luddite and radical activity of the war and post-war years and the circulation of radical and 'infidel' literature. But in Spitalfields there was a purely local cause for alarm. In the early nineteenth century the so-called Spitalfields Outrages of the 1760s and '70s were still within the living memory of the older generation.[31] From 1762 to 1773 open warfare had raged between the journeymen weavers and the largest silk manufacturers over the issue of piece-work prices.[32] All attempts to reduce these prices were met by cutting the silk on the looms, marches, riots and the burning in effigy of silk masters. Armed men were in the streets, soldiers from the Tower were quartered in Christ Church, an informer was stoned to death, and weavers were hanged in front of Bethnal Green Church; at times, it was reported, 'Spitalfields has the aspect of a town under military execution'. In the end the masters and the government were forced to give way and in 1773 an Act was passed which authorized magistrates (whose decision was binding) to 'settle regulate and declare' the wages of silk weavers, after a committee of masters and men had agreed on piece-work rates.[33] In the post-Napoleonic War period, however, the larger City men, led by Stephen Wilson, a cousin of Daniel and Joseph, began a campaign for the repeal of the Acts that was successful in 1824. Wilson wanted a free labour market, the introduction of new machinery and the opportunity to meet outside competition by extending his business to the provinces where wages were lower and the possibility of profits higher.[34] The smaller masters, however, opposed repeal; lacking the ambition of the larger men, they preferred to work in a district that enjoyed 'a state of quietude and repose' which they believed the Acts helped to ensure.[35]

The normal agencies for maintaining quietude among the poor in the pre-industrial era had been the Church and the charity school. In rural or small urban parishes the latter had been an adequate means of instructing the children of the poor in the duties of their station, while the former gave the clergy personal access to their parents. In the growing towns and cities of the early Industrial Revolution this situation was disappearing or, in places like Spitalfields, had vanished entirely, as the Rev. Richard Yates, voicing the long-felt concern of the Church, had pointed out in 1815 and again in 1817.[36] If the growth of churches and schools had kept pace with the increase in population, Yates calculated, Bethnal Green should have had fifty-two churches and Christ Church twenty-five.[37] In fact the parishes together had only three, with a total seating capacity of 4,450 for a population of some 50,000.[38] The situation in education was no less alarming; Bethnal Green had in its charity school only about one thirty-fifth of the poor children whom, according to Yates' model, it should have been educating.[39] Details of the charity school provision in Spitalfields as a whole (Table 1) confirm Yates' general thesis.

The great increase in the child population had swamped the charity schools; they were educating hundreds, while thousands roamed the streets. But the Spitalfields bourgeoisie did not see the problem purely in demographic terms, nor from the point of view of the cost in impaired intellectual growth or the restriction of life chances. William Hale,

Table 1 *Charity schools in Spitalfields*[40]

	Date of foundation	Denomination	Annual expenditure	Annual income from investments	Teacher's salary (p.a.)	Attendance Boys	Girls	Total attendance
Wheler Chapel School, Norton Folgate	1703	Anglican	£100 (1816)	£52 (1819)	?	—	36	36
Parochial Charity School, Spitalfields	1708	Anglican	£450 (1816)	£241 (1833)	£85 (master) £38 (mistress)	56	54	100
Protestant Dissenters Charity School, Wood Street, Spitalfields	1717	Dissenting	£450 (1816)	?	£60 (master) £40 (mistress)	50	50	100
Parmiter's Charity School, Bethnal Green	1720	Anglican	£216 (1816)	£338 (1818)	£65.5s	60	—	60
Parochial Charity School, Bethnal Green	1762	Anglican	£350 (1819)	£87 (1819)	£80 (master + mistress)	35	35	70
Charity School, Mile End, New Town	1785	Anglican	£230 (1819)	£28 (1819)	£60 (master) £35 (mistress)	50	30	80
Totals			£1796			251	205	456

as early as 1806, had lamented that shortage of school places increased depravity and made the children of the poor totally unfitted to enter the service of respectable families.[41] As the child population increased it was their habit of 'playing about the streets and behaving improperly' which the moralists fastened upon[42] — begging for the 'grotto', flocking to fairs, gambling at street corners, stealing apples from Spitalfields Market — and Edward Thompson has pointed out how convinced were the Evangelicals in particular of 'the intimate correlation between moral levity and political sedition' among the lower classes.[43]

The problem of education was thus seen primarily in terms of the socialization of large numbers and this not only pointed to the creation of new institutions but also determined their characteristics. Charity schools had solid and sometimes ornate buildings (Plate I), and were expensive to run; the average cost per child per year in Spitalfields was £4, largely because of the provision of clothing — it accounted for £127 in a total expenditure of £207 at Parmiter's in 1818.[44] New schools would have to be cheap and able easily to be multiplied. Charity schools were small and catered to specific categ-

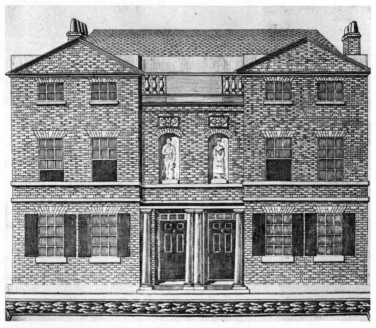

Plate I *The Charity School, Christ Church Spitalfields*

ories of children prescribed by statute.[45] New schools would need to be large and (preferably) open to all. Charity schools were rooted in eighteenth-century concepts of patronage and servitude; 'if you are humble, thankful, orderly, diligent, honest and good, you will be fit to be servants and apprentices', the children of the Protestant Dissenting Charity School were told in 1793.[46] Their subjection was exemplified by the distinctive uniform and badge the children wore on all occasions and which earned them the cry of 'charity brat' in the streets.[47] New schools would have to have the appearance of giving (or selling) education without these paternalistic appendages.

The first of the new institutions was the Sunday school which from beginnings in Gloucester in 1780 spread rapidly across the country, supported by Evangelicals and Dissenters as well as church-men. Sunday schools had first appeared in Spitalfields at the turn of the century and by 1806, according to Hale, they were educating 'some hundreds' of children.[48] Ten years later there were eighteen Sunday schools in the parishes of Christ Church and St Matthew, educating 3,936 children (Table 2), ten times as many as were in local charity schools, and a greater provision, it was believed, than in many other parts of London.[49] All except one of these schools were in the hands of Dissenters. This was symptomatic of the high proportion of Dissenters in Spitalfields; in 1812 they formed some 33 per cent of the population,[50] compared with a figure of 20 per cent for the nation as a whole. The Church had watched with apprehension their growth in Spitalfields during the previous thirty or forty years. Methodists were prominent in Bethnal Green, but Independents, Presbyterians, Calvinists, Lutherans and Anabaptists were in evidence in other parts of the district.[51]

The great advantage of Sunday schools was that they educated the largest possible number at the smallest possible expense. In Spitalfields the cost per child was roughly one shilling per year, spec-tacularly lower than that of the old charity schools. This was achiev-ed by the use of chapel or other cheap premises and the employment of volunteer teachers. Voluntary zeal not only ensured a large and regular supply of teachers and a low teacher-pupil ratio – in East London in 1824 it was one teacher to every nine pupils[52] – but also enabled personal attention to be given to the hearts and minds of the children in a way that was rare in charity schools and impossible in monitorial schools; the teachers had, in the words of the Methodist *Plan for the Establishment and Support of Sunday Schools*, 'only

Table 2   *Sunday schools in Christ Church Spitalfields and St. Matthew Bethnal Green*[53]

Christ Church Spitalfields	Denomination	Attendance Boys	Girls	Total attendance	Annual expenditure
Parochial	Anglican	70	100	170	£ 80
Raven Row	Methodist	254	227	481	–
Montague Street	Dissenting	200	200	400	–
White's Row	Dissenting	–	100	100	£ 30
Hope Street Chapel	Dissenting	100	120	220	£ 10
Artillery Street	Dissenting	--	90	90	–
Crispin Street	Dissenting	–	70	70	---
St Matthew Bethnal Green					
Friars' Mount	Methodist	486	482	968	–
Virginia Row	Dissenting	35	55	90	–
Globe Fields (1)	Dissenting	80	60	140	£ 20
Globe Fields (2)	Dissenting	40	41	81	£ 6
Darling Place	Dissenting	101	95	196	–
Bethnal Green (1)	Dissenting	–	70	70	–
Bethnal Green (2)	Dissenting	60	51	111	---
Church Street	Dissenting	–	70	70	–
Gibraltar Chapel	Dissenting	150	100	250	£ 30
Wilmot Square	Dissenting	126	103	229	--
Middlesex Chapel	Methodist	110	90	200	–
Totals		1812	2124	3936	£176

the glory of God and the good of their fellow creatures in view'.[54] Moreover, in areas where large numbers of the middle class were available, their educational attainments and refinement were believed to have had a civilizing effect on the poor; it was clear to John Daughtrey, a prominent Spitalfields social worker, that the children looked cleaner and neater after a few weeks' contact with 'young persons of well-regulated minds'.[55]

The plan of management of Spitalfields Wesleyan Methodist Sunday School, dated 1824, is apparently the only surviving evidence of the working of a Sunday school in the Spitalfields area. Its operation was probably not greatly different from that of the average school of the non-denominational Sunday School Union (whose president in 1824 was the Methodist Joseph Butterworth) to which several schools in Spitalfields were attached. In this Methodist school there was meticulous direction of the children's habits, deportment and attendance. The staple of the instruction was reading (a library of pious literature and tracts was attached to the school) and writing was considered a privilege of which about one in five of the children were allowed to partake.[56]

The prime function of the Sunday school was, of course, religious instruction;[57] the teaching of reading was merely the means to this end. Though the Spitalfields school did not employ, as others did, a corps of lecturers who took children aside in small groups to animadvert 'on the things of eternity in a close and pointed way',[58] the teachers nevertheless were adjured to inculcate 'the fear and love of God, a regard to his holy day; duty to Parents, submission to Masters and Teachers, and obedience to Governors'.[59] It is surprising to discover, however, that this was to be accomplished not by 'the subjugation of the will', which led to 'prompt and cheerful obedience' as official Methodism recommended,[60] but by letting 'the law of kindness prevail'. Love, it was pointed out to the teachers by the managers, was a more powerful motive than fear, and children, being naturally affectionate, could be brought 'to the most perfect state of discipline' without whips and rods; teachers should therefore 'lose the idea of an austere Pedagogue in the more endearing one of father and friend'.[61] This attitude to children, the teaching of writing in defiance of the decisions of the Methodist Conference,[62] and the powers which the teachers had in the management of the school,[63] all suggest an independent orientation on the part of Spitalfields Methodists. They had, in fact, a reputation for supporting radical and democratic movements within Methodism in the 1820s and '30s, one of their leaders, William Gandy, being a former member of the committee of the Sunday school.[64]

It seems likely that many of the Dissenting Sunday schools in Table 2 were in fact Methodist, for the 1818 Returns mention nine in Bethnal Green.[65] If this were so, half of the Sunday schools in Christ Church and St Matthew could have been run on lines similar to that examined above. Furthermore, the fact that none of the committee members of the Methodist Sunday school belonged (as far as can be ascertained) to the local upper and middle class suggests that this type of school expressed the interests and reflected the aspirations of 'the mechanics and labouring poor' (i.e. the skilled and semi-skilled workers) who were said to support them.[66] It could have accounted for their popularity, for they had the aura of being organized by and for the people, which the charity and monitorial schools totally lacked; this probably transcended religious differences, for in Bethnal Green many Anglican parents sent their children to Dissenting Sunday schools.[67] On the other hand they inculcated obedience and submission, which may have been the more effective for not coming from the higher social classes. The problem is complex and requires further investigation in other localities, as does the whole question of Methodism and popular education.[68]

The other new type of school was the monitorial school and this was more openly the instrument of the upper classes. Spicer Street Lancasterian School was the first in Spitalfields and the first day school to be built there for twenty-seven years. It was founded by members of the Soup Society[69] and its objects were not basically different from those of the traditional charity school; it aimed to instruct the children of the poor in 'Spelling, Reading, Writing, and Arithmetic; in the principles of piety and virtue; in the necessity of honesty, veracity and sobriety; and of having them at the same time inured to habits of subordination, industry and cleanliness'.[70] Certain features of its organization were also similar to those of charity schools: entry was by nomination, the committee kept a close watch, by visits, on the running of the school, clothing was given as prizes for good conduct, and suitable jobs were found for the most meritorious.[71] But there were fundamental differences which marked it out as a new type of institution, designed for the changing social conditions and social relationships of the nineteenth century. Fees of 1d. were charged to avoid the imputation of charity (and also to compensate for the absence of income from interest on stock), it was open 'to children of parents of every religious denomination' and the age range was extended to children between the ages of six to fourteen years.[72] Above all, it would educate far more children than the charity school at a fraction of the cost. 'The grand *feature* of this plan', explained the Spicer Street committee, 'is that one master can teach 1,000 children with as much ease as he could instruct 50 upon the usual system; that one book will serve for a whole school; and that in proportion to the numbers, the expense for the education of each child may be reduced to 10s., 7s., or even 4s. per annum.'[73]

This would, of course, be achieved by the single master instructing a corps of monitors who would in turn take groups of ten or so pupils

in learning by rote the three Rs in a strictly graded fashion. The difficulties inherent in this process were compounded by deficiencies in the
structure of the building. Francis Place visited the school in 1814 and
found it badly lit (by skylights), poorly ventilated and inadequately
heated, with a brick floor which became damp in winter. Into this
miserable hovel, 106 feet long and 39 feet wide, no fewer than thirty-
three rows of desks were crammed, each designed for twenty boys.
Fortunately for the boys' health and the master's sanity, the full
complement of 660 pupils rarely, if ever, attended on any one day.[74]

Low attendance and high initial expenditure (due to mismanage-
ment during construction)[75] pushed up the cost per pupil per year
to some £1.13s. in the first four years of the school's existence; but
given a full attendance and no expenditure beyond basic running costs,
Spicer Street could operate at a cost of 5s. per child per year.[76] Thus
without increasing the number of teachers or greatly improving their
salaries (cf. Tables 1 and 7), the monitorial system facilitated at one
and the same time a vast increase in the number of pupils and a dramatic
drop in expenditure per child. What suffered, of course, was the quality
and range of the teaching, for the system worked on the principle
that nothing could be taught beyond what the monitors could compre-
hend. But as instruments for the mass production of literacy and the
socialization of the children of the poor on the widest possible scale,
monitorial schools could hardly be bettered, superior to Sunday schools,
it was pointed out, in the degree of restraint they were able to exercise
over their pupils.[77]

That the first monitorial school in Spitalfields should be the by-product
of a soup kitchen was symptomatic of the integrated nature of charitable
and educational provision in the district, a provision which multiplied
rapidly after the crisis year of 1812, when trade depression threw many
weavers out of work. In no other place in the early nineteenth century,
observed the historian of the silk industry, were there so many benevolent
doles and charity societies as Spitalfields.[78] In addition to the Soup
Society which had been founded in 1797 and reactivated in 1812,[79]
there was the Spitalfields Benevolent Society, based on the congregation
of Wheler Chapel, which had been formed in 1811 to distribute small
sums of money to the deserving poor and additionally 'to warn and
counsel those who neglect God'.[80] The Spitalfields Association, established in 1812, sold fish, rice, oatmeal and coal at reduced prices and
distributed food and clothing.[81] In addition, several Bible societies were

formed in the district in 1813 and 1814, which sold the Scriptures cheaply or distributed them gratis.[82]

This wide range of philanthropic effort was achieved by co-operation between the various religious persuasions. It was facilitated by the growth of Clapham-style Evangelicalism among the wealthy, particularly the silk manufacturers, who used their position to introduce Evangelical preachers as evening lecturers in Christ Church[83] and to install as minister of Wheler Chapel in 1810 the Rev. Josiah Pratt, who became President of both the Benevolent Society and a local Bible society.[84] In the early nineteenth century Spitalfields was an evangelical stronghold and, unlike the great majority of orthodox Anglicans, they were prepared to co-operate with Dissenters in philanthropic and educational work. The Dissenters in this context were overwhelmingly Quakers, as is evident from the following table which sets out the religious affiliations of the committee members of the Soup Society, the Lancasterian School and the Spitalfields Association, a total of sixty-three individuals.

Table 3   *Percentage religious affiliations of membership of three organizations*[85]

Religion	%
Quaker	48
Anglican Evangelical	6
Anglican (orthodox)	5
Not known, other.	41
Total	100

The same group, analysed according to addresses, reveals a surprisingly high proportion of City men; only a minority lived or worked in Spitalfields itself (Table 4).

Merchants, bankers and large businessmen were strongly represented on these committees (Table 5). They gave considerable financial aid to Spitalfields charities and schools (Table 6), supplementing the relatively limited resources of the smaller silk manufacturers, wholesalers, warehousemen and small businessmen resident in the district. Aid on this scale can be explained partly by fear of the potentially inflammable concentration of the poor (with an insurrectionary tradition) virtually

Table 4 *Percentage distribution of addresses of membership of three organizations*[86]

Address	%
City	43
Spitalfields	33
Elsewhere	24
Total	100

Table 5 *Percentage professions of members of three organizations*[87]

Profession	%	Profession	%
Banker	5		
Brewer	13		
Silk manufacturer	13		
Merchant, wholesaler	17		
Total	48	Large business	48
		Small business	36
		Not known, other	16
		Total	100

on the City's borders; few things boosted subscription lists more than a riot. But assistance from outside was greatly facilitated by the peculiar religious and familial connections of Spitalfields capital at this period. The two most active philanthropists were Thomas Fowell Buxton, Evangelical, partner in Truman and Hanbury's Brewery in Spitalfields, criminal law reformer and leader of the anti-slavery cause after Wilberforce, and William Allen, Quaker, partner in Allen and Hanbury's the manufacturing chemists, and treasurer of the British and Foreign School Society. Allen, though he lived and worked in the City, regarded Spitalfields as his special sphere of operations.

Allen's and Buxton's connections, particularly with the great brewing and banking empires of the Hoare, Gurney, Hanbury, Barclay and Fry families (members of each of which were represented on the three committees) opened up Spitalfields philanthropy to the City. At least seventeen of the sixty-three members had family or business ties with each other, the four individuals who were active on all three committees forming a nucleus. William Allen was father-in-law of Cornelius

Table 6 *Financial aid to Spitalfields charity and education, 1812-24*[88]

Organization	Donations, financial aid, etc.
Survey of the Poor (1812)	Financed by Truman and Hanbury's Brewery.
Spitalfields Soup Society	1812: £150 per week contributed by 'bankers, fire-officers, merchants, and principal tradesmen, aided by donations from the City of London and the Bank, a committee at Lloyd's coffee-house for the relief of the Industrious Poor, the East India Company, the West India Dock and Mercers' Companies, the Royal Exchange Assurance and other corporate bodies'.
	1816: Committee at Lloyds, £300 Bank of England, £210 Truman, Hanbury and Buxton, £52.10s.
Spitalfields Benevolent Society (to general relief fund)	1816: £1300 collected by Stephen Wilson from 'silk merchants and manufacturers'
Spitalfields Association	1812: S. Hoare purchased two buildings in Spitalfields for use of Association.
	1816: East India Company admitted 200 persons as temporary labourers in warehouses.
Spicer Street Lancasterian School	1812: Anon., loan of £800
	1814: 'Messrs Hanbury, Buxton, Barclay and Sanderson, £200' Richardson & Co., £45.
Spitalfields National School	1820: Directors of the East India Company, £100 Directors of the Bank of England, £100 Donations from 'opulent among the silk merchants'.
Quaker Street Infant School	1820 onwards: Annual running cost of £120 borne by Joseph Wilson.

Hanbury (Spitalfields Association and School Committee) by his first wife, and married into the Hanbury family on her death. Buxton was a nephew and partner of Sampson Hanbury, the Quaker brewer, and brother-in-law of Samuel Hoare (treasurer of the Association and School Committee), Samuel and J.J. Gurney and Joseph Fry, brother of Charles Buxton and cousin of Charles Barclay, all committee members. John Sanderson, Quaker and China tea merchant, secretary of the School Committee, was brother-in-law of Cornelius Hanbury (by the latter's second wife) and cousin to Richard Sanderson (Soup Society and Association). Peter Bedford, a Quaker silk manufacturer, was an employee of, and later successor in business to William Allen's brother Joseph, a member of the Spitalfields Association.[89]

These merchants and financiers had grown rich on eighteenth-century trade and commerce. They were mostly of non-Anglican and middle-rank background, and their ideology, in contradistinction to that of the old regime of aristocracy, gentry and Church, was grounded on economic liberalism, utilitarianism and the Protestant-entrepreneurial ethic.[90] Inspired by Benthamite and Malthusian ideas they were critical of the operation of the Poor Laws and the criminal law, favoured private charity as a discouragement to indolence and vice among the poor, and supported undenominational education for all the children of this class as the best means of inculcating attitudes of restraint and self-control.[91]

William Allen's journal the *Philanthropist* provided a forum for these ideas. The problem of the function of charity and relief as a means of social control was thoroughly explored. The starting point, as with much social discussion at this period, was the Poor Laws. Their operation, it was asserted in 1812, was 'indiscriminate and partial', and could breed attitudes inimical to social stability:

> ... for want of a proper inspection we are now taxed, not to support the virtuous part of the poor but to maintain beggary and vice, and to foster those habits of immorality, ignorance, and insubordination, which when they rise to a certain height, endanger the existence of civilized society.[92]

'Real charity' was needed – the visiting and inspection of the poor by 'benevolent persons of the middle class of society'. If these individuals investigated the circumstances of the poor 'at their own habitations', it would be possible to distinguish between the deserving and the undeserving. Those who bore up under difficulties, who avoided seeking relief at the work-house, who did not sink to begging, would receive charity; those who succumbed, would not.[93] This strategy used the very independence of the poor man to subordinate him to the rich; the former, it was hoped, would order his conduct on the lines of 'virtuous foresight ... frugality, industry, and self-denial' and pass his life under the 'full inspection of those whose kindness it was his interest to secure'. In this way charity would operate as 'a real principle of virtue, as a motive to good conduct in the poor'.[94] Visiting was the essence of this form of social control; it enabled the middle class not only to detect imposture but also to deliver a homily to those whose conduct failed to come up to their standards, an activity at which Evangelicals and Quakers excelled (cf. Plate II).

Plate II   *The socialization of poor children: Peter Bedford, silk manufacturer, and two young thieves*

The model working man which this policy aimed to produce was
characterized by the Evangelical tract writer Hannah More as 'skilful
in his business, industrious in his calling, sober in his habits, and punctual in his engagements: laborious in earning his money and prudent in
the use he makes of it'. She was describing James Dawson, the hero of
her moral tale, 'The Delegate: with some account of Mr James Dawson
of Spitalfields', first published in 1817; he was a weaver whose moral
attitude was proof against the blandishments of a delegate from an
anonymous 'revolutionary' society but of the right kind to attract the
attention of a benevolent middle-class visitor who helped procure him a
job.[95] Hannah More, a friend of Sidmouth, wrote this and other tracts
at the request of the government, desperate for antidotes to what it
convinced itself was 'revolution' in 'all the great towns'.[96] It exemplified the fundamentally counter-revolutionary nature of the whole
charitable and educational enterprise, underlined by a pamphlet also
published in 1817 addressed to the inhabitants of Spitalfields by a

member of the Benevolent Society; it warned them of the 'secret machinations' of 'modern reformers', whose aim was to create misery in order to bring down Church and State, and it urged the poor to put their trust in Christianity and the good faith of the charitable.[97] Yet another pamphlet of the same year took the people of Spitalfields to task for Sabbath-breaking, a 'complicated crime' which included 'ingratitude, disobedience, unrighteousness, perfidiousness, rebellion . . . .'.[98]

In essence, these moral exhortations were based on the assumption that the causes of the ills of society were to be found in the individual characteristics of the working man. Remove or check his 'immorality, ignorance and insubordination' and social harmony would be achieved. The energies of the philanthropists were devoted to winning the acceptance of the population for this interpretation of reality, diverting attention from the inadequacies of the social and economic system towards the supposed psychological degeneration of the labouring poor. It was an ideology that patently operated in favour of the 'haves' as against the 'have-nots' and was legitimized by the former's economic position. A speaker at the Mansion House meeting for the relief of the Spitalfields poor in 1816 bluntly stated that a high subscription would prevent discontent from showing itself 'in a manner destructive of our happiness, if not of our ultimate security'.[99] Six years later the *Inquirer* (the successor to the *Philanthropist*), drawing heavily on the experience of Spitalfields, argued that the reduction of crime and misery among the poor by the familiar middle-class moral visitation, and the education of their children 'in habits of subordination, self-respect, economy, and reverence for religion', was the best security of 'our persons and property'.[100]

The close connection between education and charity in Spitalfields had one unfortunate result. It led to the engrafting on popular education, from the very beginning, of the strong element of social control inherent in the operations of private charity, reinforcing, sharpening, and making explicit the tendencies in this direction which instruction of the poor had always possessed, and preventing any other form of education except that of drill in the three Rs and religious indoctrination from making itself felt. Perhaps Cobbett was not far wrong in dubbing the new schools 'seminaries of slavery' which made men 'contented with a Government, under treatment which ought to urge them on . . . to lawful resistance'.[101] In Spitalfields this form of 'heddekashun', as Cobbett called it, received classical expression.

But its influence was not confined to the district; the *Philanthropist* and the *Inquirer* spread the theory to a wider audience, and Spitalfields' philanthropists strongly influenced the deliberations of the British and Foreign School Society; between 1815 and 1824 no fewer than fifteen of them served at various times on its committee.

When Spicer Street Lancasterian School was under construction an 'honest Churchman' had written to *The Times* urging the friends of the Church in Spitalfields to bestir themselves in 'rescuing their neighbours' children from danger' by a counter-proposal for a school on Dr Bell's plan.[102] Five years elapsed before Spitalfields National School was founded, but this began a period of construction during which six new schools were built, with accommodation for nearly 5,000 children (Table 7). It was part of a great increase in the number of schools in Middlesex as a whole, an area which contained the populous working-class districts of Central and East London. By 1820, 42 new monitorial schools had been built in Middlesex, one-seventh of the total for the whole country.[103]

The reasons for this building activity were social and political rather than pedagogic. The increase (or apparent increase)[104] in crime and juvenile delinquency in the post-war years stimulated a spate of investigations and prescriptions for reform of the criminal law and prison discipline on Benthamite lines, in which Buxton and Allen played a prominent role behind the acknowledged leader Romilly. Spitalfields' philanthropists gave evidence to the Parliamentary committees inquiring into crime, police and prisons in the metropolis;[105] they were well represented on the *ad hoc* committee on juvenile delinquency of 1816[106] and virtually ran the Prison Discipline and Juvenile Offenders Society.[107] The high correlation which these investigations revealed between delinquent behaviour in the young and lack of education — up to three-quarters of all juvenile offenders were 'uneducated and in a state of the grossest ignorance'[108] — seemed to point to one conclusion: greatly increased provision of education, particularly religious education, for the children of the poor.[109]

The post-war political situation — the widespread militancy of the working-class radical movement and the savage repression under Home Secretary Sidmouth — also played a part in strengthening the conviction of the upper and middle classes of the need for strong government and maximum social control, which was not without influence on popular education. In July 1817, a few months after the government

Table 7 'New' schools, Christ Church Spitalfields and St Matthew Bethnal Green, 1812-24[110]

	Date of foundation	Denomination	Annual expenditure	Teachers salary p.a.	Fees per week	Attendance Boys	Girls	Total Attendance	Capacity
Lancasterian School Spicer Street, Spitalfields.	3 Feb. 1812	Non-Denominational (Br.)	£573 (Av., 1812-16)	£126	1d	350	–	350 (1816)	660
National School, Spitalfields.	15 Oct. 1817	Anglican	£400	£70 (plus house)	1d	370	150	520 (1820)	1100
Jews' Free School, Spitalfields.	20 Apr. 1818	Non-Denominational (Br.)	?	?	F	382	140	522 (1828)	800
National School, Bethnal Green.	9 May 1819	Anglican	?	£70 (Master) £40 (Mistress)	?	304	106	410 (1820)	2000
British School, Hackney Road, Bethnal Green.	1819	Non-Denominational (Br.)	?	?	1d	–	132	132 (1821)	?
Infant School, Quaker Street, Spitalfields.	24 July 1820	Non-Denominational	£120	£80 (plus house)	F		214	214 (1823)	214
Girls' School, Spicer Street, Spitalfields.	1821	Non-Denominational (Br.)	?	?	1d	–	137	137 (1828)	?

had declared a crisis following the Spa Fields incident and subsequent radical activity, the Rev. West Wheldale, rector of Christ Church, chaired a meeting in Spitalfields which founded the National school. The meeting had adults in mind rather than children; though only a year earlier 40 per cent of Spitalfields children between the ages of six and fourteen were said to be without education and no fewer than seven-eighths of the poorest were in the same condition,[111] the reason for building a National school centred on 'the quantity and quality of population of this district'.[112] Similarly, one of the functions of Bethnal Green National School was to 'stem the torrent of the cheerless and deistical principles which have been so extensively circulated throughout the kingdom'.[113]

The National school in Christ Church opened in temporary quarters in 1817, but moved to expensive purpose-built accommodation three years later. This attractive, classically-fronted building with its three arched roofs survived until early 1973 (Plate III); it cost £2,596 to build, received grants of £300 from the National Society and was obviously intended as a counterblast to Spicer Street by a Church aroused at last from its lethargy. Significantly the Duke of York laid the

Plate III   *Spitalfields National School, shortly before its demolition in 1973*

foundation stone and Lord Sidmouth became one of the Vice-Patrons.[114] The Evangelicals, almost inevitably, got a foot in the door. Joseph Wilson signed the lease jointly with the Rev. Wheldale, and became treasurer;[115] his cousin Daniel, as we have seen, outlined the aims and the East India Company (where Evangelical influence was strong) contributed to the funds.[116] To judge by the phraseology of the first report of Bethnal Green National School, Evangelicals were probably represented on its committee also.[117]

Evangelical money founded Quaker Street Infant School, which took children under six years of age. Joseph Wilson had paid to have a building converted and maintained the school out of his own pocket for many years.[118] Modelled to some extent on Owen's New Lanark Infant School and inspired by the success of a similar school set up by Brougham and his associates at Westminster in 1819, the infant school belonged to a genre very different from the other day schools. The first master, the ebullient Swedenborgian Samuel Wilderspin, later the self-styled founder of the Infant School System, experimented with unorthodox teaching methods, introduced movement and play into the classroom, taught natural history by means of objects and pictures, and religious instruction by placing brightly coloured illustrations of Biblical scenes on the walls and letting children ask questions. Following Owen, he made the playground an integral part of the educational process.[119] 'I well remember the delight it gave me ... to see that happy school', wrote a former inhabitant of Wheler Street to Wilderspin in later years.[120] Certainly it was the only school in Spitalfields where submission was not taught. This was partly due to its Owenite pedigree, partly to Wilderspin's own educational credo (which Wilson made no attempt to influence), and partly to the greater latitude allowable in an institution which did not prepare children for the labour market.

The majority of the new schools, as might be expected from the religious configuration of the district, were British schools. The Jews' Free School and the two girls' schools did something to diversify the educational scene but little to broaden educational horizons. Only in the Jews' school did intellectual effort go beyond the three Rs; in the space of three years its pupils were expected to be able to translate prayers and passages from the Bible.[121] At Hackney Road girls' school 'advancement in learning' meant ability to read and write 'pretty well' and proficiency in needlework.[122] But success in socialization was commended more eagerly than success in teaching. The British and Foreign School Society Report of 1820 twice drew attention to the transformation of a troublesome girl of eleven, slovenly, idle, inattentive and bad-mannered, into a paragon of obedience, assiduity and neatness who moreover began to read the Bible to her sick father.[123]

Imparting religious knowledge to the young was considered to be the 'primary object' of this school; the Society, in fact, likened itself to the British and Foreign Bible Society as an institution devoted to the dissemination of religion,[124] giving some substance to Francis Place's allegation that its schools 'taught nothing else'.[125] The socializing function of the monitorial schools was based upon the assumption that the learning of Biblical texts (or texts based on the Bible) would of itself produce the desired change in children's social consciousness. Spicer Street school committee advertised that moral and religious duties were inculcated in the language of the Holy Scriptures,[126] and William Allen believed, without adducing any evidence, that by 'the constant reading of selections from the Holy Scriptures ... the soundest lessons of morality [will] be engraven on their minds'.[127] Repetition would fix the language of Holy Writ in the children's memories, 'ultimately ... to be indelibly written on their hearts'.[128] The Rev. Daniel Wilson had a more sophisticated explanation of this process, which came close to the modern doctrine of internalization:

> Conscience is the foundation of law. A doctrine of future retribution is the support of social order. No human statutes can control the heart. It is only when you inscribe an inward law -- when you erect a voluntary self-command ... when you implant a fear of that Almighty Lord ... that the frame of civil society can be cemented together.[129]

Fear of God (and presumably awe of things he could not possibly understand) once implanted in the child would thus act as a sort of general control on his behaviour. In similar fashion, it has been argued, the Anglican catechism, the product of a patriarchal age, extended the child's consciousness of filial authority in the home to the political and social order[130] (a process more likely to be effective among weavers' children than those of other trades). The duty of obedience to monarch and magistrate was structured on the analogy of the fifth commandment: honour thy father and thy mother. And honour also the King, the child was instructed, 'and all that are put in authority under him'. My duty, he was told to say, is 'to submit myself to all my governors, teachers, spiritual pastors and masters: to order myself lowly and reverently to all my betters ... and to do my duty in that state

ROYAL BRITISH SYSTEM of EDUCATION

" It is my Wish that every poor CHILD should be taught to read the BIBLE."

Spoken by His Majesty George the 3. *to Jos.* *Lancaster at Weymouth. 1805.*

Plate IV *'To honour and obey the King'; political socialization illustrated*

of life unto which it shall please God to call me'.[131] Father, magistrate, monarch, deity: all Anglican and many other children who attended school at this period had their attention drawn to this omnipresent hierarchy,[132] and few can fail to have absorbed some of its social significance.[133] It pervaded even the iconography of education. The British and Foreign School Society headed one of its leaflets with an emblem in which the robed and godlike figure of King George III hands the Bible to a white-clad child (Plate IV); a more explicit and fitting pictorial representation of political socialization could hardly have been devised.

But monitorial schools, as their structure and methods became standardized, came to rely also on the organization of the school and the teaching process to inculcate the desired attitudes. The division of labour facilitated the maximum utilization of time, orderly progression and regularity of industry, and these, an apologist for the Bell system argued, insinuated themselves into the habits of the child and had 'a proportionable influence upon his future conduct'.[134] As the committee of Bethnal Green National School observed, the method and the morality went hand-in-hand.[135] In general, the monitorial schools attempted to implant both sentiments of obedience and submission and the work-habits suited to a developing capitalist society. There is no evidence that those in Spitalfields differed in any way; in none were to be found the teaching of a skill or skills useful to weavers or artisans or indeed anything that would interest children and inspire them with a love of knowledge.

It remains to examine the ways in which the people of Spitalfields reacted to the comprehensive attempts to control their lives and thoughts and those of their children. The extent of the effort is not in doubt. In 1812 the Soup Society was selling soup at 1*d.* per quart to 7,000 persons daily.[136] In the space of eleven weeks during the slump of 1816, the Spitalfields Association organized 8,460 visits to 3,366 families.[137] Between 1812 and 1824 members of the Benevolent Society made no fewer than 158,140 visits, interviewed 116,490 individuals and distributed a total of £23,437.[138] In 1816 a meeting of representatives of these societies in the Mansion House, chaired by the Lord Mayor, opened a subscription that raised £43,369 in a few days.[139] The scale of Bible distribution may be gauged by the work of the Norton Folgate Association; between May and December 1815 it sold 173 Bibles in an area covering fifteen or twenty streets.[140] The East London organization gave away 2,000 Bibles in Spitalfields during the economic crisis of 1816.[141] In 1821 the six monitorial schools were providing places for about 60 per cent of the children between six and fourteen years of age.[142]

On the evidence of these figures and those of Table 7, and making allowances for overlapping, a large proportion of the poor purchased the cheap provisions, accepted the money, bought the Bibles, attended Church and sent their children to monitorial schools, and the examples of gratitude, acceptance and conversion quoted by the societies support this.[143] But the situation cannot be seen as one of simple acceptance or rejection. The reaction of the poor to relief was more complex than the simplicities of the James Dawson story would suggest. William Hale, among others, frequently drew attention to the almost universal horror of being forced to seek parish relief:

> A poor man will rise up early, he will sit up late, he will eat the bread of carefulness, he will undergo the most severe privations before he will take a single shilling, so long as he can keep up his head of independence, and say, 'Thank God, I have never been a pauper, thank God, not one of my family ever took anything of the parish'.[144]

On the other hand Hale observed that 'unexpected reliefs, coming from unexpected benevolence' and made at the houses of the poor were 'more thankfully received'.[145] Whether this should be construed as evidence of a move towards 'good conduct', or whether, in contrast to Poor Law relief, private charity could be accepted lightly, as possessing no stigma, is an open question. Furthermore, the disbursement of large sums of privately subscribed money, as Hale once again pointed out, did not necessarily imply, as the philanthropists maintained, a corresponding depth of suffering and consequent gratitude at its relief. The disbursement of the £43,369 relief fund in 1816, he asserted, had attracted paupers from all over London to lodgings in Spitalfields; 'in fact, it was worth something a week to become a pauper of Spitalfields at that time'. One tenth of the money, Hale believed, would have satisfied the real distress.[146]

It was, of course, widely asserted by the organizers of charity and schooling that they had been successful. In the crisis of 1816, John Daughtrey, claiming to represent the views of 'the very best informed persons, manufacturers and others', ascribed the peaceable temper of the Spitalfields poor to 'the moral influence which has been diffused among them by means of Sunday and other schools, visiting societies, etc., and to the relief which the benevolent public have afforded them under their various distresses'.[147] The Bible Society assumed the credit for the implanting of feelings of 'patience and gratitude' among the suffering poor of Spitalfields, which had foiled the 'desperate men' of Spa Fields who had allegedly counted on their active support.[148] The Rev. Josiah Pratt believed that the efforts of the Benevolent Society had helped the poor 'to bear their sufferings with submission to the will of Him who knows their wants'.[149] Both Allen and Wilderspin asserted that they noticed an improvement in the morals of children after only a few years of schooling, an improvement which in Wilderspin's opinion affected parents also.[150]

These judgments are *ex parte* and impressionistic. More significant may be the information that, in 1836, no instance was known of a former scholar of Quaker Street Infant School appearing before a magistrate,[151] or that in the late 1830s many weavers did not weave on Sundays because of their desire to keep the Sabbath a quiet day.[152] But the evidence is in any case conflicting. William Hale was of the opinion that the weavers were quiet and loyal at the time of Spa Fields and Peterloo because of the operation of the Spitalfields Acts, which kept wages comparatively high and steady.[153] He was not alone in this view;

Lord Ellenborough informed the House of Lords on the eve of the repeal of the Acts that he had always looked upon them more as a measure of police than trade, in that they preserved 'peace and good understanding' between masters and journeymen.[154] But this does not explain the fact that the repeal of the Acts was greeted by the weavers not with riots but with petitions and peaceful demonstrations.[155] Rather does it support the view that the socialization and social control measures of the previous dozen years were to some extent successful, as does the lack of any large-scale radical movement among the population as a whole in the period under review.

But should the absence or incidence of large-scale political activity be the only measure of the success or failure of social control and socialization? Perhaps the reactions of the people on a day-to-day basis over the whole period are a better indication. The weavers, for instance, maintained an underground trade union organization throughout the period of the Spitalfields Acts, despite anti-combination legislation and the existence of a union-breaking committee or the silk masters, and also combatted the latter's arguments for the repeal of the Acts based on Smithian premises of 'commercial freedom'.[156]

In the population as a whole, the reception of official Christianity, on the success of which socialization hinged, was lukewarm. In 1812 the Soup Society's survey of the poor had revealed the startling fact that 20 per cent of those interviewed confessed to having no religious beliefs at all, and that nearly half those interviewed possessed no Bible.[157] Four years later the Spitalfields Association found that nearly 30 per cent of families receiving relief were without the Scriptures.[158] To some extent this may have been a function of illiteracy, but evidence from the 1830s reveals that even taking into account the limited amount of church and chapel accommodation, attendance in Christ Church was one-third, and in Bethnal Green one-sixth, of 'what ought to be expected'.[159] Impressionistic evidence suggests that only an insignificant fraction of the population was interested in religion, and 'infidelity' was said to be widespread.[160] These attitudes are hardly likely to have been different twenty years earlier. Indeed in the early 1820s the citizens of Christ Church refused to pay church rates because the vestry had spent £6,993 on 'the meretricious decoration of churches'.[161]

This lack of enthusiasm for institutional religion was paralleled by (and was perhaps partly a cause of) a tentative response to the provision of education. Attendance at school provides a rough indication of attitudes towards education, though the evidence needs careful interpretation.[162] In 1816 all Spitalfields schools, both day and Sunday, were reported to be able to hold 'a considerably greater number' than attended them;[163] the attendance as a proportion of the capacity at the monitorial schools of Spicer Street, Christ Church, and Bethnal Green in the early 1820s was, as Table 7 shows, 53 per cent, 47 per cent, and 21 per cent respectively.[164] Poverty was one reason;[165] recognition of the insufficiency of school places another;[166] preference was often given to what were felt to be the needs and interests of the family;[167] and many working-class parents were critical of the education given in the new schools. When Wilderspin played games with the children in order to make them feel at ease on their first day at the infant school, many of the children were taken away because the mothers felt they were not 'learning their lessons',[168] an example of independence he felt was characteristic of the local people.[169]

The most significant cause of low attendance was, however, the conviction, shared by many of the poor, that the schools had been provided *for* them, by the middle classes, and were thus in some way alien to the interests of the labouring population. This was not confined to their children's schools; one of the reasons for the lack of support of Spitalfields Mechanics' Institute, founded in 1825, was the presence of silk manufacturers on its committee.[170] The poorest inhabitants were actively hostile; gangs of 'notorious characters' would gather outside Friar's Mount Sunday School in Bethnal Green to jeer and throw stones at the windows[171] and Wilderspin was pelted with filth in his early days at Quaker Street.[172]

The higher-paid sections of the working population, more positively, supported schools of their own — dame schools and common day schools. When Wilderspin's mothers removed their children they had pointed out that 'we can send them to Mrs So and So, where for 4*d*. a week they will learn something'.[173] Nothing better illustrates the class consciousness of the poor than their willingness to pay 4*d*. a week or more to have their children taught to read rather than send them to a free school teaching the three Rs (or more, in the case of Quaker Street) which was maintained by middle-class philanthropy. Allen's associate Brougham, an energetic sponsor of free schools, was surprised at this seeming perversity;[174] what he did not grasp was the deep distrust of middle-class intentions which led the poor to reject 'their' free schools in favour of 'our' expensive ones. Dame schools for children under six years and common day schools for older children have almost invariably been condemned by historians of education, and few have been recorded or described. But the evidence suggests that in some areas of East London they were educating almost as many children as the new public day schools and in some cases more.[175] One district of Bethnal Green in the late 1830s contained fifteen dame schools educating 1,662 scholars; only 662 were attending other schools.[176] The 1833 Education Returns listed twenty-nine dame and common day schools in Christ Church, eight in Bethnal Green, five in Mile End New Town and two in the Old Artillery Ground.[177] Many of these schools were in existence at an earlier date; Wilderspin refers to them and a few were mentioned in the 1818 Returns.[178] Some of the day schools taught geography and history in addition to the three Rs, had good teachers and a teacher-pupil ratio of about 1 : 30, and charged up to 1s. per week. But they had one great deficiency in the eyes of official opinion − a virtual absence of religious or moral instruction; in the words of the Education Committee of 1838 they were 'very inefficient for good purposes'.[179]

'Good purposes', in the sense of the indoctrination of children in the ideology of submission, was not seen as an essential element of education by many Spitalfields artisans; in fact the evidence suggests that the labouring population as a whole regarded education from a largely instrumental point of view. According to Wilderspin they considered that it consisted merely of the knowledge of letters[180] (i.e. reading and writing); this, though not the whole truth, was indicative of a conception of education quite different from that of the upper and middle classes.

These are parental attitudes. What can be said of children's views and experiences of education and the socialization process in Spitalfields at this time? The only material which can throw any light on these matters is contained in a lengthy footnote to one of the reports of the Hand-Loom Weavers Commission of 1840, in which W.E. Hickson set down the autobiographies of nine young apprentices born in the early 1820s in Bethnal Green, Mile End New Town and adjacent areas. As they were all in the House of Correction in Middlesex for 'disorderly conduct' (apparently in relation to their masters) they were not a representative sample of the child population, nor were all of them born within Spitalfields. But their experiences give a unique insight into what some children felt about their upbringing and education and reveal once again the existence of that spirit of independence necessary to survive in the urban jungle of the early nineteenth century.

They had few illusions about either life or education. Two had been left on the steps of the workhouse when a few months old; others had been shunted by the parish from workhouse to charity school to apprenticeship. Nearly all had had a meagre or unsatisfactory education, many were exploited by masters and not a few beaten. 'He is kind on the whole', said one boy of his master, '[he] does not beat me much.' Only one seems to have been positively affected by his education, becoming a Sunday school teacher and tract distributor. Perhaps the most moving aspect of many of the statements is the realization of the raw deal they had been given and their attempts to compensate by their own efforts. 'My master has not taught me the trade', complained one boy after two and a half years apprenticeship to a cabinet maker, 'I cannot do more than plane a piece of wood.' 'They taught nothing but reading, writing, and ciphering', said another of his charity school. 'Did not learn to read and write, am learning now to spell', was the experience of a Bethnal Green orphan who spent twelve years in 'the nursery at Edmonton'. Another boy used to learn the catechism, but 'had forgotten all about it'. 'M.L.' could not read or write after two years at Whitechapel National School so 'taught myself chiefly'. 'G.J.', also at a national school, 'did not get on well there; only boys set to teach you, who cannot teach you so well as you can teach yourself: left it because I did not get on.'[181]

'Left it because I did not get on'; here the voice of a child of the 1820s speaks directly to us; his words could serve both as a judgement on the type of education provided for the children of the poor and as a testimony to the independent attitude of many of them towards it.

NOTES

[1] Rev. D. Wilson, *The National Schools a National Blessing. A Sermon Preached at Christ Church, Middlesex ... in aid of the Spitalfields Schools* (London, 1819), pp. 32-3.
[2] Cf. Parliamentary Papers 1816 IV, Select Committee on the Education of the Lower Orders in the Metropolis, p. 208; P. P. 1817 VII, Committee on the State of the Police in the Metropolis, p. 109.
[3] L.D. Schwarz, 'Occupations and incomes in late eighteenth-century East London', *East London Papers*, Vol. 14, No. 2 (December 1972), p. 88. It would have been lower in Spitalfields but for the taxes paid by the docks, breweries and sugar refineries.
[4] P. P. 1828 IV, Report from the Select Committee on that Part of the Poor Laws Relating to the Employment or Relief of Able-Bodied Persons from the Poor Rate, p. 32.
[5] Schwarz, op. cit., p. 97.
[6] W.H. Manchée, 'Memories of Spitalfields', *Proceedings of the Huguenot Society of London*, Vol. X (1912-14), p. 310.

[7] P. P. 1840 XXIII, Reports from Assistant Hand-Loom Weavers Commissioners, Pt. II, p. 239; P. P. 1840 XXIV, Hand-Loom Weavers: Copy of Report of Mr Hickson on the Condition of the Hand-Loom Weavers, App. No. 7, p. 79.

[8] P. P. 1817, VI, Report from the Select Committee on the Poor Laws, pp. 31, 37, 42. This was one-sixth of the population of the parish.

[9] Ibid., pp. 36-7, 46; Report of the Committee of the Spitalfields Soup Society, for 1811-12 (London, 1813), pp. 11-12.

[10] This figure is taken from a survey of 1,504 poor families carried out by the Spitalfields Soup Society in 1812 (*Philanthropist* Vol. II, 1812, p. 189), and should be taken as an indicator of magnitude rather than as an accurate estimate. In Bethnal Green in 1815, 85 per cent of men and 66 per cent of women were able to sign their own names. (I am indebted to Mr Schwarz for this information.)

[11] P. P. 1828 VI, Report from the Select Committee on the Police of the Metropolis, p. 92.

[12] Ibid., p. 95; P. P. 1817 VII, Police in Metropolis, pp. 110-11.

[13] Schwarz, op. cit., p. 93.

[14] P. P. 1821 VII, Select Committee of the House of Lords, Appointed to Inquire into the Means of Extending and Securing the Foreign Trade of the Country, pp. 27, 30. This was the average for a man in work, before deductions, in two of the largest firms, and is probably somewhat high.

[15] P. P. 1818 IX, Report from Committee on Silk Weavers Petitions, pp. 46-7; P. P. 1831-2 XIX, Report of the Select Committee on the Silk Trade, pp. 730-1; P. P. 1837 LI, Distress, Spitalfields and Nottingham, p. 2; P. P. 1840 XXIV, Hand-Loom Weavers, p. 77.

[16] P. P. 1818 IX, Ribbon Weavers, p. 47; P. P. 1835 VII, Report from the Select Committee on Education in England and Wales, p. 10.

[17] P. P. 1840 XXIII, Hand-Loom Weavers, p. 271.

[18] P. P. 1840 XXIV, Hand-Loom Weavers, p. 77.

[19] Ibid., p. 78.

[20] 'All the mechanics of various descriptions, who work for their employers in the City, reside in Spitalfields; the carters, porters, and persons of every description, down to the mendicant, the man who sweeps the streets, the barrow-woman, the fishwoman, and all employed in the most servile way ...' (P. P. 1817 VI, Poor Laws, p. 41).

[21] S. Wilderspin, *On the Importance of Educating the Infant Children of the Poor* (London, 1823), pp. 3, 92-3, 101-2, 108, 123-4.

[22] Ibid., pp. 128-9.

[23] Census of 1821, *Abstract of the Answers and Returns* (1822), p. 197. The proportion for England and Wales in the 1960s was 23 per cent.

[24] It is clear from the accounts of Wilderspin and others that the different motives behind childish pranks, organized theft and stealing to keep alive were not always appreciated. Cf. Wilderspin, *Infant Poor* (1823) pp. 72-3, 117-20, 134ff, 141-3 and P. P. 1818 VII, Report from the Select Committee on the State of Gaols, p. 169.

[25] Wilderspin, *Infant Poor* (1823), pp. 216-17; S. Wilderspin, *On the Importance of Educating the Infant Poor* (London, 1824), p. 132; S. Wilderspin, *Early Discipline* (London, 1832), p. 22ff.

[26] P. P. 1816 IV, Education of Lower Orders, p. 233.

[27] For the upbringing of the middle-class child, cf. the significantly-titled manual by Louisa Hoare, wife of Samuel Hoare, *Hints for the Improvement of Early Education and Nursery Discipline* (London, 1819). This reached its eighth edition by 1824.

[28] Margaret May, 'Innocence and experience: the evolution of the concept of juvenile deliquency in the mid-nineteenth century', *Victorian Studies*, Vol. XVIII, No. 1 (September 1973), pp. 18-19, for this point.

[29] Schwarz, op. cit., p. 93. This is the average for Spitalfields, Bethnal Green and Mile End New Town in 1813.

[30] Cf. E.P. Thompson, *The Making of the English Working Class* (London, 1963), p. 603ff.

[31] Cf. P. P. 1818 IX, Ribbon Weavers, p. 57; P. P. 1840 XXIV, Hand-Loom Weavers, p. 78.

[32] The best accounts of the Spitalfields Outrages are in J.L. and B. Hammond, *The Skilled Labourer 1760-1832* (London, 1919), pp. 205ff and W.M. Jordan, The Silk Industry in London 1760-1830, unpublished M.A. thesis, University of London, 1941, on which this paragraph is based.

[33] Cf. J.H. Clapham, 'The Spitalfields Acts 1773-1824', *Economic Journal*, Vol. XXVI (December 1916), pp. 459-71. The provisions of the original Act were later extended to include fabrics mixed with silk and to cover women weavers.

[34] P. P. 1818 IX, Ribbon Weavers, p. 193; P. P. 1821 VII, Foreign Trade, pp. 40, 42.

[35] As stated in the declaration of 88 Spitalfields manufacturers in 1818 (P. P. 1818 IX, Ribbon Weavers, pp. 196-8).

[36] Rev. R. Yates, *The Church in Danger* (London 1815) and *The Basis of National Welfare* (London, 1817).

[37] Yates, *The Church in Danger*, p. 58.

[38] P. P. 1818 XVIII, Account of Benefices and Population; Churches, Chapels and their Capacity, p. 143.

[39] Yates, *The Church in Danger*, p. 112.

[40] *Sources*: P. P. 1816 IV, Education of Lower Orders, pp. 123, 189; P. P. 1818 IX, A Digest of Parochial Returns Made to the Select Committee Appointed to Inquire into the Education of the Poor, pp. 535, 543, 551; P. P. 1819 XA, First Report of the Commissioners ... Concerning Charities in England, for the Education of the Poor, pp. 196-7, 322-5; P. P. 1818 XB, Second Report, pp. 75-6, 129-30; P. P. 1835 XLII, Education Inquiry, Abstract of the Answers and Returns, pp. 555, 558; J.H. Scott, *A Short History of Spitalfields 1197-1894* (London, 1894), pp. 28-38.

[41] W. Hale, *A Letter to Samuel Whitbread, Esq. M.P. Containing*

34 *Popular education and socialization in the 19th century*

Observations on the Distresses Peculiar to the Poor of Spitalfields (London, 1806), pp. 26-7.
[42] Hale's words again (P. P. 1817 VII, Police in Metropolis, p. 111).
[43] Thompson, *English Working Class*, p. 402.
[44] P. P. 1819 XA, First Report of the Commissioners . . . Concerning Charities in England, for the Education of the Poor, p. 324.
[45] The statutes of Spitalfields Charity School prescribed the age and residence qualifications of the children, the curriculum and the religion of the teachers. Cf. Greater London Council Record Office, P93/CTC1/177-1, 'In the Matter of the Parochial Charity Schools of the Parish of Christ Church Spitalfields: Brief Petition . . . 24 April 1852'; P93/CTC1/175, 'To the Charity Commissioners of England and Wales: In the matter of the Charity called or known as the "Parochial Schools . . . Spitalfields"' (1869).
[46] Rev. H. Worthington, *The Duty of Instructing and Relieving Necessitous Children. A Sermon . . . in Behalf of the Protestant Dissenting Charity School . . . Wood Street, Spital-Fields* (London, 1793), p. 42.
[47] M.J. Fletcher, *The History of Parmiter's Foundation* (London, 1971), p. 14.
[48] Hale, *Letter to Whitbread*, pp. 26-7n.
[49] P. P. 1816 IV, Education of Lower Orders, p. 204.
[50] *Philanthropist*, Vol. II, 1812, p. 189; the percentage is derived from the 1812 survey.
[51] Guildhall Library, MS. 9559, London Diocese. Diocese Book 1766-1811, entries for Christ Church Spitalfields, St Matthew Bethnal Green and Mile End New Town.
[52] Annual Report of the Sunday School Union for the Year Ending 1 May 1824 (London, 1824), p. 22.
[53] *Source*: P. P. 1816 IV, Education of Lower Orders, pp. 123, 189.
[54] Cited in S. Grosvenor, *History of the City Road Chapel Sunday, Day, and Infant Schools* (London, 1856), p. 4.
[55] P. P. 1816 IV, Education of Lower Orders, pp. 206-7.
[56] *A Plan for the Management of the Spitalfields Wesleyan Methodist Sunday School* (London, 1824), pp. 7ff, 15-20.
[57] Moral and religious instruction was 'one essential part of the plan' of every Sunday school, according to John Cooper, steward of Spitalfields Benevolent Society (P. P. 1814-15 III, Report from Committee on the State of Mendicity in the Metropolis, p. 72).
[58] Grosvenor, *City Road Schools*, p. 13.
[59] *A Plan* . . . pp. 10-11.
[60] Cf. the series of articles on education in *Wesleyan-Methodist Magazine*, Vol. I, 3rd ser., 1822, pp. 298-300, 362-4, 643-7, 783-6; Vol. II, 3rd ser., 1823, pp. 365-8; Vol. III, 3rd ser., 1824, pp. 173-6, 243-6.
[61] *A Plan* . . . pp. 9-10.
[62] Writing in Methodist Sunday schools had been forbidden by Conference in 1814 and again in 1823 (H. F. Matthews, *Methodism and the Education of the People 1791-1857* (London, 1949), pp. 66-7).

[63] The teachers had four representatives on a committee of thirteen. The East London teachers had won this right in 1814. Cf. G.L.C.R.O., N/M14/2 London East Circuit, Minutes of the General Meetings of the Methodist Sunday School Society, 21 October 1814.

[64] *The Case of the Spitalfields Circuit* (n.d.), *passim*. This pamphlet dates from the mid-1830s.

[65] P. P. 1818 IX., Digest of Parochial Returns, p. 551.

[66] P. P. 1816 IV, Education of Lower Orders, p. 204.

[67] Ibid., p. 234.

[68] Cf. Chapter 3.

[69] *Philanthropist*, Vol. II., 1812, p. 193.

[70] Friends' Library, Tracts D/210, 'An Address to the Friends of the Education of the Poor . . .' (n.d.).

[71] Report of the Committee for Managing the School on the British System, in Spicer Street, Spitalfields, 1816 (London, 1817), p. 11ff.

[72] Ibid., p. 11; *Philanthropist*, Vol. II, 1812, p. 197.

[73] 'An Address to the Friends of the Education of the Poor . . .'

[74] B. M. Place Papers Vol. 60., Schools 1811-21, 'West London Lancasterian Association: Report of Sub-Committee Appointed to Inquire into Expense of Lancasterian and other Schools in the Metropolis'. Spicer Street did not greatly differ in size or appointment from the other schools investigated.

[75] Ibid.

[76] The master's salary, the ground rent and sundry expenses totalled £171 in 1816 (Report of Spicer Street School Committee, 1816, p. 15).

[77] P. P. 1816 IV Education of Lower Orders, p. 191.

[78] F. Warner, *The Silk Industry in the United Kingdom* (London, 1912), p. 65.

[79] G.L.C.R.O., P98/CTC1/55, Minutes of the Committee of the Society for Supplying the Poor with . . . Soup, General Meeting 1812.

[80] First Report of the Spitalfields Benevolent Society (London, 1812), *passim*.

[81] *Philanthropist*, Vol. II, 1812, pp. 239-44.

[82] British and Foreign Bible Society, Home Corres. Inwards, J. Brown to Secretary, 28 February 1823.

[83] G. L., MS. 4644/19, London Weavers Company. Court Minute Book, 21 January 1783; 18 February 1783; 1 July 1783; MS 4648, James Limborough Charity. Trustees Account Book, *passim*.

[84] Rev. G. Rigg, *A Brief History of St Mary's, Spital Square* (? 1910), pp. 14-16.

[85] *Sources*: *Philanthropist*, Vol. II, 1812, pp. 243-4; Report of Spicer Street School Committee, (1816), p. 4; 'A List of the Committee of the Spitalfields Soup Society . . . 1816-17' (Leaflet in Soup Society Minute Book). These percentages are not strictly accurate, as the dates of the committee lists differ; the error, however, is small because it is obvious from other sources that there was a great deal of continuity in charitable and educational work during the years 1812-17. Dissenters, other

than Quakers and Anglicans (both Evangelical and Orthodox), are under-represented in this table, as information of members of these denominations does not exist on the scale of that for Quakers in Friends House Library.

[86] *Sources*: as Table 3.

[87] *Sources*: as Table 3, and contemporary directories. 'Small business' includes mainly retailers and others to whom this attribution could reasonably be given on the basis of the description of their profession, but the distinction between large and small businesses was in a few cases necessarily an arbitrary one. These figures, therefore, should best be taken as indicators of magnitudes.

[88] *Sources*: *Philanthropist*, Vol. II, 1812, p. 184; Spitalfields Benevolent Society Report (1812), p. 16; Report of Spicer Street School Committee (1816), p. 12; Spitalfields Soup Society Minutes, 1 April 1816; *The Times*, 12 July 1816; P. P. 1818 IX, Ribbon Weavers, p. 192; Seventh Report of the National Society (1818), p. 232; P. P. 1835 VII, Education, pp. 30-1; W. Tallack, *Peter Bedford, The Spitalfields Philanthropist* (London, 1865), p. 31; *Life of William Allen* (London, 3 vols., 1846-7), Vol.I, p. 150.

[89] Sources for this paragraph: A.A. Locke, *The Hanbury Family* (London, 2 vols., 1916); D. Chapman-Huston and E.C. Cripps, *Through a City Archway; the Story of Allen and Hanburys* (London, 1954); A. Barnard, *The Noted Breweries of Great Britain and Ireland* (London, 4 vols., 1889-91), Vol. I; C. Buxton, *Memoir of Sir Thomas Fowell Buxton, Bt* (London, 1848); T. Geldart, *Memorials of Samuel Gurney* (London, 1857); T. Kelly, *George Birkbeck: Pioneer of Adult Education* (London, 1865); Viscount Templewood, *The Unbroken Thread* (London, 1949).

[90] The best short account of this class is in E.J. Hobsbawm, *Industry and Empire* (London, 1968), p. 63ff.

[91] For a summary of the views of Bentham and Malthus on the Poor Laws, education and charity, cf. J.R. Poynter, *Society and Pauperism: English Ideas on Poor Relief, 1795-1834* (London, 1969), pp. 117ff, 144ff.

[92] *Philanthropist*, Vol. II, 1812, pp. 190-1.

[93] Cf. the by-laws of the committee of the Spitalfields Association (*Philanthropist*, Vol. II, 1812, pp. 240-2); the Benevolent Society had a maxim: 'that street beggars are, with very few exceptions, so utterly worthless and incorrigible, as to be undeserving the attention of such a society' (P. P. 1814-15 III, Mendicity, p. 73).

[94] *Philanthropist*, Vol. III, 1813, pp. 3-5; cf. Spitalfields Benevolent Society Report (1812), p. 14.

[95] [Hannah More] 'The Delegate; with some account of Mr. James Dawson of Spitalfields' in *Cheap Repository Tracts, Suited to the Present Times* (London, 1819).

[96] M.G. Jones, *Hannah More* (Cambridge, 1952), pp. 202-3.

[97] [Irving Brock], *A Letter to the Inhabitants of Spital-Fields, on the Character and Views of our Modern Reformers* (London, 1817).

[98] *Observations on Sabbath-Breaking: Addressed to the Inhabitants of Spitalfields, and its Vicinity* (London, 1817), p. 7.

[99] *The Times*, 27 November 1816.

[100] *Inquirer*, Vol. 1, No. 1, April 1822, pp. 1-13, *passim*.

[101] *Cobbett's Weekly Political Register*, Vol. 82. No. 10, 7 December 1833, p. 598.

[102] *The Times*, 21 March 1811.

[103] P. P. 1820 XII, 'A General Table Showing the State of Education in England', p. 343.

[104] James Millar, a member of the Committee on Juvenile Deliquency, felt that increased investigation and detection might have made an increase apparent (P. P. 1816 V, Report from the Committee on the State of the Police of the Metropolis, pp. 169-70).

[105] P. P. 1814-15 III, Mendicity in the Metropolis; P. P. 1816 V, Police of Metropolis; P. P. 1817 VII, Police in Metropolis; P. P. 1819 VII, State of Gaols.

[106] The two secretaries and fourteen of the fifty committee members were Spitalfields men (Report of the Committee for Investigating the Causes of the Alarming Increase of Juvenile Delinquency in the Metropolis (London, 1816), p. 3).

[107] Peter Bedord and William Crawford were the first secretaries; in 1824 Samuel Hoare was chairman, Buxton treasurer, and William Allen and three other Spitalfields men were on the committee. (Report of the Committee of the Society for the Improvement of Prison Discipline and for the Reformation of Juvenile Offenders (London, 1818), pp. 3, 32; Sixth Report (1824), xiii.)

[108] P. P. 1816 V, Police of Metropolis, p. 171; P. P. 1817 VII, Police in Metropolis, p. 429.

[109] Cf. Reports of above Society and Committee, *passim*.

[110] *Sources*: P. P. 1816 IV, Education of Lower Orders, p. 189; Fifteenth Report of the British and Foreign School Society (London, 1820), p. 113; Sixteenth Report (1821), p. 128; *Twenty-third* Report (1828), pp. 71-2; Twenty-sixth Report (1831), pp. 67-9; Seventh Annual Report of the National Society (London, 1818), pp. 229-34; Eighth Report (1819), pp. 17-18; Ninth Report (1820), pp. 82-3; pp. 193-6; Report of Spicer Street School Committee (1816), pp. 14-15; P. P. 1835 XLI, Education Inquiry. Abstract of Answers and Returns, pp. 555, 558; Wilderspin, *Infant Poor* (1823), pp. 7, 109; P. P. 1835 VII, Education, pp. 30-1.

[111] P. P. 1816 IV, Education of Lower Orders, pp. 189-90.

[112] B. M. Add. Mss. 38268, Liverpool Papers, L. A. Anspach to Liverpool, 11 August 1817.

[113] Ninth Annual Report of the National Society (London, 1820), p. 193. The reference was to the works of William Hone.

[114] Seventh Annual Report of the National Society (London, 1818), pp. 229-34; Eighth Report (1819), p. 17; Seventeenth Report (1828), p. 66; Scott, *History of Spitalfields*, p. 30.

[115] G.L.C.R.O., P93/CTC1/163, 'Counterpart Lease of a Piece of Ground and Sch. rooms in Quaker St Spitalfields (27 May 1819)'; Wilson, *The National Schools* . . ., list of officers on fly-leaf. According to Scott, Joseph Wilson 'founded and supported' the school (*History of Spitalfields*, p. 31).

[116] Charles Grant, a member of the Clapham Sect, was Chairman of the Court of Directors of the East India Company in 1815-16 and remained, in the words of his latest biographer, 'spokesman for the Company's rule' until his death in 1823 (A. T. Embree, *Charles Grant and British Rule in India* (London, 1962), p. 261ff.).

[117] Ninth Annual Report of the National Society (London, 1820), pp. 193-6. This is noticeable in the references to the Bible, to Jesus Christ, to salvation, to vice and to the importance of the Sabbath, all familiar aspects of Evangelical theology.

[118] P. P. 1835 VII, Education, pp. 30-1.

[119] Wilderspin, *Infant Poor* (1823), *passim*.

[120] Wilderspin Papers, Elizabeth Hinton to Wilderspin, 28 February 1843. I am grateful to Dr F.A. Young, Wilderspin's great-great grandson, for allowing me access to this source.

[121] Fifteenth Report of the British and Foreign School Society (London, 1820), p. 113.

[122] Ibid., p. 112.

[123] Ibid., pp. 35-6, 111.

[124] Ibid., p. 112; Nineteenth Report (London, 1824), p. 56.

[125] P. P. 1835 VII, Education, p. 75.

[126] Report of Spicer Street School Committee (1816), p. 5.

[127] [W. Allen] *A Defence of the British and Foreign School Society* (London, 1821), p. 13.

[128] Nineteenth Report of the B.F.S.S. (1824), p. 56.

[129] Wilson, *The National Schools* . . ., pp. 32-3.

[130] G.J. Schochet, 'Patriarchalism, politics and mass attitudes in Stuart England', *Historical Journal*, Vol. XII, No. 3 (1969), pp. 413-41.

[131] The catechism is reproduced in P. Schaff, *The Creeds of Christendom* (New York, 3 vols., 1919), III, pp. 517-22.

[132] The British schools and Quaker Street Infant School were the only ones which did not teach the catechism in one form or another.

[133] Recent research suggests that children, even without overt teaching, tend to form a conception of a symbolic figure as a vaguely recognized form of external authority in society. Cf. F.I. Greenstein *et al.*, 'Queen and Prime Minister – the child's eye-view', *New Society*, Vol. 14, No. 369 (23 Oct. 1969); D. Easton and J. Dennis, 'The child's image of government', in J. Dennis (ed.), *Socialization to Politics* (New York, 1973), pp. 59-81.

[134] Rev. C. Barton, cited in A. Bell, *The Madras School or Elements of Tuition* (London, 1808), pp. 270-2.

[135] Ninth Report of National Society (1820), p. 194.

[136] *Philanthropist*, Vol. II, 1812, p. 183.

[137] Report of the Spitalfields Association, in *The Speech of Thomas Fowell Buxton Esq . . . on the Subject of Distresss in Spitalfields* (London, 1816), p. 19.

[138] Figures derived from Twelfth Report of the Spitalfields Benevolent Society (London, 1827), p. 11.

[139] Scott, *History of Spitalfields*, p. 41.

[140] Shoreditch, Norton Folgate and Old Artillery Ground Bible Association Minute Book, Committee Minutes, 19 December 1815.

[141] British and Foreign Bible Society, Home Corres. Inwards, D. Ruell *et al.* to Committee, 4 July 1818.

[142] This figure is calculated on the assumption that the proportion of children in Spitalfields between 6-14 years was the same as that of the Tower Division, i.e. 16 per cent, and that 'the poor' constituted 70 per cent of the total population. On this basis, the number of poor children between 6-14 years in Spitalfields in 1821 was 8,378. The margin of error is obvious, but the figures are a rough guide to the magnitudes involved. The statistics are taken from *Abstract of the Answers and Returns* (1822) of the 1821 Census, pp. 142, 196-7.

[143] E.g., Report of the Soup Society (1811-12), p. 12ff; Spitalfields Benevolent Society Report (1812), p. 22ff.

[144] P. P. 1828 IV, Poor Laws, p. 33.

[145] P. P. 1818 IX, Ribbon Weavers, p. 44; cf. P. P. 1817 VI Poor Laws, p. 39.

[146] H. of L. Sessional Papers 1823 XIII, Minutes of Evidence Taken Before the Lords Committee on the Silk Manufacturers' Bill, pp. 27-8.

[147] P. P. 1816 IV, Education of Lower Orders, p. 208. Hale asserted that the influence of Sunday schools was an antidote to Luddism in Spitalfields (P. P. 1814-15 III, Mendicity, p. 79).

[148] Thirteenth Report of the British and Foreign Bible Society (London, 1817), pp. 308-9.

[149] *Christian Observer*, Vol. XV, No. 11, November 1816, p. 762.

[150] P. P. 1818 IV, Select Committee on the Education of the Lower Orders, Second Report, p. 64; Wilderspin, *Infant Education* (1825), p. 168.

[151] F. Hill, *National Education; Its Present State and Prospects* (London 1836), p. 194.

[152] P. P. 1840 XXIII, Hand-Loom Weavers, p. 245.

[153] W. Hale, *An Appeal to the Public, in Defence of the Spitalfields Act* (London, 1822), pp. 15-16; P. P. 1834 X, Report from Select Committee on Hand-Loom Weavers Petitions, p. 320.

[154] Parl. Deb., N.S., Vol. IX, 16 June 1923, 987.

[155] Hammonds, *Skilled Labourer*, p. 216.

[156] For Spitalfields trade unionism, cf. S. Sholl, *A Short Historical Account of the Silk Manufacture in England* (London, 1811), pp.4-11; P. P. 1818 IX, Ribbon Weavers, pp. 55-9, 194-6. For the controversy between masters and journeyman over the Spitalfields Acts, cf. *Letters . . . Tending to Injure the Journeymen Silk Weavers . . . also, the*

Answers by the Journeymen (London, 1818); *Observations on the Ruinous Tendency of the Spitalfields Act* (London, 3rd ed., 1822).
[157] *Philanthropist*, Vol. II, 1812, p. 189.
[158] B.F.B.S., Thirteenth Report, p. 303.
[159] P. P. 1840 XXIII, Hand-Loom Weavers, p. 244.
[160] *Evidence . . . as to the Operation of Voluntary Charities* (1833; reprinted 1837), pp. 48-9; P. P. 1835 VII, Education, pp. 11-12.
[161] *Considerations on Select Vestries* (London, 1828), pp. 5-7, 29-30.
[162] Cf. Chapter 2.
[163] P. P. 1816 IV, Education of Lower Orders, p. 12.
[164] The percentages are approximate, as attendance figures fluctuated.
[165] P. P. 1816 IV, Education of Lower Orders, pp. 12, 14.
[166] In the 1830s the 'indifference' of East London parents towards the education of their children was said to have arisen largely from 'the hopelessness of being able to obtain it' (P. P. 1838 VII, Report from the Select Committee on Education of the Poorer Classes, p. 99).
[167] Child labour, particularly in the weaving industry, kept many children from school (P. P. 1816 IV, Education of Lower Orders, p. 190). Attendance at fairs usually took precedence over attendance at school (Wilderspin, *Infant Poor* (1823), p. 116).
[168] Wilderspin recalled this incident in a speech at Liverpool many years later (*Albion* (Liverpool), 5 September 1836); cf. also Place's belief that London parents were suspicious of the new schools because children 'play and learn nothing' (P. P. 1816 IV, Education of Lower Orders, p. 268).
[169] Wilderspin, *Infant Poor* (1823), pp. 106-7.
[170] P. P. 1840 XXIII, Hand-Loom Weavers, p. 249. Cf. also *A Course of Three Lectures . . . Occasioned by the Formation of Spitalfields Mechanics' Institute* (London, 1825), *passim*.
[171] P. P. 1817 VII, Police in Metropolis, p. 108.
[172] P. P. 1835 VII, Education, p. 18; Wilderspin, to do him justice, fairly soon had the local population on his side.
[173] *Albion*, 5 September 1836.
[174] [H. Brougham] 'Early moral education', *Edinburgh Review*, Vol. XXXVIII, No. 76 (May 1823), p. 441.
[175] This evidence was supplied by H. Althans, an inspector for the British and Foreign School Society, and refers to the late 1830s. In three East London parishes he investigated, Althans estimated that these schools were educating 5,000 children, as against 3,000 in public day schools (P. P. 1838 VII, Education, p. 134).
[176] Ibid., p. 97.
[177] P. P. 1835 XLII, Education Inquiry, pp. 554-8.
[178] Wilderspin, *Infant Education* (1825), pp. 80, 242, 277; P. P. 1835 VII, Education, p. 23; P. P. 1818 IX, Digest of Parochial Returns, p. 543.
[179] P. P. 1838 VII, Education, pp. 135-8.
[180] Wilderspin, *Infant Education* (1825), p. 126.
[181] P. P. 1840 XXIV, Hand-Loom Weavers, pp. 23-4.

Chapter 2:

Patterns of attendance and their social significance: Mitcham National School 1830-39

Beryl Madoc-Jones

> If I have 100 children upon the books, I shall not have 30 in regular attendance; but one third of them will come two or three days in a week, and then their parents had some little job or other by which they can earn 6*d*. or 1*s*., and they they will come again after a few days, and the children in the meantime forget a good deal of what they have learned.
>
> William Allen[1]

Amongst the obstacles which vexed those participating in the voluntary effort to provide elementary education for the lower classes was the problem of attendance. Throughout that part of the nineteenth century when the provision of such schooling remained essentially a voluntary activity, and when working-class commitment to the benefits so offered was also non-obligatory, regular and sustained attendance was consistently acknowledged to be one of the besetting organizational difficulties.

In order to estimate the scale of the problem two major questions have been raised by educational historians: first, the number and proportion of lower-class children who made contact with the various schools at their disposal through both working-class and middle-class initiative, and, second, the extent of time which these children typically spent at school. It is the intention in this paper to focus on the latter question and to examine the social implications arising from this manifestation of working-class behaviour.

Attempts to establish with any precision the average length of stay in school of lower-class children in the first half of the nineteenth century are fraught with difficulty.[2] Absence of statutory control of register-keeping in a voluntary system must have impeded the regularization of such practices. This kind of record-keeping is essentially a bureaucratic activity which would have had little priority for the schoolmaster or mistress in the relatively haphazard structure of an elementary school of the period. The problem is further aggravated by the apparent 'folk-lore' of some mistresses that it was 'unlucky' to count one's pupils.[3]

Nevertheless the question of attendance was one of considerable importance to the members of the series of Select Committees seeking to investigate the state of education between 1816 and 1838. The evidence at their disposal falls into two main categories: on the one hand they dealt with estimates of recruitment and attendance offered by returns of organizations such as the National Society, statistical societies and returns of government inquiries; on the other hand they amassed the individual opinions of well-known citizens with extensive experience of a local school (or schools). Although the later Committees of the thirties had a national mandate, the bulk of the information on length of stay related to the metropolis. Thus no national estimate of average length of attendance is available. The estimate which was most general in its frame of reference was that based on the National Society's Report for 1834. The average rate of individual attendance for children at thirty schools which returned adequate information was reported to be 3 years 3 months. (All the schools were in the London area.)[4]

The most extensive estimate of the national trend was that based on the 1851 Census Report on education when it was estimated that the average length of a working-class child's school life was about four years.[5] Professor West has come to the conclusion that 'the average school life in those days was around five years' – referring to the 1850s. He goes on to suggest that 'typically a child would spend, say, one year in a dame school, and four in a common school'.[6] It is debatable whether such national generalizations are meaningful, given the problems inherent in early nineteenth-century statistics. The more important point to make in the context of this study is that this kind of average figure may mask a large variation in habits of attendance between and within regions. To examine and account for the nature of such variation is an essential undertaking if the difficulties encountered in the process of institutionalizing working-class education are fully to be appreciated.

The second category of evidence, referred to earlier, lends substance to the point that there was considerable variation in expectations of attendance between schools. The Rev. Basil Woodd, in speaking of a day school associated with Bentinck Chapel, Mary-le-bone, claimed that the

average length of stay was three years.[7] However, a school in Blooms-
bury was reported to have received 774 children between 1813 and 1816
with never more than 200 attending, which suggests a much more rapid
turnover.[8] In 1834 Henry Dunn, secretary of the British and Foreign
School Society, referring to the central school at the Borough Road,
suggested that the average attendance of pupils was one year, but
pointed out at the same time that there was considerable variation within
the school. The first (and largest) class was said to pass through the
school in a few weeks or months; the second class remained for a period
of one to one and a half years; while the third (and smallest) class was
in school for three years or more.[9] Again John Thomas Crossley, master
of the Borough Road School, thought that the average length of stay for
children who did not become monitors was twelve months.[10] The findings of the Select Committee in 1838 provide no evidence to suggest
that there was any radical change in the situation from previous years.
Mr Dunn certainly had no grounds for changing his view and made the
following comment to reinforce previous impressions:

> In the Borough Road School, there were always in attendance from
> 500–600 children; and yet, that number of children come in and
> out every year, arising from the shifting of population or from the
> carelessness of the parents.[11]

Thus the range of variation in length of stay in schools under discussion
appeared to cover a period of months to one of more than three years.

Caution is also timely in assessing the reliability of individual opinion
and impressions. Zealous promotors of lower-class education were
prone to exaggerate the activities of their schools. On the other hand,
others motivated by a desire to convince politicians of the urgent need
to rationalize and extend educational facilities may have tended to
under-estimate educational accounts of the scope of school provision.[12]
However, two general comments on the reality of the situation can be
made with confidence. First, the length of time spent at school was always
very short judged by present-day expectations, and, second, there was
probably no significant change in the situation before 1870 and the
gradual introduction of compulsion with regard to the regulating of
attendance.[13]

A third source of information contributes to the mapping out of
patterns of attendance — case studies of the reality of the situation in
individual schools. Where such information comes to light an additional
perspective is provided, rounding out or modifying the general impres-

sions available from other sources, and may serve as one kind of check on their validity. Unfortunately, adequate records of individual schools at this early date are rare. Few are known to have survived. Indeed it is questionable, for reasons already discussed, whether many schools kept the kind of records necessary for the purpose of the present analysis. However, increasing interest currently demonstrated in the social aspects of early elementary education leads to the tapping of this kind of source, in the hope of accumulating a body of data on individual schools.[14] The direction of this study now turns to an investigation of one school for which appropriate records were kept and have survived.

The school in question is the Mitcham National School which opened its doors to boys and girls in 1813. The social structure of the parish is of interest since it provides an example of a population undergoing the transition from a primarily rural economy to an industrial structure. Through the period under examination there existed a juxtaposition of agrarian and industrial organization, so that the social context of the parish must have been a fusion of long-established rural custom and the demands of industrialization. In 1801 there was a population of 3,466 which rose by 1821 to 4,453. At this time 296 households were occupied in agriculture and 460 in trade handicraft and manufacture. The major opportunities for employment were gardening – the commercial growing of lavender, camomile and peppermint, – and employment at the cotton and silk factories established along the banks of the River Wandle. The area was particularly noted as a centre for bleaching, dyeing and calico printing.[15] The following analysis is based on records of the school, contained in Minutes of the Monthly Meetings of the School Committee.[16]

From the outset, the committee was concerned with the matter of attendance. The practice of recording the names and ages of children in the Minutes, giving the month in which they were admitted, was established immediately and continued throughout the period under discussion. Similarly, each month, the names of those pupils withdrawing were noted. Thus it is possible to calculate the length of stay in months for the children recorded. One of the frustrations of this kind of historical research is the degree of consistency of the record-keeping. It is dependent on the vagaries of those responsible for such routine behaviour. Inevitably there are gaps, and months in which the desired information becomes sparse. However, the years 1830–9 were ones in which the records were maintained with commendable care and consistency. In addition to data on length of stay and ages of children, parental occupation was also recorded. For these reasons, it has been decided to concentrate on analysing trends in this ten-year period.

The school population recorded in these years was 690 pupils: 400 boys and 290 girls. 604 of these entries have dates for both enrolment and withdrawal and therefore could be utilized as a basis for calculating attendance patterns. This amounts to 87.5 per cent of the known school population for the ten years considered.

The first question to be raised is the average length of stay of pupils. Table 1 indicates that the mean length of time in which the pupils remained on the school records was 34.5 months. An initial comment would be that this school achieved better average attendance rates than many schools of the time. It is of further interest to note that the average length of stay of girls was considerably higher than that of boys. This can be accounted for partly by the relationship between work and school, discussion of which will be deferred until later.

Table 1 *Average length of stay of pupils in months**

	Mean
Boys (No = 339)	31.0
Girls (No = 265)	38.9
All pupils (No = 604)	34.5

*Tests of statistical significance were not carried out since there was not a random sample. The degree of variance was large, the standard deviation being 24.4, 28.4, and 26.5 respectively. Furthermore the distribution was not normal but almost rectangular.

Some care is necessary in assessing the importance of this average figure. It must be remembered that the data available referred only to the length of time the children were recorded as pupils of the school and not to the actual time spent in school. A major problem in the interpretation of an arithmetic mean is that it is sensitive to the relevant spread of scores. Table 2 demonstrates that there was a very wide distribution of lengths of stay. The most significant trend emerging would appear to be that within the school population there was a very wide variation in the length of time the children attended. While it is true that the majority (61 per cent) did not stay in school for more than three years, a very substantial minority were on the books for a considerably longer period of time. The difference in average length of attendance between boys and girls has already been noted. Perhaps of more interest is the finding that a much higher proportion of girls remained at school for a long period, that is over five years. In fact, the figure of 25 per cent in the case of girls who were at school for more than five years is remarkably high.

Table 2 *Frequency distribution of pupils' length of stay*

Length of stay in months	Boys		Girls		All pupils	
	N	%	N	%	N	%
1 – 12	108	32	62	23	170	28
13 – 24	61	18	46	17	107	18
25 – 36	47	14	36	15	83	15
37 – 48	30	9	33	12	63	10
49 – 60	46	13	21	8	67	11
61 and over	47	14	67	25	114	19
Total	339	100	265	100	604	101*

*This percentage is due to rounding.

It was important that the school was able to attract numbers of this magnitude to continue at school. The organization and success of the monitorial system hinged on the ability of the school to recruit experienced pupils as monitors and assistant teachers,[17] pupils not only with a minimum acquirement of educational skills, but also familiar with the social climate and expectations of the school. One of the difficulties which could hinder masters and mistresses in the operation of their schools was encountered when parents were reluctant to permit their children to continue in attendance once they had mastered the rudimentary skills of reading and writing. At the very moment when the more able children were necessary for the school to be an ongoing concern, parents were inclined to withdraw them. At the British Girls' School in York it was the custom for members of the school committees to call on parents of promising older pupils to persuade them to allow their daughters to remain at school in the capacity of assistant teachers, with a small salary.[18] Presumably, one of the reasons for weekly payments to monitors for carrying out the responsibilities of their roles was a similar inducement to retain them and compensation for forgoing earnings to be won outside school.

One of the most important sources of information necessary in order to understand working-class attitudes towards schooling is to know under what conditions children were withdrawn from school. Table 3 classifies the reasons recorded for cessation of schooling. By far the most important reason recorded is entry into work. Interesting differences are apparent between boys and girls. Approximately twice as many boys as girls were withdrawn from school in order to enter employment (treating service and work as one employment category). Needless to say, it is hardly surprising that girls rather than boys should be kept at home to help with the exigencies of domestic life. It is impossible to know anything of the future careers of the substantial number of children in the unspecified category. But it is not an unreasonable speculation that many of them would also be heading for work or be occupied at home.

Table 3 *Frequency distribution of pupils' reasons for leaving school*

Reasons for leaving	Boys		Girls		All pupils	
	N	%	N	%	N	%
Work	197	57	26	10	217	36
Service	3	1	45	17	48	8
Helping at home and child minding	3	1	27	10	30	5
Left parish	61	18	39	15	100	17
Illness and death	12	3	3	1	15	3
Workhouse	6	2	4	1.5	7	1
Another school	–	–	7	2.5	7	1
Dismissed*	4	1	20	7.5	24	4
Unspecified	59	17	94	35.5	153	25
Total	339	100	265	100	604	101†

*Usual reasons were either bad behaviour or very poor attendance.
†Percentage due to rounding.

Perhaps of most interest is the number of children whose schooling was interrupted by their families' moving. 17 per cent of the children were known to have been withdrawn for this reason. Another 3 per cent withdrew in order to attend other schools or to be admitted to the workhouse. Thus 20 per cent of the pupils were likely to have acquired additional schooling elsewhere after entering this particular school. From this point of view, the figures available are a minimum rather than a maximum estimate of the length of the experience of schooling of the children.

The mobility of a sizeable section of the school population is pertinent also to the discussion of the significance of the average rate of attendance given earlier. For this purpose, rates of length of stay have been cross-tabulated with the reasons recorded for leaving school. From Table 4 it is quite clear that seventy-one children who left the parish account for a considerable proportion of those whose time at school

Table 4 *Length of stay by reasons recorded for leaving*

Length of stay in months	Work		Service		At home		Child minding		Left parish		Illness/ death		Work- house		Other school		Dismissed		Un- specified		Total
	B	G*	B	G	B	G	B	G	B	G	B	G	B	G	B	G	B	G	B	G	All pupils
1 – 6	17	1	–	2	–	–	–	–	22	8	3	–	1	–	–	–	2	2	22	17	97
7 – 12	21	8	–	1	–	1	–	1	11	2	2	–	–	1	–	–	1	3	6	14	72
13 – 24	31	–	–	3	1	1	1	4	14	14	1	1	2	–	–	2	–	3	11	18	107
25 – 36	26	1	–	1	1	2	–	4	5	5	2	–	–	–	–	1	1	2	12	20	83
37 – 48	21	4	–	2	–	1	–	1	3	5	2	–	1	3	–	2	–	6	4	9	64
49 – 60	40	2	3	7	–	2	–	2	2	2	–	–	1	–	–	1	–	2	3	4	70
61 and over	35	10	1	29	–	3	–	5	4	3	2	2	1	–	–	1	–	2	1	12	111
Total	191	26	4	45	2	9	1	17	61	39	12	3	6	4	–	7	4	20	59	94	604

*Boys and girls

was only two years or less. In effect, many of the very low scores on attendance were among this group of mobile children. This suggests that if the category of movers had been omitted, the calculation of the average mean attendance would have been considerably higher. The lower average for boys is accounted for not only by the high proportion of girls who were at school for a long time but also by the large number of boys who left the parish after short stays in the school.

Another point emerging from Table 4 relates to girls entering service. This was in fact their most likely future prospect (on this evidence). In this locality, it would appear that a long period in school was the path to a position in service. It is an interesting phenomenon, since one of the questions which had worried the Select Committee of 1816 was the contention that an increase in lower-class education and the benefits in its wake would tend to disrupt the natural order or social structure of society by encouraging amongst the working classes social aspirations inappropriate to their station in life. For example, the Rev. John Campbell, familiar with a British day school at Kingsland, was asked whether education would make 'females less inclined to enter upon services', to which he responded:

> No; though there are instances of females who must have been servants but for the school; by their acquiring additional knowledge of needlework, they have been able to commence milliners and mantua makers for themselves; there are various instances in which they would have been servants, had they not had this education at school.[19]

The demand for milliners and mantua makers must at all times have been limited in any locality! At least as far as Mitcham was concerned two decades later, there was little fear that 'educated' working-class girls would reject opportunities in service as not worthy of their newly acquired educational status. On the contrary, it would seem that it facilitated entry into this kind of work. There is no knowledge available of the nature of service which the majority entered but it is surmised that the ladies of wealthy domestic establishments in the neighbourhood would be interested in girls recommended by the school. Since needlework was taught, many of the girls must, after five or six years, have acquired considerable accomplishment and been well equipped to rise to the more superior positions in large households.[20] Also, a reasonable degree of literacy and numeracy would have its attractions for lady employers and would open up for the girls future prospects of promotion to house-keeping status and the higher positions in the social hierarchy of large establishments. In addition, with regard to prolonged schooling, it is possible that the socializing influences of internalizing the values promulgated by a school under the auspices of denominational societies would make these girls attractive to their prospective employers and also facilitate their acclimatization to a middle- or upper-class household. Furthermore, it is likely that members of the committee would recommend their 'successes' — girls who had remained at school and gone through the classes — for domestic positions with their own acquaintances and friends, in order to establish and maintain a reputation for the school, thereby safeguarding continuing subscriptions. Of course, it would only be the older girls who would be eligible for service. It is also necessary to remember that other kinds of employment are likely to have been more limited for girls than for boys.

Another aspect of children's attendance at school is the age thought to be appropriate for their instruction. The rules of the school stated that children should be admitted at the age of six and ought not to remain in school after the age of fourteen. Some laxity was allowed in practice and a small number of pupils was admitted at the age of five. Table 5 indicates the age structure of children on entry into school. It is seen that around half came into school at six years of age. For the remainder, it is not possible to know how many of them were embarking on their first acquaintance with school and what proportion had attended other schools previously. In spite of the range of dame schools and others organized amongst the working classes, it is likely that many of those between seven and ten years of age were entering school for the first time. It is customary in the twentieth century to take for granted the notion that the organization of schools should be based on principles of age-specificness. However, monitorial schools of the first decades of the nineteenth century did not exhibit the same degree of self-conscious treatment of age as a social category. Children were accepted at schools other than infant school at five years and on occasion remained until they were fifteen. In the Mitcham School, two children were admitted in this period whose parents were honest enough to admit they were only four years of age. In an era before the compulsory registration of birth (this legal innovation of the thirties was insignificant in its effects on enrolment before 1840), parents could without difficulty enrol children of large physical stature who had not arrived at the minimum age required by the school. A telling comment on the absence of a contemporary preoccupation with age was made by the Rector of St Clement-Danes in speaking of his Sunday school and

Table 5 *Frequency distribution of pupils' age at entry*

Age in years	Boys N	Boys %	Girls N	Girls %	All pupils N	All pupils %
5	15	4	7	3	22	4
6	175	52	124	46	299	49
7	52	15	46	17.5	98	16
8	47	14	42	16	89	15
9	19	6	21	8	40	7
10 and over	31	9	25	9.5	56	9
Total	339	100	265	100	604	100

procedures of recruitment: 'We take them as soon as even the boys have got breeches, – we do not consult their age but their size.'[21]

The organization of school classes was certainly not age-specific. Children were allocated to groups on the basis of their proficiency or lack of it, on first becoming a pupil of the school.

A further indication of the lack of concern or preoccupation with age is apparent from examining the relationship between age at entry and length of stay in school. Table 6 summarizes this data. It indicates a wide distribution of length of stay across age categories. This suggests that age would not be a particularly significant factor in determining the likely length of a child's passage through school. Presumably, when a child had reached the minimum level of accomplishment in the three Rs thought desirable by the parents, then the time had arrived for the termination of schooling, regardless of the child's age.

Other evidence of the lack of significance attached to age as a category of social identity comes from the apparent tendency, in the pattern

Table 6 *Length of stay by age at entry*

Length of stay in months	Age of entry (in years) 5 B	5 G*	6 B	6 G	7 B	7 G	8 B	8 G	9 B	9 G	10 B	10 G	Total (all pupils)
1 – 6	–	–	24	6	9	4	12	12	5	2	17	7	98
7 – 12	–	1	14	9	5	5	11	5	5	5	6	6	72
13 – 24	1	–	26	16	14	12	13	5	4	7	3	6	107
25 – 36	4	–	25	14	8	3	3	10	2	6	5	3	83
37 – 48	2	–	15	19	7	8	4	4	2	–	–	2	63
49 – 66	3	2	36	8	5	4	1	5	1	1	–	1	67
61 and over	5	4	35	52	4	10	3	1	–	–	–	–	114
Total	15	7	175	114	52	46	47	52	19	21	31	25	604

of enrolments and withdrawals, for parents to send their children to school in batches. Brothers and sisters of varying ages tended to arrive simultaneously, and correspondingly to be taken out of school at the same time. This leads into a discussion of other difficulties accounting for the variation in observed lengths of stay.

One of the difficulties in establishing regular attendance was linked with fluctuations in the economic situation of the locality and, correspondingly, of individual family fortunes. For instance the committee had observed in its report of 11 May 1818, that 'the number of children attending to receive instruction is somewhat diminished and the fluctuation may probably be expected in a manufacturing district'. The relationship between the industrial situation and attendance was not straightforward. In time of depression, some families unable to pay the weekly fees, may have felt compelled to withdraw children. At the same time, a depressed state of the 'manufactories' might well have mitigated against a tendency for other parents to withdraw their children, since the prospects of finding employment for them would have been unfavourable. Alternatively, in good times, some parents would have been tempted to withdraw their children when their chance of earning wages to contribute to the family budget was high, while other parents with a different level of commitment to education would have found it easier in such a situation to make the effort to keep their children at school.

One of the most fascinating insights into the pattern of schooling emerging from the study of the Mitcham documents is the link between school and work evident in the incidence of children having interrupted school careers. It was not uncommon for children to leave the school only to return at a later date. 107 pupils (approximately 17 per cent of the school population) were known to have returned to school. Table 7 indicates both the incidence of the phenomenon and the range of intervals of time between leaving and re-entering school. The majority who returned to school did so within a period of twelve months, but others enjoyed a gap of two to three years, while three girls were recorded as returning to school after an interval of more than four years.

This pattern of school behaviour must be explained partly in terms of attitudes to school and work. Girls were much more likely than boys to return to school. This is probably because many girls were withdrawn for domestic reasons, and would be more likely to return to school when the urgency of need for their help lessened. Some boys left one month expecting to go to work, only to come back to school a month

Table 7 *Number of pupils and frequency of re-entry by intervals of time between each withdrawal in months*

No of pupils*	Intervals of time in months					
	1–6	7–12	13–18	19–24	25–36	37 and over
First re-entry						
Boys	23	11	4	5	7	3
Girls	26	9	10	1	2	6
Second re-entry						
Boys	3	–	1	–	1	
Girls	3	2	2	1		
Third re-entry						
Boys	1					
Girls	2	1				

*The total number of pupils for whom there is information on their withdrawal and re-entry is 53 boys and 54 girls. For a further 20 pupils reference is made in the Minutes to their re-entry but no record has been made of their previous departure. However, it suggests that the information in this table is an underestimate of the tendency of children to return to school.

or two later. This suggests a working-class orientation that if work was not available, then school was a second alternative where children would be safely occupied. There would appear to be no assumptions necessarily held that schooling was a social experience which was a prerequisite to work. Although the majority of children began school at six-years old, this may be accounted for in terms of lack of suitable work available for the numbers of such young children in the area. Although there were factories, there could not have been anything like the demand for child labour known in the textile districts of the North. Also statutory control of child labour was beginning to affect the cotton mills, at least, in the area. Once children were past the stage of early childhood, either the work-world or the school were appropriate places or locations where parents who did not want their children on the streets could have them supervised. There is no evidence in this study that the order in which children were introduced to these two sets of socializing experiences was of any significance. One of the questions raised in the nineteenth-century debate over the desirability of education and the factory child was the issue of the extent to which the social nature of schooling prepared them for the discipline (and monotony?) of factory employment. Some employers clearly thought so. However it may well be that the experience of work also socialized children into an acceptance and toleration of the routine of school.

Table 8 *Parental occupation by pupils' length of stay in months*

Occupation	1–6 B	1–6 G*	7–12 B	7–12 G	13–24 B	13–24 G	25–36 B	25–36 G	37–48 B	37–48 G	49–60 B	49–60 G	61 and over B	61 and over G
Labourer	16	12	13	11	18	23	16	14	9	15	20	15	15	31
Gardener	2	1	1	2	5	3	3	3	6	1	2	–	2	8
Carpenter	3	–	3	3	1	–	1	3	–	–	1	1	6	9
Printer	7	5	8	3	5	3	1	1	2	–	7	–	4	5
Shoemaker	4	–	–	3	2	–	1	2	1	1	1	1	2	2
Tailor	3	–	3	2	3	1	–	1	–	–	–	1	1	–
Dealer (coal and tea)	3	1	–	–	1	–	–	–	–	1	–	1	–	2
Bricklayer/maker	1	1	–	1	–	2	3	2	–	2	3	1	5	4
Shopkeeper	1	–	–	–	1	–	4	1	1	–	1	–	–	1
Smith and wheelwright	1	–	–	1	1	–	–	1	–	–	2	–	1	–
Sawyer and cutter	1	1	1	–	1	–	1	–	–	–	–	–	–	–
Bleacher and dyer	1	–	–	–	–	–	2	–	–	–	–	–	–	–
Coachman, carman, carrier, carter†	2	1	–	–	2	2	1	1	3	–	4	–	–	1
Skinner and leather dresser	2	3	–	–	2	–	1	1	–	2	–	–	–	–

Cowman and milkman	—	—	—	—	—	—	—	—	1	—
Engraver and jeweller	1	1	—	1	1	—	1	—	—	—
Engineer	1	—	—	1	—	1	—	—	—	3
Watchman	2	2	—	2	1	1	1	—	1	—
Ostler	1	1	—	1	—	1	—	1	—	1
Beadle, bailiff, debt collector	1	—	1	—	1	1	—	—	—	1
Ratcatcher	—	—	—	—	1	1	1	—	—	—
Miller and baker	2	—	1	2	1	2	2	—	4	—
Hairdresser, sweep	1	—	1	—	—	—	—	—	—	—
Foreman	1	—	1	—	—	—	—	—	—	—
Sailmaker	2	—	—	—	—	—	—	—	—	—
Widow	5	2	5	7	2	1	2	6	2	3
Master/drawing master	2	1	1	—	1	—	—	—	—	—
Publican/brewer	2	1	1	1	1	—	1	—	—	3

* Boys and girls.

† Where occupations are grouped it simply denotes one parent only represented the occupation. It must be remembered that the figures relate to pupils, not parents.

One last question to be investigated on the pattern of attendance (length of stay) relates to the social composition of the pupils of the school. During the ten-year period under scrutiny, parental occupation was recorded for the majority of pupils entering the school. Table 8 presents a summary of the occupational description of the parents, cross-tabulated with the length of stay of their offspring. There are difficulties in placing too much emphasis on this information. A basic problem concerns the way in which the information on parents was arrived at. Little clue is given in the Minutes. However, it was the responsibility of the master to handle applications; parents who wanted their children admitted were expected to turn up at the schoolhouse on Monday morning to request their children's enrolment. It is assumed that the main source of the description of parental occupation was obtained from the mothers, or simply recorded on the master's 'common knowledge' of the people in the parish. Taking into consideration the unreliability of women's accounts of their husband's work and the well-known difficulties of making twentieth-century sense of the social significance of the great range of occupational labels of the nineteenth century, no attempt has been made to group the occupations arising here in any order conferring social status.

At the same time it is important to note that a wide range of occupations was represented and in this sense a cross-section of the community supported the school. The largest category was that of labourers. However, it is an undifferentiated group. It is unknown what proportion was agricultural and which was industrial. Neither can they be identified in terms of level of skill or economic status. The main point that emerges from this table is that on the basis of the limited evidence, no obvious relationship is evident between a parent's occupation and a child's length of stay. For all occupations in which there is more than a handful of children associated, the variation in terms of length of stay is wide. It would be rash to assume that the groups which might reasonably be expected to be more skilled, such as tailors and shoemakers, were necessarily representative of the more prosperous sections of the working class without more knowledge of each case. The essential point that can be made is that children from homes where fathers, on the surface evidence, were engaged in reasonably skilled occupations were no more likely than any other group of children to stay at school for a prolonged period.

So far, the main trend analysed has been the length of the school career. Any conclusions reached must be tempered by the question of

regularity of daily attendance. Far less is known about this perspective
of the issue of attendance, but it was one which worried and perplexed
the committee. Constant exhortations appear in the Minutes referring
to the over-riding importance of establishing regular attendance patterns.
It was generally recognized that the benefits accruing from school
would be seriously undermined if regular attendance did not become
the norm. It was a common practice in this school and others on the
Bell and Lancasterian Systems to offer prizes for regular attendance. In
the early days of the school the committee, at their meeting in November 1813, ordered the following letter to be printed and dispersed in
the parish:

> The Committee for conducting the schools in this parish, are sorry
> to observe the frequent complaints of the great irregularity in the
> attendance of the children, especially on Sunday, more particularly
> in the afternoon of that day, and they call on the parents to enforce
> a regular attendance, for unless order is observed in that respect, it
> is vain to hope for any permanent good effects from instruction
> which can only be partially administered.

The only kind of numerical information to throw light on this
problem is the recording of average monthly attendance. Once more
these figures need to be treated with caution. In addition to the kind of
problems previously discussed, there is the difficulty that a count for
the purposes of providing information to the committee seemed to have
taken place at the same time, the end of the month and on Fridays. It is
possible that attendance on these days may have been rather higher
than general attendance. After all, the master and mistress would
probably take all steps possible to ensure a good turn-out for these
occasions. It was also the practice on Friday at this school for clothes
to be distributed to be taken home to wear to church on Sunday (only
to be returned on the Monday!). The day on which attendance was
counted and recorded was also the day when the visitor appointed for
the month from the committee made his inspection. This could have
had two effects. It may have encouraged higher attendance, but at least
the figures subsequently presented to the committee were not entirely
dependent on the competence and integrity of the master. Table 9
gives the monthly attendance for three years in the period 1830–9.
These years were selected because they were the only ones which did
not have gaps in the data. Once more erratic behaviour is evident, attendance ranging from almost 100 per cent (girls in January 1833) to

Table 9   *Record of monthly attendance for years 1832, 1833 and 1835*

Months* and Nos. on roll, present and absent	1832		1833		1835	
	Boys	Girls	Boys	Girls	Boys	Girls
January						
Present	91	82	92	92	112	99
Absent	15	17	14	7	20	112
February						
Present	79	76	95	90	112	86
Absent	27	16	12	14	20	31
March						
Present	95	71	96	78	107	90
Absent	20	21	12	27	26	30
April						
Present	96	76	86	70	107	84
Absent	21	16	18	33	26	36
May						
Present	85	61	86	60	111	96
Absent	31	33	19	39	19	23
June						
Present	83	58	85	60	99	86
Absent	35	40	16	36	29	36
July						
Present	89	69	87	67	98	96
Absent	28	27	11	25	32	22
September						
Present	56	45	51	39	85	78
Absent	57	46	48	47	38	40
October						
Present	73	65	84	74	99	84
Absent	35	26	18	14	22	31
November						
Present	81	79	85	70	95	96
Absent	18	14	16	20	26	23
December						
Present	83	90	91	82	103	93
Absent	18	7	7	11	21	26

*August was not recorded as it was the main holiday month.

less than 50 per cent (boys and girls September 1832). On the whole it would seem that this school was relatively successful in maintaining an average attendance of between two-thirds to three-quarters of the children enrolled. The fluctuation between months must have been one of the most serious organizational problems for schools. It has already been noted that attendance was geared to the fortunes of local industry. In this area whose economy was also agricultural, attendance was controlled to some extent by seasonal fluctuation in the demand for labour. September was a notoriously bad month for attendance. Children were temporarily taken out of school for camomile picking.

Frequent mention was made of the influence of weather on attendance. In months of heavy rainfall, attendance would drop. This must be connected with the problem of inadequate clothing, and footwear in particular. It must be remembered that many children walked long distances to school. In wet weather, even for those lucky enough to have 'adequate' footwear, it must have been a practical impossibility for both school and home to cope with sodden apparel twice a day, since children were not allowed to remain in school for the lunch period but were sent home.

A different point of view on the influence of weather on attendance was expressed by the somewhat cynical Rev. Wigram referring to his own parish, south of the river (Lambeth district). Although acknowledging that bad weather must generally have accounted for low attendance he made the following comment:

> My own schools are generally lowest in point of numbers during the fine weather, that is, when the London season is at its height.[22]

The explanation given was that at such times of bustling activity children had the greatest chance of proving their usefulness in extra earnings.

The other main reason for absence recognized as legitimate by the members of the committee was sickness. There was no occasion recorded of severe epidemic in this period. However, illness must have been a common excuse for intermittent absence.[23]

The foregoing analysis of the patterns of attendance and problems encountered in the process of institutionalizing regular and — by the standards of the time — relatively prolonged schooling, demonstrates that they were, in essential ways, the product of their social context. A study of one school is clearly no basis for generalizing on trends outside its own locality. However, such studies increase in importance when they can be linked with other similar studies, and the findings compared. It is of particular interest to consider the Mitcham National School and its difficulties in establishing attendance rates thought desirable by the committee, in relation to the data on the Kennington National School of the same period, since both schools were located in South London.[24] The two social contexts had much in common: the major alternatives for work were between market gardening and the 'manufactories'.[25] The school committee at Kennington was also confronted with the problem of irregular attendance and once more believed that main social factors which influenced regularity of attendance were lack of suitable clothing and footwear, a problem aggravated in wet weather, and seasonal fluctuations in the demand for labour.

These experiences are further corroborated by the opinions expressed by the Rev. Wigram in 1835. The following comment on poor attendance gives his interpretation of the situation at his Lambeth parish (neighbouring that in which the Kennington School was located) and indicates that problems familiar to Mitcham and Kennington were shared in his schools:

> . . . their leaving school arises in some measure from change of the parents' residence, and from the necessity they feel of moving to be near their shop of work; in these cases there is a partial cessation only of the children's attendance at school; but the evil complained of arises much more extensively from the indifference of the parents to their children acquiring anything more than an ability to read and write. When this is once obtained, they have got the chief thing they want, and they do not choose to be under any restraint or to conform to the discipline arising out of settled rules. The fluctuation of wages is one great cause of the disturbance to which schools are subjected. The parents become high in their manners and difficult to manage, when the wages are very good; on the contrary, the usefulness of children at home, or the want of clothes, when times are bad, has a similar effect as to their continuance in school.[26]

Another perspective of the social implications of attendance comes from an examination of the social functions of education. One major social responsibility of the school in advanced industrial societies deals with socialization. Although the process of socialization is life-long, it is generally accepted that socializing experiences in childhood are of overwhelming importance. It has become taken for granted that the modern school is strategically located in the structure of such a society to handle this function, since its members are children. The significance of the school as a crucial arena for articulating lower-class culture with that of the Establishment was well recognized by those anxious to promote working-class education. They understood clearly that access to children through the school provided an opportunity to bring them face-to-face with values of the dominant culture. It may be said that one of the inspirations supporting the endeavour to provide education was the faith and optimism apparent in early nineteenth-century commentary, in the transformative capacity of the social institution of schooling.[27] Interests concentrated on the school as an agency for moral socialization while instrumental education was of secondary importance, provided since it facilitated the former by allowing children with reading skills to become more familiar with the moral teachings of the Bible.

Since this paper is limited to a discussion of one aspect of school behaviour — attendance — the area of social learning on which it is relevant to focus attention concerns the set of values and attitudes which shape patterns of behaviour ordered on conception of time. E.P. Thompson[28] has pointed out that one of the major re-orientations in social organization necessitated by industrialization was an adaptation to a changing interpretation of the social meaning of time as a way of making sense of the social world. The transition to factory organization depended on precision in integrating processes of manufacture which conflicted with task-oriented work-structures typical of earlier economies. The normative climate of the pre-industrial work-world had accepted irregular working days and weeks. The social phenomenon of Saint Monday and concomitant practices of heavy drinking died hard.

New time-dimensions as a basis of the structuring of the industrial work-world could not fail to carry over into domestic organization and contribute to the upheaval experienced in that area of social activity during the transition to industrialization. Where schools became significant parts of social structure, they were in a position to participate in the long-term process of adjustment to such changes. However, it is evident from the difficulties encountered in schools which tried to instil in their pupils a respect for punctuality and regularity in attendance that it was a discouraging task. Traditions like Saint Monday were resistant to change and were likely to impede the efforts of the schools. For example, the Rector of Bethnal Green described typical Sunday behaviour in his parish as the forming of 'riotous assemblages in Hare-Street fields, which consist of many hundred persons, principally boys and men, who assemble, fight dogs, hunt ducks, gamble and enter into subscriptions to fee a drover for a bullock to hunt on the Sunday evening, or for their diversion on Monday'.[29] The result of these Sunday pursuits tended to be a day lost to the work-world since 'as soon as the bullock is driven into a populous part of the parish, hundreds and thousands join in the chase, and leave their looms'.[30]

It takes little imagination to contemplate the scale of the problem of getting parents and children to accept punctuality and regularity in school attendance when such expectations challenged the traditions of their homes. The data analysed on Mitcham indicated that many of the children came from social backgrounds in which their fathers were likely to have been self-employed or were in other principally task-oriented occupations. It was demonstrated also that many of the pupils were moving between the social worlds of school and work. For some of them associated with more traditional occupations the social experience of schooling must have been confusing, when it involved conflicting expectations of behaviour with regard to the significance of time.

While it is possible to comment on the opportunities created by the structure of the school for socialization, it is impossible to venture into an evaluation in any quantitative way of the social effectiveness of schooling in this period. Even today, the difficulties with research of this kind, given the complexity of the variables involved in socialization processes, are daunting. The early inspectors were certainly dismayed by the low standards of instrumental attainment in many schools, but once more it was a matter of wide variation. In the light of lack of relevant data, little can be said about socialization outcomes even of an instrumental kind. At the same time there are some important observations to be made about the dimensions of the problem and the caution necessary to avoid rash or inadvertent interpretation of limited or inappropriate data.

The evidence available from Parliamentary accounts and local sources has in common that it has been recorded by middle-class observers of the educational scene. Thus, the only information to be gleaned from these sources of working-class opinion is indirect — interpretation by the middle class of lower-class attitudes — and not necessarily accurate. The most interesting point that emerges from these accounts is that lower-class parents and middle-class parents and middle-class providers did not apparently share the same perspective on the purpose of education. The former were thought to have been most concerned with instrumental ends — they expected the school to teach their children to read and write — while the providers thought the proper concern ought to be with moral socialization. The quotation given earlier of the opinions of the Rev. Wigram indicated that he was highly critical of parents who failed to appreciate the 'true' benefits to be gained from schooling. By 1838 he appeared to have moderated his views and come to accept that parents' predominant interest in education was secular and instrumental, so that they were more likely to support schools in which writing as well as reading were taught.[31] If he was accurate in his evaluation of working-class attitudes, then his change of tone is an interesting insight into the kind of negotiation between parents and school committees which must have become part of the social interaction of the school.

In an important sense, the situation of 'successful' schools for lower-class children (successful in that they were able to recruit adequate numbers of children and a sufficient number of subscribers to finance the schools) presented a different socialization context from that of schools today. Consider the following comment on social arrangements of the 'old world':

> It is true that the ordinary person, especially the female, never went to a gathering larger than could assemble in an ordinary house except when going to church.[32]

This kind of social structure would have given the school a power it has lost today. The main social contact for non-working children, apart from the church, was the school. The school was therefore not competing for attention with other extra-familial social institutions as is the case today when the social influence of the school is tempered by the mass-media and a welter of youth organizations. The greatest source of power and social control of the denominational schools was that they were, in effect, extensions of churches and chapels. As socializing agencies schools, churches and chapels combined to present a united front to those pupils attracted into dual membership. It was a different state of affairs from that now experienced by the secular contemporary school, confused about its social role by pluralistic value-systems and the lack of a dominant culture in the nineteenth-century tradition. On the other hand, the length of time and consistency with which children are exposed to a social climate must be important variables in assessing the socializing impact of an institution. The problem of irregular attendance must have mitigated against the influence of the school. Reasonably prolonged, and perhaps more important, regular attendance within a time span would seem to be essential conditions for successful socialization in any long-term perspective.

An increasingly popular view at the present time of the difficulties experienced by the voluntary system, particularly that of attendance, is that they are indicative of a tendency for working-class parents to reject the opportunities provided for their children by the middle classes. It is true that many National schools were frequently not filled to physical capacity. In Mitcham the initial plans for the schools had been drawn up in 1812 on the expectation of 200 boys and a similar number of girls being recruited. This was a gross over-estimate and after the first enthusiasm had died down, the school population settled down to an average figure of approximately half the original estimate. But that average figure was then sustained for decades and in the face of the sociological difficulties encountered in the process of routinizing schooling. Any estimate made in 1812 of a potential demand for schooling must have been to some extent a shot in the dark. The National Society was in its infancy and thus local school committees had little comparative experience on which to draw. Furthermore, the Mitcham School was successful in maintaining relatively stable enrolment numbers in a highly competitive situation. In 1833 the following day school provision was reported in Mitcham:

1   infant and day school (80–90 children)
11   daily schools (180 children, 10 of these being kept by women
     for young children)
1   National school (98 males and 95 females).[33]

In numerical terms the National school was obviously the most successful. It would be premature to interpret the fact that denominational schools were not always full to capacity as meaning that parents were 'voting with their feet' and opting for schools set up by working-class enterprise. It is simply not known on what basis parents interested in education and able for economic reasons to send their children to school made their selection, when an opportunity for choice arose. Common sense reasons such as proximity to a school are likely to have played a large part in such decision making. Not least of the factors accounting for the changing fortunes of individual schools was probably the local reputation of the master and mistress.

The 'rejection thesis' appears to be a reaction to an alternative interpretation of the social effects of education – that the voluntary system was utilized by the middle classes to socialize lower-class children into a docile acceptance of the dominant culture. There is little doubt that this was an acknowledged intention. However, it is not legitimate, in the absence of far more substantial evidence than the sources considered in this study, to make assumptions about attendance at school, regular or irregular, fleeting or prolonged, and the extent to which schools were successful in exercising this king of social control. The social impact of early nineteenth-century lower-class education remains a matter for speculation. The main contribution here has been to probe some complexities of the problem and its relationship to the significance of schooling.

NOTES

[1] P.P. 1834 IX, Report from the Select Committee on the State of Education, p. 80.

[2] The problems are extensively discussed in two articles in the *Economic History Review*, 2nd ser. XXIV: J.S. Hurt, 'Professor West on early nineteenth century education', and E.G. West, 'The interpretation of early nineteenth century statistics'. Both articles are reprinted in M. Drake (ed.), *Applied Historical Studies* (London, 1973) pp. 93–119.

[3] This attitude was commented on in P.P. 1837–8 VII, Report on the Select Committee on Education of the Poorer Classes in England and Wales, p. 103.

[4] Quoted in P.P. 1835 VII, Report from the Select Committee on Education in England and Wales, p. 4.

[5] This figure is quoted from P. and H. Silver, *The Education of the Poor* (London, 1974), p. 38.

[6] West, op cit., p. 114.

[7] P.P. 1816 IV, Third Report from the Select Committee on the Education of the Lower Orders of the Metropolis, p. 219.

[8] Ibid. p. 4.

[9] P.P. 1834 IX, Education, p. 19.

[10] Ibid. p. 84.

[11] P.P. 1837–8 VII, Education, p. 49.

[12] For an examination of the problem of this kind of error see E.G. West, 'Resource allocation and growth in early nineteenth-century British education', in *Applied Historical Studies*.

[13] For further discussion of this point see A.C.O. Ellis, 'Influences on school attendance in Victorian England', *British Journal of Educational Studies*, Vol. XXI, No. 3 (October 1973), pp. 313–26.

[14] One recent study of this kind is that of the Kennington National School, P. and H. Silver, op cit.

[15] Information from 1801 and 1821 Census returns.

[16] Two bound volumes (manuscript) dating from 1812–30 are in the possession of the Surrey Record Office, County Hall, Kingston.

[17] The term 'teacher' is used here as described in Dr Bell's outline of his plan for school organization. It refers to a role allocated to the more competent monitors and is to be distinguished from the role of the master which was the only adult position in the social structure of the monitorial school. For a detailed study of the monitorial system, see

A. Bell, *An Experiment in Education at the Male Asylum, Madras* (London, 1797).

[18] Minutes of the Managers, 1833—55, York British Girls' School, bound volume (manuscript) at York Public Library.

[19] P.P. 1816 IV, Education of Lower Orders, p. 325.

[20] This comment of course assumes a reasonably competent mistress. However it needs to be pointed out that a great deal of interest in needlework was taken by the lady visitors from the school committee who supervised and kept a close watch on the standard of the work produced.

[21] P.P. 1816 IV, Education of Lower Orders, p. 17.

[22] P.P. 1835 VII, Education, p. 5.

[23] A point of interest to note here is that the York British Girls' School was closed for a time in 1833 because of an outbreak of cholera — see the Report of General Meeting of Subscribers (1833), York Public Library.

[24] For an account of attendance at Kennington, see P. and H. Silver, op cit., pp. 38—48.

[25] Ibid, p. 18.

[26] P.P. 1835 VII, Education, p. 4.

[27] For a discussion of the response of the Church and motivation to tackle the task of transforming society, see R.A. Soloway, *Prelates and People. Ecclesiastical Social Thought in England 1783—1852* (London, 1969). Of particular interest is chapter 10, 'Education and social order 1783—1830'.

[28] E.P. Thompson, 'Time, work-discipline and industrial capitalism', *Past and Present*, No. 38 (December 1967).

[29] P.P. 1816 IV, p. 229, Rev. J. King.

[30] Ibid.

[31] P.P. 1837—8, VII, Education, pp. 77, 838.

[32] P. Laslett, *The World We Have Lost* (London, 1965), p. 9.

[33] P.P. 1835 XLIII, Abstract of Returns Relative to the State of Education in England and Wales.

Chapter 3:

Socialization and rational schooling: elementary education in Leeds before 1870

Simon Frith

One salutary effect of the current 'deschooling' debate has been the reminder that 'schooling' – the rational organization of children in an institution based on teachers and a formal curriculum – is only one method of education. I think it is especially easy for historians of nineteenth-century education to take for granted in their investigations of educational growth, industrialization and social control, that they are dealing with the development of schooling, a particular *form* of socialization. The general relationships between education and the labour market, between education and class struggle, meant, in local terms, the creation of institutions that faced *immediate* problems – problems revolving around the central reality of the school as an institution: the power of the educators over the educated. The schooling of working-class children in nineteenth-century England, whether by charitable individuals, by religious organizations, or by the State, involved the exercise of *authority*. And that raises questions not just about the educators' motives, not just about the content of the education they provided, but also about their *rights* as educators. How was their educational power legitimated? Why did working-class children accept it (and how did they resist it)? What rights did their parents claim?

In this essay, by concentrating on what happened in one local situation, Leeds, I want to reverse the general approach to the history of education. I shall take for granted educational ideologies, the role of elementary education in the economy, its social control function. My concern is with how 'rational schooling' developed as a *form* of socialization, with the problems this created (and solved) for the relationships between educators and educated.

At the end of the eighteenth century, formal education in Leeds was confined to those who could afford to use private academies and, at the other extreme, to the very poor, who were educated in the work-house or the charity school.[1] Most children were educated by their parents at home or during the course of an apprenticeship. This was a straightforward process in an economy of domestic hand-loom weaving. A family, together with an apprentice or two in some cases, worked on the cloth as a unit; the father as head of the family directed activities and supervised not only the children's labour but also their morals and discipline.[2]

These families were educationally autonomous because of their economic autonomy. It was because such domestic manufacturers were able 'to maintain their families in comfort by their own industry and frugality' that a Parliamentary commission of inquiry into the state of hand-loom weavers could praise their system for 'the encouragement it thus holds out to domestic habits and virtues', for 'its favourable tendencies on the health and morals of a large and important class of the community'.[3]

Other educational arrangements only became necessary when families could not cope economically. Public education was confined to the children of those families who were unable to maintain themselves in comfort, who could not educate their children in domestic habits and virtues or get them apprenticed. The parish fulfilled its obligations to the very poorest, the orphans and the destitute, in the workhouse, where they were educated as well as maintained. Rule 22 ordered

> That the Nurses shall have all the Children under the Care washed, combed and cleaned by Ten O'Clock every Morning, and that such Children be taught to read, and work (as their several capacities will bear), in such Manufactures as may be most useful and beneficial for the public Good; and that the Nurses repair their own and Children's Linen and Cloathes, to keep them decent and clean; and in case of Disobedience or Misbehaviour of any of the Children, such Children shall be corrected by the Master.[4]

The social function of workhouse education was to give the children the preparation for a useful economic role that they could not get from their families. Rule 13 ordered

> That the Churchwardens and Overseers in the Month of November in Every Year, shall make a Return of such Inhabitants in their several Divisions, as are proper to have poor Apprentices put out to.[5]

The Leeds Charity School had a similar educational purpose. Its original legacy, in 1705, was for the maintenance of forty poor children and their education in the doctrines of the Church of England and in the necessary skills for 'honest trades and professions'.[6] These aims were firmly maintained in the daily life of the school in 1800. For forty-nine weeks a year, eight hours a day, 120 children (aged eight to thirteen) were 'clothed and taught English and writing and to spin worsted', the girls being 'also taught to sew, spin, line and knit and to wash and clean a house'. They were 'given Church of England instruction, brought to church and catechised', and afterwards 'put to husbandry or to the cloathing industry or to service'. It was agreed that the children should 'be enured to some early labour, in order the better to qualifie them for Service, when they go out Apprentices' and the master and mistress had to

take care that the Children come Decently to Church on all Sundays and Sermon-Days, and see that they behave themselves with Reverence (as such Charity-Children ought to do) both to GOD and all Mankind.[7]

The Charity School provided its pupils with much the same education as their contemporaries got at home. Moral and academic education were integrated with real work (the school's workshop made a profit) and the school had no examinations or formal curriculum. There were no certificates to brand school learning — what branded the charity school children was their decent blue uniform, the ever-present symbol (the children had to wear the clothes the school provided at all times) of the school's authority.

This authority was claimed over the pupils' lives out of school as well as in it. There were rules for parents, who had to send their children to school 'clean Washed and Combed' and to control their behaviour at home and to take particular care to prevent them joining with 'a Mob in a tumultuous manner' or begging for money in the streets.[8] Parents were told to 'freely submit their Children to be Chastised for their Faults' and to 'forbear coming to School on such Occasions, that the Master may not be interrupted or discouraged in the performance of his Duty'. They were expected to get their children at home to repeat the catechism 'frequently', to read the Bible to them, to say family prayers morning and evening, so that they and their children would 'the better be informed of their Duty' and by sincere and constant practice of it get God's blessings. Any parents failing to obey these rules had their children dismissed and their clothes forfeited. No parent could 'presume' to put a child out to be apprenticed without the consent of the committee of trustees of the school.[9]

Poor parents, in admitting they were unable to educate their children, were compelled to yield their 'natural' authority over them. This was obviously true in the workhouse, where the authority of the overseers over the children was absolute (and legally sanctioned) but it was equally true of the 'voluntary' charity school, where the children were under constant obligation to their patrons, who had got them into the school (admission depended on sponsorship) and would get them into an occupation. Uriah Heep expressed most graphically what this sort of education meant. At his 'sort of charitable institution': 'they taught us all a deal of 'umbleness — not much else that I know of, from morning to night'.

Charity education depended on a society in which everyone knew their place. The Leeds school's trustees, drawn from the well-off members of the community, chaired by the vicar of the parish church, represented the traditional authority of property and the established church. The school's master and mistress depended for their jobs on their relationship with the patrons who had voted for them, with those who had supplied their recommendations. They did not have any specifically educational qualifications, no credentials or certificates; their quality was to be respectable, religious, upright. The school was not organized in terms of competition or individual achievement — a pupil was 'ready' to leave when his behaviour was suitably obedient, when he had a 'recommendation' from his patron and there was a place for him to go. There were conflicts (which usually culminated in an argument over who owned the charity clothes, the family or the school); parents were reluctant to give up their power to put their children to work, to keep them at home, to replace them at the school with a sibling, as family and economic circumstances changed, but on the whole the school's authority was accepted. It got its meaning from traditional values and skills, from traditional relationships; it was, after all, a substitute for the most traditional authority of all: that of a father over his children.

But if in the last decades of the eighteenth century the Leeds Charity School was a secure and successful institution, by the second decade of the nineteenth century it was facing a crisis, as its traditional assumptions were challenged first by the rise of Dissent[10] and, second and even more important, by industrialization.

One of the most immediately-noticed effects of the factory system was that factory children were not being educated at home, morally, usefully, or for literacy. Richard Oastler summed up what was supposed to have happened. He referred to the domestic system of the West Riding during his own childhood, when children 'mixed learning their trades with other instruction and with amusement' under the immediate care of their parents. Now children worked in the mills which dominated the industry and scarcely learnt anything at all from their parents.[11]

The exploitation of children in factories raised two problems for charity schooling. Firstly, there were now far more children lacking parental education than the traditional institutions could cope with (and it was partly this problem of sheer numbers that the monitorial systems of Bell and Lancaster were devised to solve) but, secondly, these children, whatever their ignorance and suffering, were not dependent on charity or the parish for their livelihoods, present or future. The old equation between economic and educational autonomy was no longer a simple one. Oastler himself noted the decline of filial respect:

> It is a very common system, as soon as a child is enabled to earn a little more money than its board wages, for it to strike a bargain with its parents; when it gets to be 13 or 14 years old it will threaten to leave if they will not let it have so much of its wages; and they consider themselves quite free agents and under no control.[12]

The old mechanisms of charity education could not be applied to these working children; if the authority of the family itself was shaken by industrialization so was that of the 'substitute family', so were the ties of patronage and charity and gratitude. I can best show this paradoxically, by looking at the educational institutions that did continue to claim an extensive authority over the lives of children.

In 1848 the Poor Law Guardians of Leeds opened a Moral and Industrial School for the workhouse children; its object was to qualify pauper children for apprenticeships that they might ultimately become useful and respectable members of society.[13] The ideology was more utilitarian but the workhouse children's experience of education was much the same in 1848 as it had been in 1800. The institution could still claim complete authority over their destinies because these children were otherwise helpless.

In 1859 the Leeds Ragged School and Shoe-Black Society opened its first school; two years later it was registered under the Certified Industrial School Act and began to receive children sent by magistrates' orders. It was a 'school in which industrial training is provided, and in which children are clothed, lodged, and fed, as well as taught'. The object was 'to train for lives of honest industry and Christian purity children who by early neglect, criminal associations, or their own proclivities, are growing up as criminals or outcasts'. Children were detained in the school for 'begging or receiving alms', 'wandering and not having any home', being 'orphans, or having a surviving parent in gaol', 'frequenting the company of reputed criminals', as well as for specific crimes. The school's management committee commented that it was a matter of the utmost moment to give them 'habits of regular industry' and to accustom their minds to daily and continuous labour.[14] The school employed a tailor and shoemaker to teach selected pupils their crafts; other children were kept busy with wood-chopping or house-cleaning or out with the shoe-black brigade. The girls were taken into private houses to be trained as servants while the boys were sent to live as apprentices with masters who would send them to Sunday or night schools as well as teach them a trade.[15]

For these children education meant confinement in an institution making an extensive series of demands over their present and future lives. The similarity to the purposes of the old Charity School is obvious: the Industrial School children were similarly being socialized to take their lowly place in the occupational structure. But their school's authority rested on the impersonal demands of the law — patronage did not come into it. These children had *already* been a nuisance to society, their threat was not just a potential one. Charity, and the attempt to prevent children becoming, because of their families' material circumstances, an expense to society, had become (except in the workhouse) reform, and an attempt to reclaim children who were already an expense. The traditional authority of kinship and the social hierarchy had been replaced by the rational authority of the law. And by 1870 this was a minor aspect of the schooling of the working class in Leeds — in 1869 there were about 1,000 children under the authority of the magistrates or the Poor Law Guardians, the total elementary school population was over 28,000.[16]

The major educational problem for the middle class in nineteenth-century England was the schooling of the non-criminal, non-destitute, working-class child. Because of the effects of industrialization, educational need could no longer be subsumed under other sorts of need. Except in special cases, elementary schools could not claim an extensive authority over their pupils' lives. Let me give one further example of how things changed.

In 1802, in one of the earliest responses to the factory 'problem' in Leeds, a committee of 'benevolent ladies' opened an Industrial School for girls who could be personally recommended as 'proper objects of charity'. The school was open in the evenings for girls 'employed in manufactories, or otherwise during the day' and its pupils were taught to read, write, knit and sew and prepared for work as domestic servants — this was considered necessary in a district where the girls' employment in factories often unfitted them for servants' duties.[17]

Fifty years later, in 1852, some equally benevolent ladies opened the Leeds Factory Girls' Sewing School. It was also to give lessons to factory girls in the evenings, but there were differences from the previous school. It was open to all factory girls, whether or not they were proper objects; its aim was not to train servants but to prepare wives and mothers. The school wanted not only to teach the girls dressmaking but, by allowing the teachers to mix freely and easily with the pupils and to 'sympathize with them in their stories of their families and their work, and the joys and griefs of their everyday life', to raise the moral and religious tone of the pupils and to show them 'what better educated people would do or say under similar circumstances'.[18]

Between 1800 and 1850 the benevolent middle class had had to adjust its notions of education as charity in the face of the working class's marked 'independence of feeling'. At the centre of this process of adjustment were the schools set up by the British and National Societies.

The Leeds National Society was founded in December 1811, by a group of 'the Town's Churchmen' as a response to two related problems: the increasing population of poor children in the Leeds district — 'in the 20 Parishes which it contains, abounding in manufactures, and very populous, the number of uneducated Children must be very great'; and the increasing population of Dissenters — 'in the Manufacturing part and of those that are under Instruction, the largest proportion belong to the Institutions of Dissenters, who are industriously training them up in their own principles'.[19]

The aims of the Leeds National School were the same as those of the Leeds Royal Lancasterian School, which had opened a few months earlier; its committee considered that the formation of habits of decency, regularity, attention and subordination were as important as the communication of useful knowledge.[20] But whereas the Lancasterian School was designed 'to embrace all denominations of Christians as its supporters, and to admit the children of the poor without discrimination',[21] the National School reflected Anglicanism's new-found aggression. The Church had run Sunday schools in Leeds since the late 1780s but in the face of dissenting competition it had now determined that they should be supplemented by a day school using the Madras system, so that its improvement of the understanding and regulation of morals might be extended to those children who attended only Sunday schools.[22]

Both schools were conceived as charity schools. Their aims were similarly extensive: to prepare poor children for their place in society by instructing them in 'suitable Learning, Works of Industry and in the Principles of the Christian Religion'.[23] Their trustees were equally 'the Principal Gentlemen, possessing property in the borough of Leeds',[24] whose task it was to recommend children for admission, 'who might otherwise have passed their lives in idleness and mendicity', and find them 'stations of usefulness and respectability'.[25] In 1815 all the boy pupils and most of the girls were transferred from the Charity to the National School and the charity atmosphere of the new monitorial schools is well evoked by the 1829 report of the Leeds Lancasterian School, which pointed out that the sight of five hundred children of poor parents actively employed in acquiring 'the first principles of religion, the rudiments of useful knowledge, and habits of cleanliness and order' could not fail to gratify 'every benevolent mind'.[26]

But monitorial education differed from charity education in several important respects. Firstly, these schools were not free – between 1815 and 1840 the average fee was 1*d.* a week, thereafter 2*d.* and sometimes 3*d.* in the top classes. The schools' managers (and subsequent historians) stressed the cheapness of this education but the fact remains that the children's school pence provided half of the schools' incomes throughout the period 1815 to 1870. Regular attendance, the obsession of these schools (as the mistreatment of the blue clothes had been of the charity school), was necessary not only for the pupils' educational progress but also for the schools' economic survival. The increasing amount of government money involved after 1833 was a substitute for local subscriptions not for school pence – the hundreds of thousands of pounds pumped into schooling by the Treasury were always matched by those trickling in from 'poor' parents. It was local subscribers who gradually faded from the educational scene.[27]

The trouble was, as the Leeds National Society noted in 1842, that 'these schools are established in the poorest district of the parish where no subscribers can be obtained', in areas where 'no one except the Clergyman lives above the condition of a builder' — if the inhabitants 'rise in the world they go to live in a better part of town'.[28] Urbanization — the geographical division of Leeds along class lines — severed the social ties of patronage as effectively as industrialization undermined the patron's role in the job market.

The Leeds Lancasterian School was quick to stress the practicality of its education — its provision of skills as well as character. The 1829 report that I have already quoted as an example of charitable claims equally boasted of the pupils' 'efficiency in writing and accounts, such as to qualify them for stations in shops, warehouses and counting houses'.[29] The school's curriculum was consciously made relevant to the needs of local employers[30] and by 1867 the Committee was writing of its pupils 'raising themselves' by their education.[31]

The National Society was less willing to drop its charitable assumptions but the decline of patronage was not the only problem for its authority. National school pupils' independence was given force by educational competition. Even before the Leeds Society opened its first school in 1813, it had come to an agreement with the Lancasterians that their schools should exchange lists of children dismissed for any reason and make sure that they did not admit each other's delinquents. But competition was not just between these two schools. As the National Society expanded its activities (four schools in Leeds by 1839, twenty-nine by 1851)[32] so did other educators. A common complaint was that voiced by one school in 1838. It explained its decline in numbers by referring to the opening of a Dissenting school in the neighbourhood, the novelty of which had 'allured several of our Scholars'; in some instances, the Report continued, the children had attended without prior knowledge of their parents, who had subsequently acquiesced. To build schools where they were not wanted would create 'a competition of the most injurious kind'.[33]

Some competition was even more direct. At one Leeds school, in 1851, after a mistress was sacked 'most of the girls followed her to a school which she is carrying on on her own account'.[34]

Some National school managers revelled in the competition and enjoyed responding to the threat of 'opposition schools'[35] but even when they were confident of providing a better education than any of their rivals, they could not be sure of keeping their pupils. As the Leeds National Society explained to its subscribers in 1830:

In a commercial town, the description of children sent out to acquire habits of discipline and rules of learning in a scholastic institution like yours, will always be of a very tender age, because as soon as they are capable of being employed in any branch of trade, their labour becomes too valuable to admit of any relaxation from it and the rapid succession with which they pass through the school, occasioned by the nature of the trade, and the variations incident to a dense population must always cause great fluctuations in attendance.[36]

The schools were in double-bind. When trade was good children left school to work, when it was bad they left, unable to afford the fees. Thus, for example, in 1849 the Yorkshire Inspector of Schools reported that Christ Church School's boys' department had considerably decreased in numbers during the past year in consequence of a mill owner discontinuing 'short-timers', leaving only six instead of seventy-five mill children in the school.[37] Two years later he reported that the girls' department of the same school had experienced a similar fall in numbers, partly because improved trade had caused parents to put their children to work at home or in the mill.[38] Various devices were used to try to keep the children at school. In 1833 the Leeds National Society opened a lending library, hoping that this would strengthen their pupils' connection with the school, and a year later the Committee was claiming some success in that books were often taken home and read by parents.[39]

Over the next few years the library was joined by a clothing society and savings bank, and 'a society for the relief of persons educated in the Schools', which 'promises to be of advantage'.[40] But the real significance of these activities was not for attendance at the National Schools (turnover continued to be rapid), but for their ideology. In 1831 the metropolitan National Society had warned its local branches of the danger

of attracting the children to the schools, encouraging them to stay and to continue the connection: the scholars should never be permitted to forget the benefit they themselves derive, or to imagine that their attendance confers a favour on the conductors of the school.[41]

The warning fell on deaf ears. A gap had opened between the ideology of National education and the practical realities of running a working-class school. In an industrial city like Leeds the mechanism of charity were, as I have tried to illustrate, inapplicable. The result was a crisis of legitimacy — the traditional authority claims of the National schools were rejected by their pupils' parents; the continual conflicts over attendance reflected the implicit assumption of working-class families that they could educate their children where and how they liked. Parents could not be expected to be 'grateful' when it was their pence which provided an essential part of the schools' incomes; schooling could not be treated as a 'gift' to otherwise educationally destitute families when pupils could, without notice, be removed to competing educators; the 'benefits' of National education were not obvious in an economy in which the state of trade (and not 'the state of character') determined job availability.

It was increasingly impossible for the National Society to ignore the reality of working-class autonomy — by 1838 the General Committee was even commenting on the importance of school pence for *preserving* 'a right spirit of independence and responsibility'.[42] Schools began to justify themselves as efficient means to the *secular* end of literacy, to stress the efficiency of their pedagogical methods, the superiority of their teachers. The Leeds Society showed the way in its 1833 report which pointed out that the high standard of the half-yearly examination results was due to 'the excellence of the system and to its being so well-organized'.[43]

By the 1860s the better National schools in Leeds were attracting the children of 'small shop-keepers, clerks and superior workmen', who realized that National education was 'better suited to their needs than that which is to be purchased in small private academies'.[44] The Leeds Parish Church National School even had an upper department and offered latin, geometry and algebra — an education which can hardly be called elementary.[45]

It is tempting, faced with such evidence, to analyse the mid-nineteenth-century history of National schooling as a straightforward process of secularization, the replacement of a moral by a secular curriculum. But I think this would be wrong. There is counter evidence that the primary purpose of these schools continued to be 'that greatest of blessings, a sound religious education'[46] and one of the effects of the lack of local patrons was, in fact, to *increase* the importance of the local clergy in National schools — one constant theme of Watkins' reports on Yorkshire schools in the 1850s was the importance of the local vicar's involvement for the success of a school.[47]

If National schools were no longer a charity, their aim was still to educate working-class children for their subordinate place, for their 'duty in that state of life unto which it pleases God to call them'.[48] Working-class parents might have made an important financial contribution to National education, might have been free to enrol and withdraw their children at will, but they certainly did not have any *power* in the schools. National education remained something that was *provided* for them and secular instruction had to be accompanied by religious instruction because, as the National Society often emphasized, the presence of the latter stopped the pupils becoming over-ambitious as a result of the former.

The problem for the National schools in a place like Leeds was how to maintain their authority as *providers* of education when the old trappings of patronage and charity were no longer available. Secularization was part of the solution − National education could be offered for its usefulness − but only part, because on the one hand this useful education was still education for subordination (Leeds National schools rarely echoed the Lancasterian School's pride in their pupils 'raising themselves') and, on the other hand, *National* education still had to differentiate itself from the education offered by other institutions − if there was educational competition, it was a competition that the National Society was determined to win. The solution to these problems revolved around the *method* of National education; the history of Leeds National schools is a history of rationalization.

British and National schools were based on a methodical system of instruction from their origins. Their education was devised for application to a large population; it had to be well organized and cheap. The Leeds Lancasterian School, for example, had 500 pupils by 1812, and was teaching them at a cost of only five shillings per pupil per year.[49] The oft noted parallels between factory organization and the monitorial system were less the result of a conscious attempt to socialize children for work than a shared rational solution to a similar organizational problem. Hence the Lancasterian (and virtually identical Bell) system of instruction − the use of monitors and trained teachers, of text-books and formal lessons, of a time-table and curriculum, of competition, rewards and sanctions.[50]

But if the original aims of this process − to educate as many children as cheaply as possible − were clear, the use of rational organization had other implications. First, where there is competition, there is achievement. National schools (unlike charity schools) differentiated their pupils according to their ability — children took tests and moved groups accordingly; the cleverer pupils were raised above their fellows through their employment as monitors; success was measured and rewarded.

Second, though, if the children could now be examined for 'progress', their results were no longer simply attributable to their own moral or intellectual qualities — the 'efficiency' of the schools themselves was in question. The committees of both the Leeds Lancasterian and National Societies regularly put their pupils on 'public exhibit'[51] — when things went well the schools got useful publicity ('To see so many boys go through their school exercises, with military precision and yet lighthearted ease, is very pleasing.'[52]); when things went badly, blame was cast upon the teachers.

Teaching was now regarded as a skill (in applying the Bell or Lancaster system) which required training. The first Leeds National schoolmaster, for example, was appointed on the basis of an examination as well as references and was immediately sent off 'to be instructed in the Madras System of teaching'. Twelve months later he was sacked — his results were bad and 'the school has greatly fallen off in all the essential points of Dr Bell's system during the last half year'.[53] From then on Leeds recruited its teachers from the National Society's Central School.[54]

The rationalization of education, the increasing use of systematic criteria of 'efficiency' — whether the efficiency of pupils, teachers or the schools themselves — was accelerated by the involvement of the government in education after 1839 — treasury funds had to be 'accounted for', aided education justified. The response of the National Society to the Committee of Council and its Inspectorate was to build the National Training School (to give local National schools a ready supply of certified teachers), to appoint National Society inspectors (to supervise existing schools) and Organizing Masters (to help establish new ones). The introduction of the pupil-teacher system in 1846 established the principle that government money could be used for maintaining as well as establishing schools and gave the government's inspectors considerable influence over National education. I do not need to go into the details of how they affected the development of the curriculum, of examinations, of teacher training; it is enough to cite the case of one of her Majesty's Inspectors of Schools who, writing in 1860, stated that whereas his duties in the early days consisted mainly of driving from school to school to examine in a few elementary subjects or inspect the buildings and accounts, now they involved examining Normal Schools, preparing examination papers, holding collective examinations of pupil teachers, settling and revising Teachers' Certificates and examining large schools in a thorough and detailed manner.[55]

Between 1840 and 1870 National education became rational schooling, 'the age-specific, teacher related process requiring full-time attendance at an obligatory curriculum'.[56] Rational organization replaced charity at the centre of National schools' justification of their role. They were superior to other schools because their organization was superior; their pupils were kept in place by the rules of time-table and curriculum and examination. Individual working-class ambition and achievement was possible but, with the right organization, could be controlled and limited — the secularization of the curriculum was balanced by the moral lessons of rational school discipline.

This was still a system of social control but to appreciate this it is not enough to look at the history of National education only from the top. Despite the suggestions of the Whiggish history of education which traces the steady progress from 1839 to 1870 to 1944, there were alternatives to rational education and resistance to it.

Victorian education reformers assumed that if children were not at school they were not being educated, and they had doubts even if the children were at school. Was all schooling — public and private, day and Sunday, evening and adult — equally valuable? By 1870 the consensus among middle-class educators was that the only schooling worthy of the name was the rational type to be found in the inspected public day schools — other types of education were devalued. The educational tradition of the dissenting, respectable, working class suffered this fate; its mixture of Sunday schools, self-help, evening classes and reading rooms provided an alternative to rational schooling, an alternative which is worth describing in some detail.

In Leeds the Dissenters broke away from the original Sunday school movement at the end of the eighteenth century and set up 'Schools for the instruction of their own poor'.[57] Dissenting schools taught writing as well as religious dogma (an innovation) but they also expressed a much greater religious fervour than the Church Sunday schools — their aim was conversion. The Wesleyan Methodists, for example, had a 'Select Class' for the children who were converted to the sect and drew most of their teachers from it. The teachers were, in turn, enthusiastic and organized, holding regular meetings together to hear educational papers and discuss the progress of their teaching. Progress was measured in religious terms: 'Several Children converted to God last year and several died happy'; 'the work of God has revived among the Children – one of them obtained a sense of Pardon on the 7th February at their Prayer Meeting and two more last week'; '6 or 8 know the Lord and the School generally improving.'[58]

The teachers' religious ideology was the basis of a self-righteousness that was sufficient, on occasion, to support opposition to their ministers and superintendents. In 1821, for example, the Wesleyan Methodist teachers objected to the form of the annual anniversary meeting, at which a few children were selected to recite their lessons to the public. The teachers did not like having to pick these children from their classmates, thus 'exciting in the former Ambition and in the latter Envy and Ill Will'.[59] Earlier, in 1819, a running row between a teacher and a superintendent had resulted in the teacher being dismissed. The other teachers immediately called a meeting and demanded, successfully, their colleague's reinstatement.[60]

These incidents suggest that the Wesleyan Sunday school teachers (who were, in fact, simply the older and more zealous pupils) had at least a small measure of independence and organization – something of which there is no evidence in the Leeds Anglican educational system at this time. At any rate, the latent tension between the Wesleyan teachers, on the one hand, and the ministers and superintendents, on the other, became an overt conflict in 1827 over the issue of the teaching of writing.

The terms of this debate reflect a split between the middle-class members of the sect who, with their preachers, had an ideology of education similar to that of the Church schools, and the working-class community (including the teachers) who by now relied on the Sunday schools as the only possible source of secular learning. As one of them remembered:

> When we had work we had not time to go to school; and when we had not work we had nothing with which to pay school wages: so that a Sunday School was our only resource. What little learning, therefore, I did get, I got it at home from my brothers and sisters, and at the Sunday School.[61]

And he also remembered that:

> Neither the preachers nor the leading members among the Methodists appear to have had the least desire to spread knowledge or to make people intelligent or wise.[62]

The 'leading members'' decision to cease teaching writing on Sundays was, admittedly, accompanied by a decision to set up evening, day and infant schools ('to obviate the prejudice likely to be made in the minds of the poor by the abolition of Sunday writing'[63]) and the preachers denied that they had been 'actuated by a love of power; and excited disturbance where all before was peace'.[64] But by 1833 the secretary of the Leeds Sunday School Union was reporting that the New Connexion and Protestant Methodists still taught writing on the Sabbath; this was one reason for the flourishing state of their schools, which frequently attracted children from those which did not teach writing.[65]

The importance of these continuing secular Sunday schools was that they offered their pupils an opportunity of literacy (without the sacrifice of jobs and wages) in institutions that were rooted in the local community rather than being provided from above. There were Dissenting day schools in Leeds (differing from National schools only in their refusal to accept government funds) but J.G. Fitch commented in his 1869 survey of Leeds education that with the exception of the Wesleyans and the Unitarians, he had been unable to find a single Nonconformist congregation which was doing anything to forward primary education in the city.[66]

What these congregations did do can be illustrated by the history of Zion School. In 1832 a number of 'honest, hard-working, good-minded men' rented 'a small, dark, ill-ventilated room adjoining the old Blacksmith's shop in Wortley Lane' and opened a Sunday school, with pupils aged from seven to thirty joining in prayers, singing, reading and writing. The immediate problem was the size of the premises and public meetings were held to discuss the availability of funds, the need for a new school and the form it should take. New premises were eventually opened in 1835, big enough to hold 850 children and adults of all denominations. After some dispute it was agreed that writing should be taught, as 'it was evident to most people, that to learn to write was one of the most important things to the majority of the scholars who came to our new school'. They were working-class children, who worked daily from 5 a.m. to 7 p.m. and a free Sunday school was their only chance 'to gather up the fragments of instruction so necessary to their future comfort and enjoyment'.[67]

The school's teachers were local volunteers and it soon became the centre of local eductional life. A library was opened and a public reading room; there was a Mechanics Institute with evening classes for adults, and a Mutual Improvement Society with classes early on Sunday

mornings (in English and elocution and optics and Euclid) and discussions and lectures during the week.[68] There was even a day school:

> But it was a poor affair. I remember going to the Day School at this
> time and I can truly say that I learned little or nothing . . . the Day
> School appears to have been managed more with regard to giving a
> few shillings relief, by the school pence, to the master than for the
> fitness of the work in which he was engaged.[69]

And in 1846 an H.M.I. commented that the Zion Day School's
departments were 'very feeble' and ought to be considered essentially
as village schools, struggling for existence in the midst of a factory
population which patronized only 'the great Sunday Schools', held in
the same rooms.[70] The Sunday schools were the community's social
centre, the place for the Penny Readings and tea meetings, for the concerts and excursions, the Christmas plays and entertainments, the annual
Children's Festival, when the schools' younger pupils walked in proces-
sion from house to house, singing hymns and collecting money before
returning to Zion for tea and games.[71]

Education at Zion School differed in significant ways from the
rational process that was being developed contemporaneously in
Leeds' National schools. It was not age-specific − children and adults
attended the Sunday and evening schools, the library and the readings,
together. It did not require full-time attendance − it was an education
designed for people in full-time occupations. There was no obligatory
curriculum − the variety of educational activities (three Rs teaching,
mutual improvement, religious instruction, newspaper reading, etc.)
meant a variety of subject matter; the evening classes, for instance, were
given in whatever subject an available teacher could teach.[72] And, any-
way, the education provided by Zion School was not only teacher-
related: the stress on mutual improvement, the natural progression
from older pupil to younger teacher, the joint activities like the concerts
and the plays, the flexibility of the system (for teachers and students)
gave the school an atmosphere of independence and community control.

This sort of education was the response of one local working-class
community to its situation. It did not involve a theoretical rejection of
any other educational system; there was no explicit Chartist vision of
national secular education. Rather, Zion's pattern of Sunday and evening
schools, of mutual improvement and discussion, was the necessary result
of a production system that meant the daily occupation of both adult
and child. The element of community control reflected the effects of

urbanization — as the middle class moved into Leeds' suburbs, it was inevitable that the working class would take control of its own education. This process occurred, if at different speeds, for many Sunday schools. A Sunday school superintendent stated in 1860 that whereas twenty years earlier he had had forty middle-class candidates for Sunday school teaching, he now had the greatest difficulty in getting one, the duties being assumed by 'the moral and intelligent portion' of the labouring class.[73]

At Zion a community education was uncommonly flourishing, but its elements were present in all the working-class neighbourhoods of Leeds. What were common to the resulting institutions (whatever their varieties of achievement) were a breadth of ambition and a sense of self-respect. The success of a school like Zion showed that working-class education did not have to be restricted to basic literacy, the Bible and a bit of sewing; the community could educate itself, working-class children did not have to be dependent on the charity or efficiency of a superior class. These beliefs were given public expression by the Chartist movement[74] — this, for example, was the dream of Joseph Barker, a Leeds Knowledge Chartist (who had himself been educated in the Dissenting tradition): he wished to see people in possession of books 'on every important subject, in every branch of useful and interesting knowledge', from astronomy to chemistry, from philology to mechanics, he wished them to have the means of obtaining instruction in 'reading and writing, in mathematics and languages, in music and drawing'. In this way the industrious masses would become 'an intellectual and literary brotherhood' and their houses 'so many schools and colleges'.[75]

Measured against this vision National schooling was puny and degrading. For Barker education was a matter not of social control but of personal liberation. He remembered his own experience with a local preacher:

> Though Mr Hill was but poor at that time, yet, being a stranger and something of a scholar, he was generally much respected even by the richer portion of the people. And when I found myself noticed and cared for by him, and even treated with brotherly respect, it made me feel I can scarcely tell how. I felt as if I had risen from the rank of nothingness to that of being: I felt as if I really was a man, or destined to be one, and as if the world had not been made in vain. I felt as if I had been an outcast from the world before, an outcast from the world of thoughtful, intellectual, honourable men, and as if I were now admitted within its circle.[76]

The important point to make about Barker's experience is not that it was 'typical', but that it was possible. National education was not (despite the Leeds Committee's constant claims to its subscribers) simply a matter of providing an elementary education to a class that was otherwise intellectually and morally destitute; it was, rather, a matter of providing a particular *form* of education to a class which had (however unsystematically) alternative *forms* of learning available. I can illustrate the importance of the *form* of National education another way, by giving some evidence of how it was treated by those working-class children who did attend Leeds' public schools.

The Revised Code of 1862, with its rules of attendance, reduction of education to Standards, and reliance on measurements and examinations, marked a new stage in the rationalization of education. One of its requirements was that every school receiving government money should keep a log book of its daily life. It is this source which, ironically, gives us a clear picture of the resistance of the working class to rational schooling.[77]

The schools' first and most basic problem was to ensure their pupils' regular attendance; to impose the schools' rational organization of time on children whose lives still revolved around the rhythms of their homes. When the two systems clashed, the schools were the losers. Children stayed at home for a variety of domestic reasons — the girls to help with washing or nursing or extra housework, the boys whenever their fathers were on holiday or strike, when there was a political meeting to attend, or festival to celebrate. Even when the children did attend, they would arrive late and leave early according to their domestic duties — when they had 'Fathers', brothers' or sisters' dinners to carry' from home to the factories, for example.[78]

A new series of problems arose once the children were at school. Many parents disliked the age classifications used: on the one hand children were sent off with younger brothers and sisters in tow ('Admitted eleven boys; one boy only 1½ years old, his mother wants him to come with his brother'[79]), on the other hand parents objected to their children being placed in infants' departments, believing that these were not proper schools.[80]

There were clashes over rules of behaviour and dress ('Dismissed a girl — her grandmother insisting in sending her with her hair in papers, when told time after time it was contrary to rules sent extremely saucy messages.'[81]) and, especially, over punishments. Parents did not accept that teachers (and especially not pupil teachers) had the right to punish their children:

A boy, who was caught in a theft, and telling lies, has been taken from our school, simply because his *parents* will not *allow* their children to be punished *even* for such an offence.[82]

Mrs Rhodes came and caused a great disturbance in School because her daughter had been slightly punished for talking in class.[83]

Complaints about the schools' curricula were common but varied in detail from parent to parent; all were concerned about their children's educational progress, but they used different criteria of this both from each other and from those of the schools themselves — teachers had constant arguments about the use of copy-books and home work, about the place of arithmetic and knitting. Taking it all together — the flaunting of attendance regulations, the complaints about age-groups and lessons, the refusals to allow punishment — they must have shared this view of one of their colleagues:

Such is the *animus* of these people; that the arrangements of the Committee, and the interests of the School are nothing to them if they may not have their own way.[84]

Behind this cry of despair lay the realization that 'if they may not have their own way' parents were willing and able to withdraw their children altogether. All the schools experienced a constant turnover of pupils and for a great mixture of reasons:

some for change merely; others for work; others again to support a poor neighbour who has begun a dame school close by. Another family removing — Few really stay a whole year.[85]

And children leaving were a threat to the schools' survival because of the payment-by-results system — government funds were at risk as well as the children's pence. Parents had to be begged first to keep their children at school long enough for them to clock up their 200 attendances and second (if they then withdrew them) to let them back for the day of Inspection. There is a revealing entry in one school log book in 1864:

the Mistress asked all those children who were afraid of the Examination to put up their hands — the only hands held up were the Teachers'.[86]

The pupils at Leeds National schools in the 1860s were in an odd situation. The schools made a series of rational demands of them: they had to attend regularly, be classified by age and ability, learn a given curriculum in a given order and at a given speed, be examined and display their abilities for measurement. They were expected to accept these demands because of the schools' organization as systematic means to the end of basic literacy. The implication was that unless a child followed the rules and regulations (and took the rewards and sanctions that went with them) he would learn nothing. Yet much of this system, as I have tried to illustrate, was rejected by the pupils' parents; the schools' authority was tenuous because there was no agreement as to what end schooling was an efficient means. For their working-class pupils the schools filled up a waiting period before employment (and were abandoned as soon as there was a job going), they were not seen as providing a *necessary* preparation for work. There were no shared criteria of what schooling was for.

This was made equally clear by J.G. Fitch's investigation of working-class parents in Leeds who rejected the public schools altogether. In 1869 about a fifth of Leeds working-class school children were at private schools.[87] This was not a matter of apathy or neglect – parents preferred private to public schools for good reasons. Dame schools, for example, were often nearer home and smaller than the public infant schools, and mothers were happier about leaving their 'babies' there. Some parents resented the public schools' restraints, their insistence on regular attendance and punctuality, their fixed curricula and discipline; others rejected any education that smacked of charity and there was a strong element of anti-religious feeling.[88]

Fitch himself believed that the main reason for these parents' preference of private schools was their educational ignorance: 'Many of them', he wrote, 'look upon "learning" as a marketable commodity, and value it at exactly what it costs.'[89] He believed that most working-class parents were unable to appreciate the value of trained teachers and a pedagogical *system*, were too easily impressed by the superficialities of education – by schools styling themselves 'Academy', offering a choice of subjects, humouring parental whims.[90]

In 1800 there had been at least a measure of educational consensus. Parents educated their children themselves and only if they could not did the workhouse or charity school do it for them, taking on parental authority in the process. By 1869 there was not even this amount of educational agreement. Those children who were criminal or destitute still became the responsibility of the State but the 'ordinary' Leeds working-class child, even when he could not be educated at home, did not necessarily accept the authority of the public school system to educate him instead. Some children were educated without any schooling, some relied on private adventure schools, and even those who did experience rational schooling were quick to reject it 'if they may not have their own way'.

The history of education before 1870 is not simply the history of educational growth. It is also the history of the development of a particular *form* of socialization, rational schooling. And the evidence for Leeds, at least, suggests that this form of schooling, despite the efforts of the educators (and particularly of the National schools and of the government's inspectors) was not readily accepted by the educated. Certainly Fitch, in assessing the state of elementary education in Leeds for the Department of Education, was as much concerned with the quality as with the quantity of schools. He judged private schools by rational criteria and found them wanting. They lacked 'careful or systematic teaching in any subject whatever' and any 'knowledge of method', and such classification as existed depended on the children's payments rather than on their knowledge or mental requirements.[91]

Fitch's conclusion was categorical: private adventure schools could not be regarded as contributing to 'National Education' because nineteen out of twenty of them could not provide proof of their self-appointed teachers' qualifications.[92]

Fitch's judgements (and the criteria for them) were confirmed by the 1870 Education Act —firstly by its own equation of elementary education and rational schooling and, secondly, by its underpinning of the shaky authority of the inspected public schools by legislation (and the power of the State was fully mobilized behind schooling in 1884, when it was made compulsory). These Acts of Parliament were not, of course, an instant solution to the problems I have been describing — board schools had their own problems of authority[93] and the attitudes and responses of working-class children and their parents to State education have been the recurrent concern of educationalists and sociologists ever since. But the point with which I want to conclude is this: the development of elementary education in Britain can and must be related to technological changes, to the evolution of the occupational structure, to class conflicts and ideologies, to social control, but whatever conclusions we come to about the functions of education in a capitalist society, they must bear upon the actual *experience* of children in schools.[94] Unless we can relate our 'macro' analyses of State education to 'micro' analyses of children's experience, our understanding of the educational process is incomplete. The point of connection is schooling: the State makes its educational demands and exercises its educational authority through schools and it is schools' demands and claims and logic that children experience. In this essay I have only given a partial account of elementary education in nineteenth-century Leeds (I made no attempt to place the schools in their 'macro' context) but I hope I have done enough to show that the history of *schooling* is an illuminating and vital aspect of the history of education.

NOTES

[1] Leeds Grammar School, although free, taught Latin and Greek only to those who could read and write sufficiently well to pass the entrance requirements – this usually meant children who had been prepared by tutors or academies.

[2] R.M. Hartwell, The Yorkshire Woollen and Worsted Industry, 1800–1850, Oxford D.Phil.Thesis, 1955, pp.444–5.

[3] Quoted in ibid., pp. 295, 310–11.

[4] Rules and Orders for Relieving and Employing the Poor of the Township of Leeds: and for the Government of the Workhouse There (1771).

[5] Ibid.

[6] Subscription Roll of the Leeds Charity School, Leeds City Archive, DB197/5.

[7] Leeds Parish Return to the Archbishop of York's Visitation, 1764; Leeds Charity School General Book, Leeds City Archive, DB196/1.

[8] Ibid; Minutes of the Leeds Charity School Committee, Leeds City Archive, DB196/5.

[9] Ibid.

[10] See below.

[11] P.P. 1831–2 XV, Richard Oastler's Evidence to the Select Committee on the 'Bill to Regulate the Labour of Children in Mills and Factories'.

[12] Ibid.

[13] H. Schroeder, *The Annals of Yorkshire* (Leeds, 1852), Vol. 2, pp. 19–20.

[14] *A Few Plain Facts about the Leeds Ragged and Certified Industrial Schools* (Leeds, ?1867); 9th Annual Report of the Leeds Ragged School and Shoe-Black Society (1868).

[15] *A Few Plain Facts about the Leeds Ragged and Certified Industrial Schools.*

[16] J.G. Fitch 'Report on Leeds' in Returns and Commissioners' Reports on the Schools of Birmingham, Leeds, Liverpool and Manchester (London, 1870), p. 120.

[17] T. Bernard in Reports of the Society for Bettering the Condition and Increasing the Comforts of the Poor (London, 1805), Vol. IV, pp. 112–20; E. Baines, *History, Directory and Gazeteer of the County of York* (Leeds, 1822), Vol. 1, pp. 28–9.

[18] J. Hole, *Light, More Light!* (Leeds, 1860), pp. 48–9; Minutes of the Committee of Council, 1856–7, Rev. F. Watkins' Report, pp. 313–14.

[19] Report of the Leeds National Society (Appendix I to the 3rd Annual Report of the National Society, 1814). Minutes of the Leeds National Society, 20 December 1811 and 10 May 1815.

[20] Report of the Royal Lancasterian School, Leeds (in the Annual Report of the British and Foreign School Society, 1815).

[21] J. Pearson, *The Life of William Hey* (Leeds, 1822), p. 191.

[22] Report of the Leeds N.S. (Appendix I of the 2nd Annual Report of the N.S., 1813).

[23] Minutes of the Leeds N.S., 20 December 1811.

[24] T.D. Whitaker, *Loidis and Elmete* (Leeds, 1816), p. 74.

[25] Report of the Leeds Lancasterian School (in the 1825 Report of the B.F.S.S.).

[26] Report of the Leeds Lancasterian School (in the 1829 Report of the B.F.S.S.).

[27] This refers to the schools' running costs – local donations remained important for the initial building costs. For detailed figures see the Leeds and District N.S. Minute Book, 1811–45, and the Records of the Trustees of the Charity School Funds, 1850–84, Leeds City Archive DB 196/19–55. Fitch calculated the 1869 income of the National Schools in the whole borough as £11,452.6s.7d., of which 20.7 per cent came from subscriptions and endowments, 41.5 per cent from fees and 37.8 per cent from the government (Fitch, op.cit., p. 81).

[28] Leeds N.S. Minute Book, 25 January 1842, and see the individual school files held by the metropolitan N.S. – schools were in continuous correspondence about their lack of local subscribers.

[29] Report of the Leeds Lancasterian School (1829) (included in the Annual Report of the B.F.S.S.).

[30] See, for example, the Report of the School in 1838 (in the Annual Report of the B.F.S.S.).

[31] Report of the Leeds Lancasterian School (1867) (in the Annual Report of the B.F.S.S.).

[32] Hole, op. cit., pp. 29–30; Fitch, op cit., pp. 80–1; The Census of Population, 1851.

[33] 26th Annual Report of the Leeds and District National Society (1838).

[34] Minutes of the Committee of Council, 1841–2, Vol. 2 (Rev. F. Watkins' Report on the Girls' School at Woodhouse, Nether Green, Leeds).

[35] See the National Society's School Files for Leeds – for example, Christ Church, 1841, 1843 and 1844, or Trinity, 1846.

[36] 18th Annual Report of the Leeds N.S. (1830).

[37] Minutes of the Committee of Council on Education, 1848–9–50, Vol. 1, Rev. F. Watkins' report, p. 217.

[38] Ibid., 1850–1, Rev. F. Watkins' report, p. 336.

[39] Appendix VII to the 22nd and 23rd Annual Reports of the N.S. (1833 and 1834).

40 Appendix XI to the 26th Annual Report of the N.S. (1837).

41 Appendix IX of the 20th Annual Report of the N.S. (1831).

42 27th Report of the N.S. (1838 Report of the General Committee).

43 21st Annual Report of the Leeds N.S. (1833).

44 Report of the Endowed Schools Inquiry Commission (1868), pp. 246–7.

45 Ibid.

46 A phrase used in the 20th Annual Report of the Leeds N.S. (1832).

47 Minutes of the Committee of Council. See, for example, 1850–1, pp. 288, 335, or 1851–2, Vol. 2, p. 119.

48 A phrase used in the 21st Annual Report of the Leeds N.S. (1833).

49 Whitaker, op. cit., p. 74; Annual Report of the B.F.S.S. (1816).

50 Cf. D. Wardle, *English Popular Education, 1780–1970* (Cambridge, 1970), p. 86.

51 A phrase used in the Minutes of the Leeds N.S., 1 December 1815.

52 From an account of the public examination of the Leeds Lancasterian School in the *Leeds Mercury*, 20 December 1839.

53 Minutes of the Leeds N.S., 26 and 31 October 1812; and 7 May and 27 June 1814.

54 Minutes of the Leeds N.S., 12 July 1814 and 13 June 1816.

55 Rev. F. Watkins, *A Letter to His Grace the Archbishop of York on the State of Education in the Church Schools of Yorkshire* (1860), pp. 8–9.

56 Ivan Illich's definition – *Deschooling Society* (London, 1971), pp. 25–6.

57 J. Ryley, *The Leeds Guide* (Leeds, 1808), p. 52.

58 Quotes from the Wesleyan Methodists' Sunday Schools Minute Book, 1816–21.

59 Ibid.

60 Ibid.

61 J. Barker, *The History and Confessions of a Man, as Put Forth By Himself* (Leeds, 1846), p. 62.

62 Ibid, p. 79.

63 V. Ward, *Observations on Sunday Schools* (Leeds, 1827), p. 30; and see the Wesleyan Methodists' Sunday Schools Minute Book, 1827–8.

64 Ward, op. cit., p. 30.

65 P.P. 1833 XX, George Haigh's evidence to the Commission for Inquiry into the Employment of Children in Factories, p. 115A.

66 Fitch, op. cit., p. 89.

67 See B.A. Kilburn, *Annals of Zion School* (Leeds, c. 1878) and A. Richardson, *Zion Sunday School* (Leeds, 1935).

68 Ibid.

69 Kilburn, op. cit., pp. 17–18.

70 Minutes of the Committee of Council, 1846 (J. Fletcher's Report on Zion).

71 Kilburn, op. cit., *passim.*

72 Samuel Smiles, for example, taught Comparative Anatomy, Natural History and Geography, during his brief association with the school. See Richardson, op. cit., *passim.*

[73] Quoted in H. Fligg, A History of Elementary Education in Leeds Prior to 1870, M.Ed.Thesis, Leeds, 1938, p. 54.

[74] See for example the *Northern Star*, 22 June 1839: 'The government wish to build schools, to select teachers, and to teach "spelling, writing and arithmetic" to the young of all willing . . . The people, oppressed as they now are, *will* not accept the offered "schooling" . . . The true and profitable education will be that which is voluntarily sought by men rendered peaceful in mind and free in action . . . Let the people have their rights and they will instruct themselves.'

[75] Joseph Barker in *The People* (Leeds, 1849), Vol. 1, p. 322.

[76] Barker, *The History and Confessions of a Man, as Put Forth By Himself*, p. 141.

[77] The information for the following discussion was drawn from the collection of 28 school log books held in the Leeds City Library Archives and from the two books held by St George's C. of E. Primary School, Leeds.

[78] Quote from St Mark's National School for Girls, 13 January 1863.

[79] Quote from St Simon's Boys' School, 20 August 1866.

[80] The best examples of this can be found throughout the log book of St Andrew's Infant School.

[81] Quote from St Andrew's Girls' School, 22 February 1866.

[82] Quote from New Wortley Boys' National School, 14 December 1863.

[83] Quote from New Wortley Girls' National School, 21 February 1866.

[84] Quote from New Wortley Boys' National School, 11 June 1866.

[85] Quote from St Saviour's Girls' School, 27 January 1863.

[86] Quote from St Simon's Girls' School, 2 September 1864.

[87] Fitch defined working-class private schools as those which charged five pence a week or less — Fitch, op. cit., p. 110.

[88] 'It is certain that there is a strong and very general feeling amongst the working people against any devices which seem designed to make the school an instrument for promoting what they regard as clerical or sectarian as opposed to purely educational interests.' Fitch, op. cit., p. 106.

[89] Ibid., p. 106.

[90] Ibid.

[91] Ibid., pp. 94–105 (quote from p. 97).

[92] Ibid., p. 107.

[93] See, for example, D. Rubinstein, *School Attendance in London, 1870–1904* (Hull, 1969).

[94] See P. Corrigan, *Smash Street Kids* (London, 1977).

Chapter 4:

The content of education and the socialization of the working-class child 1830-1860

J. M. Goldstrom

Not until the 1780s did the idea that working-class children should have an education receive serious consideration. Charity schools existed before this time, but in insignificant numbers. The Sunday School Movement that gathered momentum at this time was a first brave attempt to teach basic reading and writing to large numbers of children. Day school education was the logical development and in 1808 the British and Foreign School Society was established, followed by the National Society for Promoting the Education of the Poor in the Principles of the Established Church in 1811. These two religious societies were to dominate the field of education for the poor until 1870 and the coming of the Education Act.

For the first twenty years of their existence their day schools provided an education that was centered around the Scriptures. But by the 1830s the Bible-based system of education was meeting with challenge and by the 1850s it had been practically supplanted by a new orthodoxy, that of political economy. The period taken for discussion here, from 1830 to 1860, presents us with the phenomenon of a rigidly devised system of education that was made to change over a relatively short space of time in response to acute economic and social pressures.

The moral and religious identity of the societies' schools, so important to them, remained intact over the whole period, in spite of the fact that the schools were funded increasingly by the government and had to comply with certain minimum standards once they submitted themselves to government inspection. The 1851 Census of Education in fact distinguishes between twenty-six types of denominational schools, not counting the various types of secular school, but the only two organizations of major influence over the period were the National Society and the much smaller British and Foreign School Society.[1]

These two societies had taken the responsibility upon themselves from their founding years of nothing less than the education of every working-class child in the country. With limited resources, particularly financial resources, to deploy, it was of crucial importance to them to concentrate on the control of the ideas and attitudes they wished to disseminate in the schools. After an initial helping hand from head-quarters in the setting up of a new school, fund raising and the day-to-day running of it was delegated to the local branch. Direction of educational ideology came from the central organization and the local branch ran its school in accordance with the rules of the parent society.

At the society's headquarters a set of readers embodying the 'correct' moral and religious tenets was prepared with the utmost care, then distributed to schools at subsidized prices. Any other set of readers was discouraged or forbidden, thus the only additional printed material to find its way into the classroom would be Bibles, religious tracts and moralizing tales. To accompany the set of readers there was a teacher's manual which instructed in minute detail how the lessons should be conducted. Given the low level of ability of teachers at that time, the school reader played a crucial role. Most teachers were untrained, and those few who received instruction beyond their own school years would have obtained it from their society's training college, where the stress was on conformity to a rigid system rather than on a broadening of views. Piety and conscientiousness, not independence of mind, were the qualities sought in the teacher of that period. So of necessity, since children stayed just a short time at school and saw very little other than their set of readers, the ideas to which they were exposed were very limited.

The monitorial system of teaching, expounded by Dr Andrew Bell, was the keystone of Anglican eduction in the National schools. His system's greatest virtue lay in its economical deployment of teachers. Only one need be employed for the parish school, no matter how big it was, a large portion of the teacher's work being systematically delegated to unpaid child monitors. The series of school readers prepared for use in National schools was prepared in 1812 and published by the Society for Promoting Christian Knowledge. The basis of the series was a 154-page publication of Mrs Sarah Trimmer's, called *The Charity Spelling Book*, and first published in 1791. The book was taken to pieces and reconstructed as the National Society Central School Book series. 'Book One' consisted of twelve sheet cards of words and phrases, 'Book Two' was a twelve-page booklet of little stories. When the third book was printed the National Society felt the series was quite adequate. A simplified version of Bell's *Instructions for Conducting Schools* accompanied the series. At no stage could a teacher or his monitors be in doubt as to how they should proceed:

> Q. How is the National School Book, No. 2, that is, the collection of stories of words of one syllable, begun?
>
> A. By a repeating lesson from the mouth of the teacher, in the following manner: the teacher says, 'The way', class says the same after him; teacher, 'Of God', class, 'Of God'; teacher, 'is', class the like; teacher, 'a good way', class, ditto. Then the assistant, and the boys after him, as before in the cards.
>
> Q. What is done next?
>
> A. The first boys say, 'The way'; next 'of God'; next, 'is'; next, 'a good way'. Each child repeating to itself in a whispering or low voice what is said aloud by the child whose turn it is to read ...[2]

The reading material referred to in the manual does not mention Mrs Trimmer's various instructive tales, which were available to the schools, but the list nevertheless gives a fair indication of how limited reading materials were in National schools until the 1840s.

Joseph Lancaster was the driving force behind the Nonconformist education system embodied in the British and Foreign School Society. He was a campaigning schoolmaster, of Quaker background, and he passionately wanted to rescue the children who roamed the city streets, illiterate and a prey to any corrupt ideas that came their way. The education he envisaged would instil in them the virtues of thrift, temperance and industry, respect for property, law and order as well as the Christian morals. But he could not commit his teachers and schools (the first of which was established in 1798) to a particular religious doctrine as was the practice in National Society schools, since he was determined to teach children of all religions. What he needed was an educational system quite free of sectarian overtones.

The selection of suitable material for such a reader was fraught with difficulties. If the Bible itself were used critics were not satisfied that the interpretation could be impartial; if a selection of texts taken from the Bible were the basis, then the nature of the selection itself was vulnerable to criticism. The uneasy compromise on which he eventually settled was an early eighteenth-century Bible catechism.[3] Lancaster was just as mindful of economy in the running of a school as was the National

Society, and he too applied the monitorial system. He argued however that the book was an inefficient tool of education, and pointed out that only a small part of a book could be in use at any one time. At first experimenting with book pages torn out from the catechism and pasted on cards, he then had large reading sheets printed. Around these groups of children could gather, under the supervision of monitors. One set of sheets would serve an entire school, and thus in Lancasterian schools it was possible for a child to learn to read without ever touching a book.

Lancaster's system had won wide acclaim by the opening years of the new century, although he had constant financial troubles. When his connections with the British and Foreign School Society came to an end in 1814 his methods were taken over in entirety by his best pupils, and were incorporated eventually in the Society's training manuals. Although extracts from the Scriptures formed the staple, indeed the only reading material employed in British and Foreign School Society schools until 1839, there was some opposition to the use of the old eighteenth-century catechism in some quarters because of its vulnerability to different interpretations, which might be offensive to parents of particular denominations. So in 1820 William Allen, a leading administrator in the Society, compiled a manual which he called *Scripture Lessons for Schools on the British System for Mutual Instruction.* The book was broken into sections illustrating the various duties and responsibilities of the Christian. Under section headings like 'The Duty of Parents towards their Children', 'Duties of Masters and Servants', 'Of Anger and Malice', were listed relevant quotations taken direct from the Bible. There was no comment or interpretation which might provoke accusations of bias towards any particular denomination, as he was to explain later to a Select Committee:

> We have made them (the Scripture Lessons) to bear upon those duties in a very striking and prominent way without any comment whatever; but merely in the words of the Scripture; such as the duties of subjects to government in the words of Scripture; the duties of servants to masters in the words of Scripture; the relative duties of husbands and wives, and parents and children in the words of Scripture. They were most anxiously calculated to bring out those great and important duties, and to engrave them upon the minds of the children . . . .[4]

Taking the two societies together, if one looks at the teaching matter to be found in the schools it is not surprising, since so much of it came direct from the Bible, that the lessons look thoroughly indigestible. In the Anglican books there are references on most pages to the Commandments, God, the Thirty-Nine Articles and the Life Hereafter. And William Allen, in the preface to his *Scripture Lessons* which went into all Nonconformist schools in 1820, remarked that no other work of ethics or moral reasoning could equal the Holy Scriptures since God was the author, Salvation was the end, and Truth the subject.[5]

But whilst many pages in many of the books have biblical texts down one side with questions on meaning down the other, different techniques were employed to instruct in the Christian way of life. For example, a story is given of a farmer who carried about with him in his fields a notebook containing his own selection of scriptural texts for guidance in his duties as farmer and head of the family. The child is given the picture of a man whose every task and decision is influenced by Christian principle. A series of appropriate texts follows the story.[6] A variant on the straightforward catechism is the tale of Tom Bowles:

LESSON V

In what way was Tom Bowles brought up?

What were all the days in the week to him?

What day ought he to have considered different from the rest?

A. Sunday.

Why?

LESSON V

Tom Bowles was a poor boy, who was brought up so bad, that he did not know what a church was for, and all the days in the week were the same to him; he did not know how to serve God, he had not thought of God, and yet he took the name of God in his mouth, but it was to swear and curse by. In this sad way Tom Bowles went on . . .[7]

There was an earnest desire on the part of the compilers that the Bible should be seen to have relevance to everyday life:

Though this worthy woman had such pious thoughts, it was not her wish to be reading and praying all day long, because she knew that it was the duty of poor people to labour for their food and raiment: she therefore resolved to continue to be industrious, and to go out washing and ironing, as she used to do.[8]

Instruction in conduct and morality have a decidedly Calvinist tone in the Nonconformist books, with biblical quotations on the sins of in-

temperance, malice, pride, avarice etc. The Nonconformist child was
required to digest the implications of

> MATT.CHAP.XIII.40 As therefore the tares are gathered and burned
> in the fire; so shall it be in the end of this world.
> 41 The Son of man shall send forth his angels, and they shall gather
> out of his kingdom all things that offend, and them which do
> iniquity; . . . .[9]

The Anglican books instructed through sermons, moral fables and hymns
as well as through the Bible text:

> My good Child,
>   The vi-ces which child-ren of your age are most u-su-al-ly tempt-ed
> to com-mit, are ly-ing, tak-ing God's name in vain, and steal-ing.
>   Ly-ing, and pro-fan-ing God's name, are faults which ap-pear
> ve-ry early: these are found in child-ren al-most as soon as they can
> speak, and are chief-ly ow-ing to the bad ex-am-ple of their pa-rents,
> or o-thers of their own fa-mi-ly . . . .[10]

Both societies wished the children to learn through their readers
about the demarcations between rich and poor, and the mutual depen-
dence of each in a harmonious society. Contentment in the station of
life to which God had assigned them was an important precept. Also
important was that a child should grow up to take his place as a member
of the respectable, devout and hard-working poor, and not allow himself to become one of the contemptible 'undeserving poor'. To reconcile
the working-class child to his lot, there is thorough discussion of the
duties and obligations of the rich towards him. The rich man is described as having a positive duty to be charitable, to make available
rewards, encouragement and advice to the less fortunate, and to treat
his servants with consideration. In such sentiments the two societies do
not differ. But the Nonconformist *Scripture Lessons* is interesting for
the much less patronizing tone it adopts when discussing the social
place of the poor person. When the question of bettering oneself is
raised, the Nonconformist view is that a thrifty and diligent person may
well be able to improve his lot. The National Society books on the other
hand tend to discourage such ideas as impracticable. Far better that the
poor should devote themselves to work, relaxation in simple pleasures,
and avoidance of the shameful workhouse.
    One would not expect there to be very much vocationally instructive
matter in the books, given that children were trained to know their place

in life, and that only limited occupations would be available to them. Mrs Trimmer plainly expected her readers to assume the duties of servants and labourers, and concentrated her advice on their proper deportment as such when they had left school. The British schools taught some needlework, but no other practical skills.

That the vast majority of children did not have access to books beyond those described, that is *Scripture Lessons* and the Bible in British schools, the National Society reader series, biblical tracts and S.P.C.K. publications in the National schools, may be fairly assumed. Further, it must be remembered that very little of the material had been written after 1820, most of the tracts and stories in the National schools in fact dating from between 1780 and 1800. The influence of the S.P.C.K. in these schools was enormous, partly because it was their publications that the schools purchased, partly by nature of the monitorial system that was so widely used. British schools also followed the monitorial system faithfully but perhaps ideas in their classrooms were less exclusively scriptural. During the 1820s and 1830s teachers at the Borough Road model school in London evolved a technique of elaborating on the associations that could be drawn from a word taken from the Bible, ostensibly for spelling practice. Thus a smattering of history and geography was introduced.

> FERTILIZE. What is the meaning? To make fruitful. What is this applied to? The ground. What makes the ground fertile? Sun and the rain. What country is very fertile? Egypt. What is the cause of that? The overflowing of the Nile.[11]

The British and Foreign School Society claimed that they could in fact give a broad education whilst still confining themselves to Bible extracts. However the senior pupils had access to a handful of geography and history books which they were permitted to draw on for use with the younger children. There is evidence here that the British and Foreign School Society administrators were straining against their own self-imposed limitations.[12]

Educationists remained satisfied with a religious-monitorial system in schools over a long period, and only the Radicals complained. Their agitation for secular education went unheeded. The students at training colleges continued to study Iremonger's *Dr Bell's System of Instruction* and the children continued with their scriptural texts. General feeling among teachers was that the average length of stay at school was so short it would be positively dangerous to divert precious time from study of the Bible. But such complacency disappeared as the 1830s wore on and as working-class unrest grew. A struggle began for control of the schools and with it demands for a sweeping revision of the curriculum.

The Radicals, particularly those that were associated with the Society for the Diffusion of Useful Knowledge, had been the most assertive from the start. They had launched their *Quarterly Journal of Education* in 1831, to campaign for a state controlled, secular education. They did not make much impact at first and they were naturally much resented by the religious societies. However, their criticisms were increasingly endorsed by witnesses talking to the government Select Committees, and by the findings of the statistical societies. One such witness depicts vividly the deficiencies of the system:

> I know schools, with well-meaning but imperfectly-educated directors, where the Bible is the school-book, the only school-book; where a large Bible is selected and placed upon a stand in the middle of the school, impressing, at least leaving the impression to take effect, upon the minds of the young, that the Bible is the only book in the world, and addressing to it something almost of an idolatrous respect. In those schools every lesson, however secular, arises out of, and comes back to the Bible: for example, if the lesson should be the natural history of the bear, it will not be permitted to be entered into till the passage is read about the bears that tore the children that mocked Elijah . . . in the great majority of cases (these methods) will operate in the way of disgust, by over-doing religious instruction, and the Bible and the reiterated instructions will be all thrown away whenever the pupil escapes into freedom . . . .[13]

One provincial statistical society concluded that in the schools they examined 'little worthy of the name of moral education exists, the subject being very imperfectly understood'.[14]

Criticisms began to bite more painfully when they came from professional educationists, from churchmen and from leaders within the religious societies themselves. The argument swung round, to question whether the Bible could be properly understood in the absence of any knowledge of secular subjects. Moreover, were immature monitors fit to supervise Bible readings and to give moral instruction to young children?

The religious societies started to employ inspectors during the 1830s and in their reports they had suggestions to make for widening the educational material. The Rev. Edward Feild reported in his capacity as inspector for the National Society:

> I found an increasing conviction that it is right and necessary to introduce more books of secular and general knowledge into our schools, if only for the purpose of elucidating and applying the Holy Scriptures. And I observed that where such books and subjects had actually been introduced there was no apparent deficiency of instruction, or knowledge in religious truths.[15]

Government inspectors were making similar points in the 1840s. In the view of the Rev. Baptist Noel the poor should be taught how to set about their shopping in an economical way, how to keep out of the hands of the pawnbroker, and how to look after their health. Another inspector considered poor children should learn about cottage economy and political economy, and in 1845 yet another wrote 'the right use of good secular reading-books appears to contribute to the more reverent use, as well as to the better understanding, of the Bible'.[16]

By the middle of the century all the religious societies had conceded these points and had set themselves, albeit grudgingly in many cases, to creating secular readers. It was a slow process for most of them because the enthusiasts for change were slowed by the forces of conservatism and inertia. But quite independently of English developments a set of non-denominational readers financed by the English government had been published in Ireland by the Irish Commissioners. The books were secular in approach and had been written by people who believed in the tenets of political economy. They were produced in vast numbers for schools all over Ireland and because they were both cheap and completely non-sectarian they found a ready market in English schools.[17]

The religious societies were thus provided with tailor-made models and in the main took advantage of them. The first English series of significance was brought out by the British and Foreign School Society as *Daily Lesson Books* (1840–2), written by Henry Dunn and J.T. Crossley. This was followed by the S.P.C.K. *Reading Books* (1851–6) for the National Society, the Congregationals' *Training School Reader* by W.J. Unwin (1851), and the Catholic *Reading Book Series* in 1862. Resemblance to the Irish books is close; the sets are almost identical in number of pages, size, bindings and illustrations; even the titles and chapter headings are modelled on the Irish books. Different denominations contrived to retain denominational character in their own sets through the selection of hymns, prayers, sermons, stories, biographies and church histories they included.

The really striking difference between these and the old readers is the shrinking of the space accorded to religion. There is a total shift of focus. The Bible is still there, but its importance is secondary, and it is the fashionable laws of political economy that have usurped its role. When William Allen wrote in his preface to *Scripture Lessons* in 1820 that there could be no book to equal the Bible as an educational text he spoke for a whole generation of educational thinking. Contrast his sentiments with the Newcastle Commission in 1861 which might pay lip service still to the part religion had to play, but at the same time argued:

> ... the knowledge most important to a labouring man is that of the causes which regulate the amount of his wages, the hours of his work, the regularity of his employment, and the prices of what he consumes.[18]

When the British and Foreign School Society series appeared in 1840 it had a special section on political economy with a lesson on wages written by Archbishop Whately. This lesson was considered so important by the Society that it was reproduced from the Irish books in entirety (and was to appear in the readers of all the other denominations).[19] It combined remarks about good habits to cultivate — diligence, forethought, temperance, frugality — and all the dangers of neglecting them — with stern warnings of the dangers to the working man of challenging the economic order. The laws of political economy were invoked to demonstrate the futility of trade unions and of government intervention in wage bargaining. In short, it contained all the essentials of teaching that the middle classes desired to imprint upon the working man. Dunn and Crossley added revision notes to assist understanding of the rather difficult concepts:

1. Folly of thinking it unjust that one man should receive more than another for his labour.
2. Impossibility of regulating wages by law — has been attempted — always failed — why (see above).
3. Way in which labourer can improve his lot — increased skill — knowledge of best markets for labour — habits of forethought, temperance — economy.[20]

The direct lecture was by no means the only format used in the readers for teaching political economy. There were a number of fictional biographies and some straightforward biographies, too, in style fore-shadowing the works of Samuel Smiles. Rather ponderous fairy stories appeared from time to time, a political economy cast being given to the conventional moral ending. Less incongruous were the fables, one example of which showed what disaster would befall if the various organs of the human body went on strike in protest at the seeming greed and selfishness of the stomach. The fable explains that the stomach is to the body what the rich man is to the poor man in society, and concludes that 'a rich man, even though he may care for no one but himself, can hardly avoid benefiting his neighbours'.[21]

Another marked change in the character of the new secular books was the rather self-conscious attempts they showed at widening the range of teaching material. Compilers included a range of short excerpts, not necessarily written with the young child in mind, covering such mis-cellaneous subjects as grammar, hygiene, art, chemistry, philosophy and so forth. The editors boasted that their books provided a compendium of useful knowledge. (It was still the assumption that a child could master the skill of reading and absorb the message of the text at one and the same time.) A suggested curriculum for schools put forward in 1848 by a training college inspector was typical:

> biography (of good men); natural history; the preservation of health; cottage economy; horticulture; mechanism; agriculture; geography; history; grammar; natural and experimental philosophy; money matters; political economy; popular astronomy.[22]

Although there had been elaborate and protracted discussion of what should go into their new series the various religious societies emerged with practically indistinguishable sets. Nor was the uniformity con-fined to school readers; in the training colleges the manuals were virtually interchangeable, as were the courses, and from 1854 the students all sat the same government examination. A consensus of opinion on the constituent ingredients of education for the poor had been reached. Just as, at an earlier stage, the Bible was considered as embodying all a child need know to equip him for life, now it was his school reader that was to fulfil the purpose. It had to be 'comprehensive', and the schoolteacher's understanding of it total. From the day he began his apprenticeship in his school, the pupil teacher would be most unlikely to read any book during his working day that was not immediately concerned with the instruction of his pupils — the volume of facts he was expected to acquire in the advanced readers simply would not permit of it. If he went on to training college, though his horizons inevitably expanded with the stimulus of fellow students and more adult literature, he went on in the laborious business of acquiring facts, and mastering techniques for expounding them. Once back in the schools, fully trained, he expected of his set of readers that it should provide him with teaching matter for most of the day, and be organized so as to last for months, or for the full school year. And the technique of eking out material was brought to a fine art:

> *Do not permit too much to be read at one time.* A good teacher can profitably occupy twenty or thirty minutes over a page, without at all wearying his children. He will often say, 'I perceive you do not understand that passage; read it again.' Then he will require defin- itions of leading words, their synonyms and their opposites: then perhaps he will have the sentence analysed or paraphrased; and after this he will thoroughly explain every incidental allusion, whether geographical, historical, or biographical, which may be involved in the passage. All this, it may be, must be done before that which is read can be thoroughly understood; and he knows, (to return to the point whence we set out) that until it is understood it can never be properly read.[23]

There are a number of questions that can be asked about the effective- ness of education over this period. The question of literacy lies in an area that lends itself up to a point to quantification, and is a logical one to begin with. What evidence we have suggests that at least one half, prob- ably two thirds of working-class adults could read (though the number who could write was always substantially less) in the 1830s.[24] This was largely the work of the Sunday and the monitorial schools. Over the next two decades the Registrar General's figures are ample evidence of a steady rise in literacy.[25] If further evidence is needed we have only to look at the vast increase of books, periodicals and newspapers bought by working-class people.[26] Years before the 1870 Education Act illiteracy had ceased to be a major problem.

However, at no time had literacy been regarded by the educationists as a sufficient end in itself; their concern was to use literacy for en- couraging church attendance, for reducing crime, for curbing strikes and riots, and implanting the virtues of self-help, thrift, sobriety and cleanli- ness. Periodic surveys expressed general satisfaction with the achieve- ment of such aims, so that the labouring poor were judged to be patient in adversity, to be law-abiding and devout largely because they had been educated to be so. The claims were extravagant, sometimes 'substantiated' by tables, but do not stand up to close scrutiny.[27]

Just what it was that contributed to the easing of social tensions is far from clear. No one is in any doubt that the mid-Victorian period was a calm time compared with the upheavals of the thirties and forties. The peaceable and good natured character of the working classes was the envy of other European countries, and historians describe this as a golden era. It was to be expected that educationists of the period should claim that such a happy state of affairs was the doing of the schools; there were more school places, children attended for longer periods, there were more teachers, better trained than in the earlier days, the government was helping with finance and the new curriculum showed an awareness of the problems presented by an industrial society. One cannot say the schools had played no part, but their effectiveness must be assessed with caution, if not with scepticism. Given that the number of children educated under the new methods before the middle of the century were few in number, the proportion of adults in the mid-Victorian period to have profited must have been small. They would either have received the older monitorial kind of education, or they would have had no education at all. And no educationist from 1840 had shown any confidence that the monitorial system was producing the kind of citizen they would like to see. One could not expect the new secular education to have borne fruit in the attitudes and behaviour of adults before the 1870s and by that time the golden era had gone.

If we cannot accord a significant role to education as contributing to harmony, we must look elsewhere for explanations. Life for the working classes was improving in the most fundamental ways. Sanitary and housing standards changed for the better and the number of people having to accept poor relief was dropping. For younger people there were now more job opportunities as the demand for skilled labour in the towns rose. It was a time when wages were increasing and living standards in general looking up. People could not help but see how much better off they were than their parents had been, and they were able to see their children's future in an optimistic light.

This was now the second generation of town dwellers, and they were much better adapted to town conditions than their parents. They were more confident and self-reliant too, and less dependent on middle-class charity. We can see this if we look at the institutions that developed. Burial societies and friendly societies were organized institutions for self-help; less formally, pubs acted as focal centres for help and companionship, and relatives and neighbours came to rely on each other in times of need. Trade unions had by this time been accorded recognition and this, together with the working-class franchise, meant that working men need not resort to violence to exert political pressure.

It is all too easy to forget, when we are looking at the influence of schools on children, that school was one influence among many in a child's life. The nineteenth-century schoolchild spent only a few hours of each day there, and probably left when he was twelve. He came to school from a working-class home where values were often different from those the schools were so assiduously trying to instil in him. With his schooldays behind him he would encounter ideas through clubs, pubs, the working-class press, Sunday papers, trade union meetings and street corner discussion with his friends. Such ideas would be bound to modify the precepts that had been dinned into him at school, and probably only half understood. Of one fact only we may be absolutely confident, and that is that children could not have committed crimes while they were in the classroom and to this extent schools contributed to the fall in juvenile crime!

One claim made through the first half of the century by the advocates of denominational schools was that church attendance was affected for the good. But the 1851 Religious Census revealed that for the majority ties with the Church were at best nominal. Funerals and marriages apart, the church did not appear to have very much appeal for the average working man and his family. There was an inverse relationship as the century went on between the number of school places provided and the number of church worshippers.[28] If we consider why working-class people went to church at all a common reason would have been social ambition. Upward social mobility was very often accompanied by a move from chapel to church, and the poorest people, when times began to improve, would assert their new 'respectability' by joining a chapel and a temperance society. A minority of places of worship had high attendances among the working classes but these were generally the churches that catered for the tightly-knit communities of Roman Catholics or primitive nonconformist sects — groups for whom the church was traditionally the centre of social life.[29]

In modern times we think of education as a means of working towards a society where class barriers are removed and opportunities are as easily available to the working-class child as to any other. The Victorians never thought of education in such a way; they saw it as their duty to provide 'appropriate' education for the different classes, and working-class schools could never be mistaken for anything but establishments for the lower orders. The classics, the fine arts, the drawing-room accomplishments played little part in their curriculum, and their teachers did not hail from a ladies' college or from Oxford or Cambridge. True, a really bright child would be encouraged to use his talents to lift himself out of his class but the average child was firmly taught his place in the social hierarchy. Whilst we cannot hold the school system responsible for the rigid class divisions of the Victorian era, there is little doubt that it helped to perpetuate them.

The spreading of literacy was the most solid and unequivocal achievement of the system, and it was literacy that laid the foundation for the country's rising standard of wealth. No industrial nation could have gone forward without a work force that could build up its skills on basic literacy. The idea that you could increase a country's wealth through investing in education was a concept unknown to the mid-Victorians; the measure of success for them was a contented industrial labour force. The religious societies may have failed in what they set out to do but we can judge them today as having unwittingly contributed in a rather more material way to the well-being of society.

NOTES

[1] P.P. 1852–53 XC, Census of Great Britain, Education, England and Wales, Table B, cxxiii.
[2] F. Iremonger, *Dr Bell's System of Instruction, Broken into Short Questions and Answers for the Use of Masters and Teachers in the National Schools* (new ed., London, 1825), p. 15.
[3] J. Freame, *Scripture Instructions, in the Form of Question and Answer, as Taught in the Royal Lancasterian Schools: being a selection designed to promote piety and virtue, and to discourage vice and immorality. Originally compiled. . . in 1713* (London, 1813).
[4] P.P. 1834 IX, Report from Select Committee on the State of Education, p. 72.
[5] W. Allen, *Scripture Lessons for Schools on the British System of Mutual Instruction* (London, 1820), Preface.
[6] Sarah Trimmer, *The Two Farmers, an Exemplary Tale; designed to recommend the practice of benevolence towards mankind, and all other living creatures; and the religious observance of the Sabbath day* (London, 1826), pp. 6–7.
[7] F. Iremonger, *Questions for the Different Elementary Books used in National Schools* (5th ed., London, 1826), p. 7.

[8] Sarah Trimmer, *The Servant's Friend, an Exemplary Tale; designed to enforce the religious instructions given at Sunday and other charity schools; by pointing out the practical application of them in a state of service* (new ed., London, 1824), p. 7.

[9] Allen, *Scripture Lessons*, p. 91.

[10] *The Child's First Book*, Society for Promoting Christian Knowledge, (London, 1820), pp. 14–15.

[11] H. Dunn, *The Principles of Teaching or, the Normal School Manual: containing practical suggestions on the government and instruction of children* (9th ed., London, ?1850), p. 256.

[12] J.M. Goldstrom, *The Social Content of Education 1808–1870, A Study of the Working-Class School Reader in England and Ireland* (Shannon, 1972), pp. 108–11.

[13] The evidence of J. Simpson, a Scottish educationist, before the Select Committee on Education in Ireland (1835), and reprinted in P.P. 1835 VII, Report from the Select Committee on Education in England and Wales, p. 185.

[14] 'Report of the Birmingham Statistical Society on the state of education in Birmingham', *Journal of the Statistical Society*, Vol. III (1840), p. 37.

[15] Edward Feild, quoted in *English Journal of Education*, Vol. I, 1843, p. 214.

[16] Minutes of the Committee of Council on Education, 1845, Vol. I, p. 92.

[17] For an account of the activities of the Commissioners of National Education in Ireland see D. H. Akenson, *The Irish Education Experiment: The National System of Education in the Nineteenth Century* (London, 1970) and Goldstrom, *The Social Content of Education* pp. 61–90.

[18] P.P. 1861 XXI, Report of the Commissioners Appointed to Inquire into the State of Popular Education in England, p. 127.

[19] J.M. Goldstrom, 'Richard Whately and political economy in school books, 1833–1880', *Irish Historical Studies*, Vol. XV, no. 58 (1966), pp. 131–46.

[20] H. Dunn and J.T. Crossley, *Daily Lesson Book No. III* (London, 1840), p. 103.

[21] Commissioners of National Education in Ireland, *Fourth Book of Lessons* (London, 1834), p. 229.

[22] Minutes of the Committee of Council on Education, 1847–8, Vol. I, p. 30.

[23] Dunn, *Principles of Teaching*, pp. 80–1.

[24] R.K. Webb, *The British Working Class Reader 1790–1848* (London, 1955).

[25] G.R. Porter, *The Progress of the Nation* (London, 1912 ed.), p. 22.

[26] R.D. Altick, *The English Common Reader: a Social History of the Mass Reading Public 1800–1900* (Chicago, 1963).

[27] See for example J. Fletcher, *Education, National, Voluntary and Free* (London, 1851) or the 37th Annual Report of the National Society (1848).

[28] K.S. Inglis, *Churches and the Working Classes in Victorian England* (London, 1963).

[29] E. Halévy, *England in 1815. A History of the English People in the Nineteenth Century,* Vol. 1 (London, 1961), pp. 389–485; E.J. Hobsbawm, *Primitive Rebels: Studies in Archaic Forms of Social Movement in the 19th and 20th Centuries* (Manchester, 1959), ch. VIII.

Chapter 5:

Socialization and social science: Manchester Model Secular School 1854-1861

Donald K. Jones

The foundation of the school

'The education afforded to the poor must be substantial', wrote Dr James Phillips Kay (later Sir James Kay-Shuttleworth) in 1832. It should include, he continued, 'elevating' knowledge, those parts of the exact sciences connected with occupations, 'the ascertained truths of political economy', '*correct* political information' and the relationship between capital and labour. 'The misery which the working classes have brought upon themselves by their mistaken notions on this subject', he concluded, 'is incalculable, not to mention the injury which has accrued to capitalists and to the trade of this country.'[1]

In calling for a broader, more efficient means of socializing the working class than had hitherto been available, Kay-Shuttleworth was giving voice to sentiments which generally found favour with the rising industrial middle class. The ruling classes, and particularly the Evangelicals, had used education as a counter-revolutionary force during the period of the French wars and the depression which followed it, concentrating on inoculating the lower classes against 'infidelity' and subversive ideas by means of religious indoctrination.[2] By the early 1830s, however, in face of the growing problems of crime, urbanization and class strife, something more seemed to be needed. The conviction grew, therefore, that, in true utilitarian fashion, the lower classes must be taught where their true interests lay, in order to integrate them into a capitalist society from which, as a result of the upheaval of the post-war years, they had become alienated. It was this conviction which Kay-Shuttleworth articulated, anticipating at the same time the process of 'industrial' socialization, with its emphasis on science, industrial skill and political economy which, as will be seen, was adopted in the 1840s by the industrial bourgeoisie.

Meanwhile, inspired by Jeremy Bentham's *Chrestomathia*, radicals and agnostics, under the auspices of the Society for the Diffusion of Useful Knowledge, were already engaged in disseminating political economic theory among the working classes. Originally the S.D.U.K. envisaged an adult readership for its numerous pamphlets, but towards the end of the 1830s its policy of promoting secular knowledge was adopted even by the voluntary societies themselves, notably the British and Foreign School Society. The inclusion of such 'useful knowledge' in the elementary school curriculum was greatly facilitated by the publication of numerous cheap school books by the Kildare Place Society and by its successors, the Commissioners of National Education in Ireland. Their reproduction in the Irish readers, between 1834 and 1880, of extracts from the booklet *Easy Lessons in Money Matters*, written in 1833 by Archbishop Richard Whately, an Irish Commissioner himself, enabled it to become the staple reading matter on political economy for generations of British and colonial school children.[3]

Two other promoters of this type of curriculum were William Ellis, the wealthy insurance manager turned educationalist, and George Combe, the influential Scottish educationalist and Britain's most eminent phrenologist. Ellis, who had become interested in education after reading Combe's essay *Constitution of Man* (1828), in which the latter had stressed the importance of propagating 'a rational restraint upon population', was convinced that this could be promoted through the teaching of political economy.[4] He also believed that if only the working classes could be informed about the principles of 'commercial and social phenomena' a great deal of social distress would be alleviated by enabling them to 'understand their own position in society and their duties towards it'.[5]

With this object in view, in 1848 Ellis opened the first of his seven London Birkbeck schools, patronized William Lovett's National Hall School in Holborn, and helped to finance George Combe's Edinburgh Secular School. All of these schools were unashamedly agencies of social control, teaching political economy and physiology, under the heading of social science, to working-class children, and excluding doctrinal religion. Combe also taught phrenology in his Edinburgh school. Both he and Ellis actively promoted similar schools in Glasgow, Blandford in Dorset and, as will be seen, in Manchester.[6]

During the 1830s, alongside demands for curriculum reform, there developed a body of radical opinion, supported by the revelations of the statistical societies in the large urban centres, which alleged that the voluntary system of educational provision was failing to cope with the task of extending universal elementary education to the industrial masses; a task which it had never been intended to perform. This was accompanied by demands for state control, with the object of freeing educational provision from the wrangling of the rival religious voluntary societies, which between 1833 and 1839 administered the government building grant. Consequently, in 1836 the influential Central Society for Education, led by Thomas Wyse, M.P. for Waterford, demanded the establishment of a centralized system of national secular education in England and Wales[7] and two years later an associated body, The Manchester Society for Promoting National Education, opened three schools to which children of all religious creeds were admitted.[8]

These demands for a secular, as distinct from a denominational, solution to the perceived crisis in elementary education reflect not only the growing radical-nonconformist alarm at the increasing domination of the Anglican Church over elementary school provision, but also the demands of the industrial and commercial middle classes for an efficient, coherent, and uniform system of national education supportive of Britain's role as the leading industrial nation. The point was made very clearly some years later by Sir Thomas Bazley, Chairman of the Manchester Chamber of Commerce: 'The State has a deep interest in well-informed and well-trained subjects, and as all classes pay taxes, without favour, so ought, in my humble opinion, all classes to be permitted, without hindrance, to share in funds gathered from a common source, which are devoted to the instruction of the ignorant.'[9] Significantly, both Richard Cobden and John Bright, the Lancashire cotton manufacturers, were prominent members of the Society for Promoting National Education. It is not surprising, therefore, to find Manchester providing a powerful initiative for a secular solution to the educational problem in the aftermath of the repeal of the Corn Laws in 1846.

The settlement of the 'greatest radical issue' enabled the Radicals to turn their attention to other reform issues. Accordingly, in 1847 a group of former Anti-Corn Law League members, led by Samuel Lucas, John Bright's brother-in-law, established in Manchester the Lancashire Public School Association (L.P.S.A.).[10] Inspired by George Combe's description of the Massachusetts Common School system, published in the *Edinburgh Review* of July 1841, they drew up a plan, in close

Plate V *Sir Thomas Bazley, cotton spinner and chairman of Manchester Chamber of Commerce*

consultation with Combe, for the establishment in Lancashire of what was to be the prototype of a national system of free, secular, locally controlled, rate-supported education, based explicitly on the Massachusetts model.[11] When, in 1850, the L.P.S.A. was converted into a national pressure group, the National Public School Association (N.P.S.A.), under the leadership of Richard Cobden, these principles were embodied in the Association's Free Schools Bill, which, although unsuccessful in Parliament, enabled the N.P.S.A. to make a valuable contribution to the long debate which finally determined the shape of W.E. Forster's Elementary Education Act of 1870.

One of the main contentions of the N.P.S.A. was that a large stratum of working-class children was excluded from elementary schools because they could not pay school pence. Its leaders alleged that in Manchester alone there were 20,000 children between the ages of three and fourteen who went neither to school nor to work, some of whom would have gone to school had they been able to pay fees.[12] Admittedly, calculations such as these, based on Horace Mann's educational census of 1851, have been shown to have exaggerated the number of children who could have been expected to be in school. Nevertheless, the urban crisis was real enough, being symptomatic of the peculiarly nineteenth-century problem of child unemployment, resulting from a changing industrial structure. The situation was further aggravated by the movement of migrants into large towns, an influx which between 1821 and 1831 had increased Manchester's population by 45 per cent.[13] It was in order to exert some form of social control over this section of the urban population that the N.P.S.A. argued for the establishment of free secular schools, untrammelled by religious and financial restrictions and, therefore, eminently suited to the needs of this particular class of children.

In 1855 an N.P.S.A. delegation presented these views to Lord John Russell, urging him at the same time to adopt its secular plan instead of his recently introduced Borough Bill, by which he proposed to leave elementary education in the hands of the voluntary societies. He replied that before contemplating such an action he would need evidence of the viability of the N.P.S.A.'s plan. Taking his remark as a challenge, the delegation returned to Manchester and immediately set about providing the necessary evidence in the form of a school, to serve as a model of those which the Association hoped to establish on a national scale. For this reason it was named the Manchester Model Secular School, a name which it retained from its opening in 1854 until 1861, when as a result of a financial crisis a change of policy necessitated a change of name. Consequently, from 1861 until its final closure in 1887, the school went under the name of the Manchester Free School.[14]

What kind of school?

From the outset it was no ordinary school. As James Newbold, a member of the Manchester School Board, wrote in 1887, its promoters were unusually eminent, being a 'band of men distinguished above their fellow citizens even in a city which has long been famous for the enlightened educational zeal of its leading citizens'.[15] A sample of twenty-five of its most active promoters comprised ten cotton manufacturers, two calico printers, six merchants, one engineer, four ministers of religion, one solicitor, and a former Owenite socialist lecturer. Of sixteen of these people whose religious affiliations can be ascertained,

ten were Unitarians. There were also two Anglicans, two Congrega-
tionalists, one Free Presbyterian, and one Baptist.[16] Clearly then, the
school was the creation of the rising nonconformist provincial manufacturing and mercantile middle class, the representatives of 'big capital'
in South Lancashire. For example, Thomas Bazley, one of the biggest
cotton spinners in the area, had been a Royal Commissioner for the
1851 Exhibition. He was also president of the Manchester Chamber of
Commerce, became M.P. for the borough in 1858 and received a
baronetcy in 1869. Sir John Potter, head of the firm of Potter and

Plate VI. *Sir John Potter, M.P., Manchester merchant and three times
Mayor of Manchester*

Norris, the largest mercantile firm in the area, besides being an M.P. shared with Ivie Mackie, another promoter, the distinction of being three times mayor of Manchester; Elkanah Armytage and the machine-tool manufacturer Joseph Whitworth both received knighthoods, the latter founding the Whitworth scholarships;[17] Dr John Watts, the former organizer of the Owenite Hall of Science, was sometime president of the Manchester School Board; and, of course, there was Richard Cobden,

Plate VII *Sir Joseph Whitworth, engineer and founder of Whitworth scholarships*

architect of the borough's incorporation in 1838, but better known nationally as the leader of the most advanced pressure group to date, the Anti-Corn Law League. The significance of the predominance of Unitarians among the promoters will become clear when the teaching of practical and rationalistic, as distinct from doctrinal religion at the school is considered below.

A second unusual feature was derived from the school's role as an integral element in the N.P.S.A.'s campaign. It was designed to demonstrate first that, contrary to the prevailing opinion of churchmen, later expressed in the Newcastle Report,[18] the working classes would not despise free education, and secondly that it was possible to provide an essentially religious education without recourse to the Bible and the teaching of religious doctrine.

A third unusual feature is its organization along the lines of the Birkbeck schools. This was no accident. In 1850, when the N.P.S.A. was founded with all the expertise of the Anti-Corn Law League at its disposal, both Combe and Ellis regarded it as a means of propagating the Birkbeck system nationally. Combe wrote to R.W. Smiles, the N.P.S.A. secretary and brother to the more famous Samuel, urging the association to establish a model school to act as a counterblast against the allegations of 'godlessness' made by churchmen and other detractors of secular schools. Moreover, he included a rationale of secular education which obviously accorded with the views of the N.P.S.A.[19]

Reiterating some of Kay-Shuttleworth's comments of eighteen years before, he stressed the need for the meagre diet of the three Rs to be supplemented with the useful information so that 'the people should be so taught and trained as to know *how to work out their own well-being*'. Accordingly school children must be made aware of certain fundamental truths: the study of political economy would inform them that abundant supplies of food, clothing, fuel and shelter could only be obtained by the agency of such 'mental qualities' as industry, order, knowledge, economy, punctuality and honesty, and that 'good wages and provision for sickness and old age are equally dependent on the same qualities'; physiology meanwhile would acquaint them with 'the laws of temperance, cleanliness, well regulated exercise of mind and body, ventilation and other conditions of health'. Unfortunately, he explained, reflecting on the current debate on economic theory, such a utilitarian curriculum would invite opposition:

> These truths in nature are disliked by some because they are supposed to originate in Political Economy and Physiology. Carlyle, that great disturber and condemner of everything and rectifier of nothing, calls Political Economy 'the dismal science', and Physiology is objected to by persons who say that it makes morality and intelligence dependent on physical causes.[20]

Despite these apparent difficulties, Combe was confident that an efficiently-conducted school, based upon the above rationale, would 'speak trumpet-tongued and as no human voice could speak, in favour of the reality and efficiency' of secular education. The effect of this letter was later reinforced by a visit paid by Richard Cobden to the Birkbeck school in Southampton Buildings in 1852, accompanied by George Combe. So struck was he by the curriculum and teaching methods that he remarked: 'One half of the House of Commons might listen to these lessons with advantage.'[21] For these reasons, between 1854 and 1861 the Model Secular School operated virtually as a Birkbeck school. Significantly, William Ellis promised to finance it to the tune of £500 and proved to be one of its most generous supporters in the difficult years prior to the school's receipt of the government grant.

Providing a rationale and the initial finance was, however, only part of the business of founding a school, for teachers capable of coping with the desired curriculum were scarce. The choice of headmaster was, therefore, of crucial importance for the success of the venture. Fortunately, the Model Secular School's management committee fully appreciated this and travelled vast distances in order to examine not only the applicants for the post but also their schools. Their final choice fell on Benjamin Templar, a former student of the Borough Road College and Master of a British School in Bridport, Dorset.[22] A school which had a central hall and six classrooms was leased from the Society of Friends, and Templar was able to stock it with the most modern equipment, having visited the educational exhibition promoted by the Society of Arts in St Martin's Hall, London, in August 1854.[23]

Socializing the parents

There is little doubt that the appointment of Benjamin Templar was the managers' greatest service to the school, for its success during the first few difficult years was largely due to his charisma, patience, foresight and ability as an organizer. His first task was to find a method of choosing his pupils. At the Birkbeck schools, William Ellis selected from among children whose parents could afford to pay 6*d*. a week; 'a charge which', stated the Taunton Commissioners, 'while it is within the means of provident parents, necessarily renders the school inaccessible to the children of the destitute, or of the improvident.'[24] George Combe similarly insulated the Edinburgh Secular School from the 'undeserving poor' by charging a fee of 4*d*.[25] Aiming at a lower social stratum and charging no fees, the Model Secular School had no similar pecuniary measure with which to determine the 'worthiness' of its clientele. Consequently, in order to avoid exploitation by either the 'improvident' or the relatively affluent, Templar discriminated among the numerous respondents to the placards which advertized the opening of the school according to the following criteria: 'Honest poverty in the parents, and the probability that the applicants will attend school regularly and for sufficient time to render real advantage from the instruction possible.'[26]

The school's location in a poor and overcrowded quarter of the town ensured that there was no shortage of impoverished applicants for whom payment of school fees was an impossibility. Examples of the unfortunate condition of some of these people appear in the early reports: 'No. 7. An old woman who is guardian of her four grand-children, whose father died of cholera in 1849, . . . No. 12. A seamstress with five children, . . . No. 21. A deserted wife with two children, husband a fustian cutter.'[27] Attention was particularly drawn to the large number of heads of families whom poverty had made 'utterly incompetent' to provide for the education of their children.[28]

An analysis of sixty-three very hard-pressed parents or guardians of applicants given in the first and second annual reports reveals that 23 were employed men who nevertheless could not pay school pence; 18 were deserted wives, widows and others responsible for children; 8 were men out of work; 4 were grandparents and other elderly people responsible for children; 3 were people caring for orphans and a further 7 were disabled fathers. Of great significance, and probably the most crucial factor determining inability to pay fees, is the size of the families involved. Admittedly the sample may not be fully representative of the whole, but the following gives some indication of the numbers involved:

No. of children in the family	No. of families of this size
10	2
9	3
7	3
6	10
5	11
4	11
3	8
2	2
1	7[29]

The comment of the railway labourer's wife, a mother of five children, adequately describes the situation, albeit somewhat tersely. Upon being asked whether her husband could afford to pay school pence, she replied, 'Meat's too dear and we've got too many on 'um for us to spare brass for schulin.'[30] A clearer insight into the difficulties of living in a society unprotected by a system of state welfare is given by the following letter from one of the more literate parents:

To the Master of the Free School:
Sir, My son informs me that upon his arrival at school this morning you told him that he could not be admitted, as I was able to pay for his education. That I am totally unable to do, having had several heavy losses as well as from the present price of provisions. There are seven of us to keep out of my earnings, which I can assure you is no easy thing to do, therefore I hope you will kindly take my case into consideration. I should tell you that, besides daily expenses for the maintenance of my family, I have a doctor's bill that I am compelled to continue paying by instalments incurred by my late wife's illness. Throwing myself upon your generosity.[31]

The report for 1855 provides the following analysis of the parental occupations of 260 children in attendance at the school in that year, showing that 40 per cent were skilled, 30 per cent semi-skilled, 22 per cent unskilled, and a further 8 per cent women in various degrees of destitution:

Labourers	25	Porters	24
Cobblers	21	Widows, deserted wives	
Tailors	15	and other females	21
Joiners	12	Makers up and packers	11
Weavers	10	Carters	10
Spinners	6	Fustian cutters	9
Mechanics	5	Plasterers	9
Dyers	4	Painters, etc.	9
Policemen and		Smiths	4
watchmen	5	Cabmen and ostlers	6
Plumbers, etc.	4	Bricklayers, etc.	6
Coachmakers	3	Sawyers	2
Overlookers	2	Butchers	2
Bookkeepers	2		
Miscellaneous, chiefly unskilled labourers, street hawkers,			
chimney sweeps, boatmen, greengrocers, etc.			33[32]

From this analysis it can be appreciated that not all pupils who attended the school warranted the description of 'gutter children', a term which was used by the committee when emphasizing the philanthropic nature of its activities, and also by the Bishop of Manchester in 1879 when eulogizing over the school's impressive record. Nevertheless, insecurity and casual employment were common to many of the parents, for even skilled men beset by illness could quickly become destitute. They were, therefore, hardly the most promising people to qualify for Templar's second criterion of 'worthiness'; that they should send their children regularly to school. He therefore decided that the parents themselves should be socialized into the value system of the school. Nothing reveals the outstanding qualities of this man more clearly than his appreciation of the crucial importance of parental co-operation and his method of communicating a sense of obligation to them. The insistence on regular attendance also sheds light on the managers' conception of the function of the school: the initiation of its pupils into habits appropriate to an industrial society. Punctuality at school, it was assumed, would lead to punctuality in the factory and warehouse.

Accordingly, faced during the first year with a certain amount of absenteeism, although the average attendance of 90 per cent would have delighted the masters of many other schools, Templar devised a procedure for making parents aware of the need for good attendance. This consisted of sending a series of letters to the homes of absent boys, the tone of which fully reveals his paternalistic attitude to parents and pupils alike. The first one demanded: 'Please state the reason for your son's absence from school this morning/or afternoon as the case may be.' If no satisfactory response was received a second admonitory letter, threatening dismissal, was sent.[33] Finally, if still no communication were received a final exhortation was sent, indicating the consequence of poor attendance − 'habits of irregularity' which would endanger future success in life − and stressing that nothing less than 'serious sickness' should constitute grounds for absence. If no improvement took place, dismissal followed.[34]

By such means Templar attempted to extend the normative influence of the school into the homes of his pupils. Even when writing proved abortive he invariably visited a boy's home in a final attempt to elicit some parental response before ultimately dismissing him. He also paid home visits in the process of ascertaining the 'honest poverty' of new applicants. As the following extract shows, these were not always the most enjoyable of experiences: 'No. 28. A power-loom weaver with four children. One of the most wretched houses visited − stench horrible. Feel certain that if the boy proved moderately intelligent he will, after a short time in the school, do duty at home as a sanitary missionary.'[35] Nevertheless, the remarkable fact is that by such diligence he was able to maintain an average attendance of 92 per cent. (The number of boys on the roll was 330 in 1855, a figure which remained fairly stable throughout the school's existence.) His successor actually improved Templar's attendance figure, raising it to 96 per cent, which the report for 1880 proudly declared to be some 30 per cent above the average for fee-paying schools.[36] The average number dismissed each year for non-attendance between 1856 and 1860 was only fourteen, which bears further testimony to the success of his policy of co-operation with parents.

Templar's admonitory letters elicited some revealing explanations for pupils' absences or withdrawal from school. The nineteen replies published in the first, second and fifth reports, though not a representative sample, eloquently record the opinions and experiences of a largely inarticulate section of the population, as the following examples show:

Sir – his father has been out of work since Christmas and his bit of wages is of use to me and if so kind for to keep his place for the course of a fortnight and I will send him as soon as father gets into work.

To Mr timpler
Sir I sarah —— wish to let you know that when my boy robert is absent he is nursing while I am claring a livlihood for my family for my partner is out of employ and I cannot afford to pay for it.

James —— 's father had no work and I could not get shoes for them as soon as I can it is very hard for poor people to get everything for children.

Mr. temple   Please William —— will have to stop at home on account of the overseer Comeing for I want to try to get some Clothing for him Stop at home all week Plese will you give me a note for a suit of Clotheing to show the gardins.

Mary ——
a widder with 5 children[37]

The last letter is particularly interesting, indicating the diffuse nature of Templar's role as a headmaster and his involvement in the lives of the parents.

Despite Templar's success with the school attendance record, no amount of hard work could overcome the economic difficulties which shortened the school life of his pupils. Although their ages ranged from six to twelve years, their average stay, according to the report for 1860, was only one year to ten months, a disappointing record compared with the probably exaggerated average of five years reported by the Newcastle Commission. Nevertheless, the committee claimed that 'considering the poverty of the parents' this was 'highly satisfactory'.[38] The picture is brightened slightly by the fact that on average each boy had received one year four months' schooling prior to entry, bringing the average school life of the Model Secular School pupil to three years three months. However, of those leaving to start work, 16 per cent were aged ten or below and 60 per cent between the ages of ten and twelve, which meant that the pupil turnover was very high. During seven years 1854 to 1861, of the 1500 boys admitted 1148, or just over 75 per cent, had withdrawn.[39] In such circumstances, therefore, beset by poverty, illness and, in many cases, parental neglect, the boy from the lower end of the working class had little hope of social mobility when even the most favoured of his peers received, on average, three and a quarter years' schooling. It is little wonder that Templar insisted on a high rate of attendance in order to ensure the optimum use of this brief period. Yet some of the boys appear to have made good use of the meagre life chance presented to them.

The report for 1860 contains a schedule of forty-three returns from the employers of boys from the school. It reveals a depressing number of thirteen errand boys who, one suspects, might end their days in the pool of casual labour, but also a further twelve who had entered skilled occupations, the rest being in a mixture of trades the future of which is difficult to discern.[40] The possibility of social mobility is further emphasized by the report for 1864 in which a description of a tea-party, held in Templar's honour upon his leaving to take up a private school of his own in Cheetham Hill, refers to a large gathering of former pupils 'largely composed of well dressed, gentlemanly young men, many of whom were holding situations as clerks, shopmen, draftsmen, machinists, warehousemen, etc., who were ready and grateful in acknowledging their deep indebtedness to the school and their teacher'.[41]

Templar's exercise in enlisting parental co-operation did not end with attendance. Realizing that the unconventional nature of the school required some explanation, he called a meeting in December

1856 which was attended by about two hundred parents. Describing the curriculum, he explained that despite its secular character the school was a religious institution, for the 'moral duties which contributed the main part of practical religion were sedulously inculcated and enforced'.[42] As for the three Rs, they were not ends in themselves but, as Combe had stated, the means of acquiring knowledge of the 'common things' which the boys saw around them, such as food and clothing, furniture, merchandise and manufactures. He then described the more unusual subjects: the 'laws of health', the 'civil laws', and the laws which 'regulate the value of labour and commodities, . . . things not often taught in schools . . . although of great practical importance and likely to prove of value . . . in after life'. The parents' duty, he explained, was 'to feed, clothe, shelter, advise, reprove and educate their children', but they should also take an interest in their school work and ensure that they came to school 'regularly, punctually, and as clean as possible'. Finally, he invited them to communicate with him as often as they wished in order to make suggestions, or merely to enquire about their children's progress.

How did parents react to such paternalism? If any disapproved there is no evidence. It would, of course, be too much to expect the committee to have published letters which criticized the school adversely. The available evidence, however, provided by the attendance record and constant stream of applicants for entry to the school implies their approval. Probably the following letter, although somewhat eulogistic, expresses the feelings of the majority of the parents of Templar's pupils:

> Dear Sir: We cannot explain in words how much pleased we was to be at your Meeting Last Night. We fell Greatly thankfull to you, for the good education of our son Joseph, Which we are happy to say that he has improved a great deal in his Reding and writing zince he came to school this time we feel surprized at the answers to the question we aske's him.[43]

Socializing the pupils: the curriculum

The curriculum of the Model Secular School illustrates the logical conclusion of the mid-nineteenth century trend towards secularism.[44] It represents the apotheosis of utilitarianism; the ideology of the 'Manchester School' of political economy expressed in educational terms. Comprising the three Rs, original composition, 'common things',

British manufactures, drawing and physical science,[45] it was especially notable for the inclusion of a group of subjects which provided the element of social control, consisting of history, geography, social ethics (practical morality), physiology and social economy; the last-named subject being a combination of ethics and Ricardian political economy. George Combe gave this second group the collective name of 'social science' probably to disguise the fact that it included political economy. Each subject was taught in the order of its greatest utility and, as no-one was allowed to proceed to the higher subjects until 'usefully proficient' in the three Rs, about 60 per cent of the boys, as shown in the report for 1856, were engaged in the basic subjects; a further 20 per cent were studying grammar, geography and drawing and British manufactures, while the remainder, comprising the most advanced pupils, unravelled the mysteries of history, political economy, human physiology and physical science. The methods of presentation were nothing if not progressive. Arithmetic dealt with problems in 'shop accounts', physics was illustrated by experiments with syphons, syringes, air pumps, barometers and thermometers, and chemistry with experimental demonstrations. Whenever possible specimens, objects, charts, diagrams and demonstrations were used to illustrate lessons; a lesson on respiration, for example, being illustrated by the dissection of a sheep's thorax.[46]

For teaching the three Rs Templar was obliged to use the monitorial method, which was currently declining in popularity, but, as he explained in the report for 1856, this was combined with the acquisition of 'a large amount of useful knowledge concerning the materials of dress, food and dwellings; the world's various climates, animal and vegetable productions, races of men, and general physical and ethnological features'.[47] Pupils were made to write a description of their dress, followed by a description of the materials of which it was made, and their origin, after which they would write an account of a typical school day. The reading books used were the *Second Book of Lessons* and its *Sequel*, published by the Irish Commissioners of Education, Chambers' *Rudiments of Knowledge* and *Introduction to the Sciences*, and Templar's own textbook, *Reading Lessons in Social Economy*.

Public pressure for the inclusion of religion as an integral part of education in the mid-nineteenth century was too great for any school to survive without some form of religious component in the curriculum. For this reason, and the fact that the Model Secular School enjoyed the support of a number of ministers of religion, the managers were most anxious to emphasize in their reports, and later in correspondence with the Committee of Council on the question of grants, that the course of instruction in the school was 'decidedly religious in its tendency'. They were particularly eager' to stress, in the report for 1856, the superior normative influence exerted by the Model Secular School in comparison with the paltry efforts of the schools, reported on by H.M.I. J.C. Symons, whose pupils began the Lord's Prayer, 'Our father charter hevn', and laboured under the illusion that John the Baptist was the son of Jesus Christ. Accordingly, the religious component was provided by Templar's socratic discourses on practical morality, which all the pupils attended. His object was to inculcate 'a love of truth, honesty, temperance, cleanliness, diligence, punctuality and order; obedience and love of parents, respect for teachers and kindness to each other',[48] a task which he approached in a colloquial rather than didactic style, enabling him to make full use of the boys' own experience and moral awareness.

Such lessons, Templar believed, had made a visible impact upon his pupils 'who have begun to feel the pleasure consequent upon cleanly habits, and by the daily practice of them, showing a feeling of self-respect to which they were previously strangers'.[49] They could also be used as a vehicle for instilling them with the habit of using 'correct' middle-class English as distinct from their own demotic style, an example of which appears in the Second Report, exemplifying perfectly Templar's paternalistic and normative influence over his pupils. During the course of a lesson on lying, an attempt is being made to decide which of two imaginary boys had lied. One pupil, explaining that the 'first boy' had told a lie in that he had consciously stated a falsehood, said 'Th' furst know'd it warn't true', to which Templar quickly interjected, 'He knew it was not true, you intended to say'; a statement which completely epitomizes the school's ethos. It is worth reflecting what William Cobbett would have thought of this. If it was the boy's accent and pronunciation that Templar was trying to change he would have disagreed. On the other hand he would have approved of his correcting his grammar.[50] As will be seen, this process of inculcation of middle-class norms, speech forms and even ideology was further reinforced by the means of exercises written from memory.

The school's moral ethos was further reinforced by the method of maintaining discipline, for corporal punishment was completely abandoned, much to the astonishment of many visitors. As the report for 1856 explains, 'it is dispensed with as being less powerful for purposes of discipline and control than other means, and as destructive of the master's moral influence over the boys'.[51] This was particularly impressive, the report emphasizes, considering that 'the class of boys attending are the most unlikely possible it may be supposed for government by "moral suasion" and "the power of gentleness", but the master has the best reason to be satisfied with the results of his treatment in this respect'. Yet one must bear in mind that, in the last resort, Templar had the power of expulsion at his disposal when dealing with recalcitrant pupils.

Of the other subjects, Templar considered physiology to be very important. Redolent of 'self-help' and emphasizing the individual's responsibility for his own health, which was dependent on certain intractable laws, it obviously fitted the school's ethos, although much of it was indistinguishable from a modern biology course. Consisting of lessons on digestion and blood circulation it had, nevertheless, a strong practical bias, emphasizing the need for a good diet and a plentiful supply of fresh air.

Of far greater relevance to the Nonconformist, capitalist ideology of the school's promoters, however, and to the environment of industrial Manchester, was the study of social economy, Templar's favourite subject. Giving more than a hint of the urban social cleavage which was more obvious in Manchester than most towns in England,[52] the Second Report explains that social economy was included in the curriculum 'from a conviction that it should form an important part of every child's education, and especially so in such a *thoroughly manufacturing* city as Manchester, where the results of ignorance of its principles have been so fearful'.[53] Accordingly lessons were given on industry, knowledge, skill and economy 'as wealth producers', the functions of capital, division of labour, exchange, value, money, supply and demand, taxation, trade fluctuations, stikes and combinations. 'Great care has been taken', explains the report, 'to impart such knowledge of these as will satisfactorily account for the obvious unequal distribution of wealth.'[54]

The subject therefore presented an essentially functionalist view of society, emphasizing the advantage to all of the maintenance of the *status quo*, idolizing self-sufficiency and stressing the immutability of the Panglossian laws of political economy, which proved that this was the best of all possible worlds. Templar's teaching followed this pattern, as demonstrated by the following examples of pupils' work, written entirely from memory and indicating clearly the brain-washing techniques employed by exponents of political economy. The following extract on the 'iron law of wages' was written by E. Swithenbank, at the tender age of nine years, a former dame school pupil in attendance at the Model Secular School a mere ten months. The spelling makes an interesting contrast with that of the parents' letters:

> If all the cotton workers were to strike for more wages the masters would have to give them; that he may keep his former profits, he would have to raise the price of his goods. This rise in price would cause people to buy less, that is the demand would decrease, and the manufacturers finding the demand small would decrease the supply and would have to put their men upon short time; and although they were getting the high rate of wages upon short time, they would not be earning as much as they would upon full time at their former rate of wages.
>
> Generally the results of a strike are that the people become poor, run into debt, spend all they have saved, and are thrown out of work, because their places are filled up by the other people who are willing to work for the wages they refused and by machinery.[55]

Another nine-year old, Charles Ingle, with four years' schooling behind him, only one of which was at the Model Secular School, expounded on the definition of capital: 'Capital is wealth employed for getting more wealth . . . . A manufacturer's capital may be machinery, his factory, manufactured goods, skill and knowledge. A working man's is his skill, strength and knowledge.' It is unlikely that he would have been made aware of the following vital distinction between capital and labour, drawn by a Manchester silk-weaver before the Select Committee on Hand-Loom Weavers' Petitions of 1834: 'Labour is always sold by the poor, and always bought by the rich (therefore) labour cannot by any possibility be stored, but must be every instant sold or every instant lost',[56] the result being that the labourer was at a constant dis-advantage in his dealings with the capitalist, at least in a situation governed by the laws of political economy.

Similarly, the ten-year old E. Crookell, with six years' previous schooling, deliberated on the nature of taxation, stating that 'rates are money paid for protection, comfort and keeping the poor'. Taxes, on the other hand, were 'for the support of the army and navy and Government, and for the interest of the national debt'. Moreover, it was quite fair for the rich people to pay more than the poor, 'because they have more to protect'. He then went on to distinguish between indirect and direct taxes, explaining that the former were paid by rich and poor alike and the latter by the rich. Finally, he concluded, 'All taxes are not direct taxes because poor people do not like them, they think they are paying money for nothing.' He obviously had not been told that poor people did not like indirect taxes either and that had it not been for the regressive nature of nineteenth-century taxation his parents might have been able to have afforded to pay school pence.

By means of his correspondence with Combe and the publication of his text-book, which Combe considered 'a valuable contribution to education',[57] Templar quickly established a reputation for himself as an expert in the teaching of political economy. In 1858 he was invited to read a paper to the National Association for the Promotion of Social Science at its Liverpool conference on *The Importance of Teaching Social Economy in Elementary Schools*, in which he presented his personal rationale of the subject. He considered that its two main virtues were the usefulness of the information and its suitability for education. It was useful in that it taught the working man to make his labour as remunerative as possible, to spend its proceeds wisely, and that payment 'would depend on the quantity and quality of his work which will bear exact proportion to his industry, knowledge and skill.' It also defined the 'conditions of industrial success' against which nothing militated more than strikes and trade unions. As Swithenbank's written exercise reflects, Templar had an obsession with strikes. Whether this was as a result of some particular event such as the Preston lock-out which took place in 1853, and upon which Dickens based *Hard Times*, is not known. What is clear is that as far as he was concerned they were inimical to the well-being not only of his pupils but of the whole of industrial society. Accordingly he was convinced that the function of the teacher of political economy was to warn his pupils of their attendant dangers:

> ... when so instructed and not till then, will they see that since trade combinations cannot alter the conditions upon which the value of their labour depends they cannot permanently alter wages.[58]

Taking a Baconian line, Templar also recognized qualities of a religious, moral and intellectual nature in the subject. It was religious 'because none can reflect upon its teaching without having their veneration for and gratitude and love towards God strongly excited', and moral because it taught that the conditions of industrial success depended on the possession of 'a good moral character [and] a well-deserved reputation for honesty, truthfulness, industry, sobriety and punctuality'. His explanation of its intellectual qualities is derived from phrenology, which, as a disciple and regular correspondent of George Combe, he embraced with enthusiasm. Phrenological theory assumed that the mind was composed of numerous faculties, each of which could be developed by a wise teacher by means of the appropriate subject matter. Accordingly he described social economy as 'a fine extensive field for the exercise of the *perceptive* and *reflective* faculties . . . by a careful consideration of the advantages that arise from a division of labour, commerce, the uses of money and credit, the production of wealth . . .'.[59]

The teaching of social science, therefore, was not an attempt to introduce school children to the processes of inductive thought, but to instil into them certain basic premises based on middle-class values, which, by process of deduction, would lead inevitably to 'correct' conclusions, with regard to their political and economic behaviour; correct, that is, so far as the preservation of capitalism was concerned. It is not difficult to conclude that in denying the right to strike to the working classes, their only weapon against the capitalist employer, such teaching was inimical to their better interests. On the other hand, up to the time that Templar was writing, the progress of militant trade unionism had hardly been auspicious, and he was not short of evidence to support his arguments. Moreover, in the case of the Model Secular School, the exercise did not remain purely negative. Much of what was taught under the heading of 'social economy' was akin to the modern subject of 'civics'. A very positive effort was also made to give the pupils an education relevant to living in an industrial and commercial society, an example of which were the lessons in phonography (shorthand) given free of charge to promising pupils by Henry Pitman, brother of Sir Isaac Pitman, and reporter on the *Manchester Examiner and Times*, the journal of the Anti-Corn Law League faction. Certainly the parents appear to have been grateful for these efforts, as their letters show. Not only is the following writer appreciative of the practical nature of the curriculum and its relevance to industrial employment, but also of Templar's efforts to impose socially acceptable norms of behaviour on his pupils:

Dear Sir: I cannot find words to express my gratitude to you for the education my son has received while in the Secular School. He has received instruction not only in ordinary school learning, but how to conduct himself in society . . . I thank you for the extra attention you paid to him in teaching him [mechanical] drawing. I thank you for the good character you gave him; I thank you for the many books you have presented to him; and I thank you for your general kindness and goodwill towards him.[60]

Nevertheless, it cannot be denied that the socialization process carried on by the Model Secular School consisted of superimposing the authority of one social class upon another; the inevitable function of a nineteenth-century elementary school in search of state recognition. Despite this, as will be seen, the school failed to meet with the approval of the Committee of Council on Education.

The price of secularism

As its name implies, the Model Secular School was the prototype of the state-supported secular school envisaged by the N.P.S.A. In reality, however, it was a voluntary school and therefore dependent on voluntary subscriptions. Originally its early expenses had been guaranteed by the generosity of the promoters, but in 1855 the addition of amenities such as a library, a playground, and improved sanitary facilities, raised the possibility of a financial crisis, despite an annual subscription of £390. Moreover, the inability to pay pupil-teacher stipends was causing Templar to lose promising pupils to industry. Consequently, on Cobden's advice, in February 1856 a memorial, supported by testimonials and stressing the 'salutary and moral and religious influence' of the school, was sent to the Committee of Council requesting to participate in the pupil-teacher system.[61] In addition a report from H.M.I. J.D. Morell testified to its valuable services to the neighbourhood and the sound teaching, good moral influence and encouragement given to the children to attend Sunday school. After a delay of four months the school secretary's reminder elicited a negative response from R.R.W. Lingen, Secretary to the Committee of Council on Education, referring the managers to the case of the Williams' Secular School in Edinburgh, opened by George Combe in 1848 with the aid of William Ellis, which had been refused a grant on the grounds of the lack of biblical instruction. Lingen emphasized that in the absence of any guarantee of 'the opportunity of instruction in revealed religion' in the rules of the Model Secular School, no grant would be forthcoming; a principle which he claimed to be in accordance with the majority of school promoters throughout the country.

A month later, Templar's request that service at the Model Secular School of one of his assistant teachers, who had completed his appren-

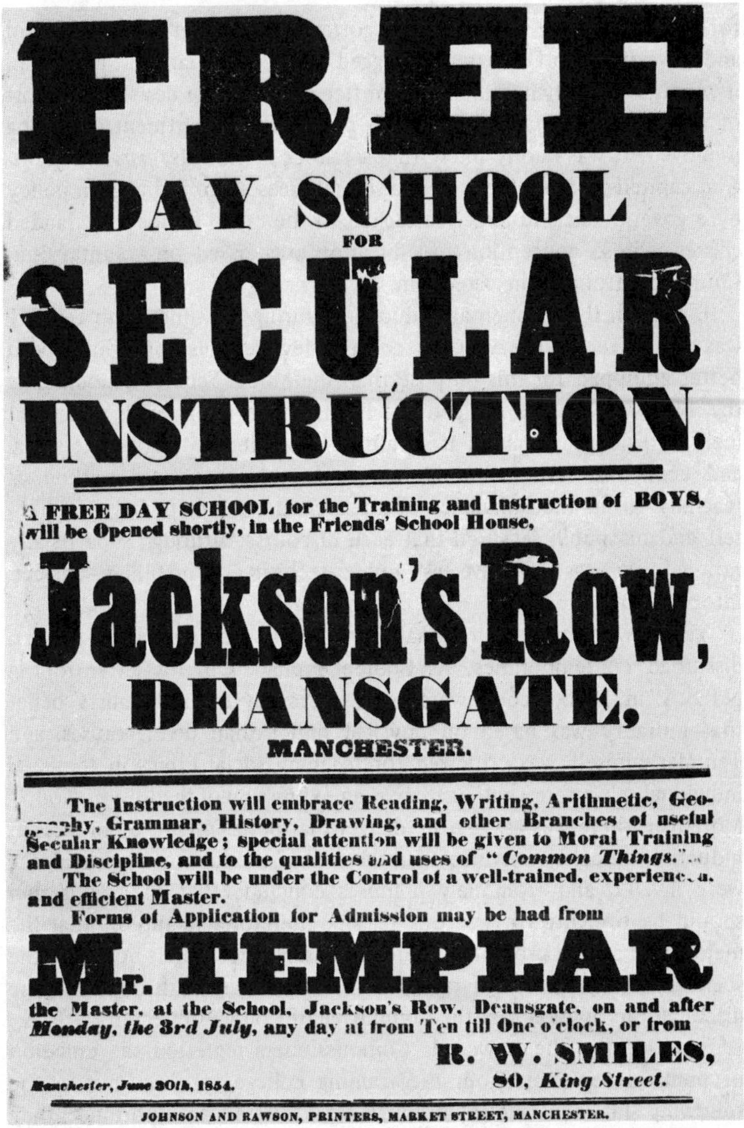

FREE
DAY SCHOOL
FOR
SECULAR
INSTRUCTION.

A FREE DAY SCHOOL, for the Training and Instruction of BOYS, will be Opened shortly, in the Friends' School House,

Jackson's Row,
DEANSGATE,
MANCHESTER.

The Instruction will embrace Reading, Writing, Arithmetic, Geography, Grammar, History, Drawing, and other Branches of useful Secular Knowledge; special attention will be given to Moral Training and Discipline, and to the qualities and uses of "*Common Things.*"

The School will be under the Control of a well-trained, experienced, and efficient Master.

Forms of Application for Admission may be had from

Mr. TEMPLAR

the Master, at the School, Jackson's Row, Deansgate, on and after **Monday, the 3rd July,** any day at from Ten till One o'clock, or from

R. W. SMILES,
80, King Street.

Manchester, June 30th, 1854.

JOHNSON AND RAWSON, PRINTERS, MARKET STREET, MANCHESTER.

Plate VIII *Poster advertising Manchester Model Secular School*

ticeship at the Warrington British School, should entitle him to sit his certificate examination after three years, met with similar intransigence. Lingen replied that despite Templar's previous experience in training pupil teachers the school was uninspected and therefore did not qualify for teacher-training purposes. The correspondence between the school and the Education Department dragged on for two years, but in the end it was the school management committee, by that time desperately short of money, which had to change its policy, the Department remaining unmoved. It was hardly likely that a school founded by *parvenu* industrial capitalists would be seen as a suitable reason for a change in policy by a government still largely attached to the credo of the 'old' landed classes, whose conception of education was based on voluntaryism, Church control and the catechism.

But given that elementary education during the nineteenth century was mainly a matter of social control, few schools could have been better equipped for this purpose than the Model Secular School. Like the Birkbeck schools it filled the heads of its pupils with masses of inert knowledge, much of it carefully calculated to justify the social and economic *status quo*. Moreover, Templar's socratic method of teaching, given the imbalance of intellectual attainment between himself and his pupils, ensured that each discourse, although superficially rational, was as effective as any catechism in instilling 'correct' information.

Yet it was this very rationalism, false though it might be, which disturbed contemporaries. As Combe explained in his letter to the N.P.S.A. in 1850, people were made uneasy by the rationalists' belief that morality was based on physical rather than divine causes, and Templar himself was criticized for teaching social ethics in terms of individual self-interest rather than as an expression of the love of God.[62] Moreover, there was always the danger that pupils might, by process of inductive thought, convince themselves that the laws of social science were invalid, and from new premises conclude that the *status quo* should be overthrown. For this reason, therefore, it appears that the majority of school promoters preferred to have their pupils bound to the social order by catechism rather than by persuasion through socratic discourse; an opinion that the Committee of Council reflected.

Significantly, the Newcastle Commissioners regretted the omission of political economy from the training college syllabus, but as the following statement shows, although they stressed its importance, they firmly believed that it should occupy a secondary role to the teaching of religion: 'Next to religion, the knowledge most important to a labouring man is that of the causes which regulate the amount of his wages, the hours of his work, the regularity of his employment, and the prices of what he consumes.'[63]

The effect of the Committee of Council's decision was to bring to an end the secular phase of the school's history. Yet rather than close it and deprive over three hundred children of an education, the management committee, after a great deal of heart searching, reluctantly agreed to permit the reading of selected scriptural passages, in order to qualify for the government grant. The reaction of the parents to the change of policy is most interesting.

Since its foundation the school had succeeded in proving that children of a variety of religious persuasions, including Roman Catholics, could be educated together. For example, of the 193 children admitted to the school in 1860 there were eighty-three Anglicans, forty-five Methodists, ten Roman Catholics and fifty-five of other dissenting congregations such as Quakers and Swedenborgians. The Committee, therefore, was anxious lest the Catholic children should be driven away by the change of policy. Once again Templar handled the situation with consummate skill. Having failed to reach any agreement with the Roman Catholic canon, he called a meeting of some thirty Catholic parents and read to them extracts from the scriptural passages selected for school use. Their comments were most favourable and they resolved to continue to send their children to the school. In the event only one Catholic family withdrew their child, despite several such intimations prior to the meeting.

There could be no more obvious demonstration of the working-class parent's lack of concern for religious teaching in elementary schools. Middle-class preoccupation with this aspect of education, which so hindered progress towards a unified system of elementary schools, is clearly revealed as something completely alien to working-class interests; a mere function of the determination of the voluntary societies to maintain their vested interests in education. This fact was not lost on Templar, as he revealed in his paper *The Religious Difficulty in National Education* (1858).

> Knowing what I do of the wishes of parents concerning education, I cannot help feeling that all the clamour that is being made about giving biblical instruction in the day schools is a noisy mistake . . . . Of my certain knowledge, I can assert that parents do not care to have their children religiously taught in the day schools . . . and in many cases their *sole* object in sending them to day school is that they may get good secular instruction.

This statement was fully supported three years later by the revelations of the Newcastle Commission.[64]

What Templar did not say was that they probably viewed the teaching of political economy with a similar lack of interest. Certainly none of the letters published in the reports makes a reference to it, except by the vaguest implication. On this point, however, the behaviour of the Model Secular School parents contrasts with that of the skilled artisan parents of the Edinburgh Secular School pupils, who accused the head-master, W.M. Williams, of indoctrinating their children with the capitalist ethic.[65] The reason for this may be that the Edinburgh parents, all of whom could pay 4*d.* a week in school fees, were economically less dependent than the Manchester parents and therefore were all the more ready to make demands on the school. The latter were probably only too glad to take the free education and job opportunities that the school could offer their children to feel any desire to criticize.

For some boys it probably had the long-term effect of providing them with a means of social mobility via skilled trades into the ranks of the 'labour aristocracy'. For a larger number it had some immediate effect on their speech and writing through the imposition of 'correct', middle-class forms of expression and there was some immediate incul-cation of an ideology inimical to the Labour movement. Yet the durability of the indoctrination process would almost certainly depend, not so much on the efficiency of Templar's teaching, but on the experi-ences of his former pupils, fortunate or otherwise, in the free-for-all of the labour market. It is probable that for most of them the practical, as distinct from the ideological content of the curriculum made the more lasting impact.

As for the parents, their willingness to send their children regularly to school is clear evidence that it was able to provide them with much of what they wanted for their children, for which many of them, as their letters reveal, were extremely grateful. It is therefore reasonable to suppose that the general effect was to bind them closer to the existing social order and to increase their empathy with the industrial middle-class. Yet the evidence that the Model Secular School provides in the light of the subsequent history of the labour movement suggests that elementary schools, despite the intentions of their promoters, never became particularly efficient instruments for the control of one social class by another. Rather does it seem that despite the propaganda and brainwashing a proportion of the working classes took what they wanted from the system and discarded the rest.

NOTES

[1] J. Kay-Shuttleworth, *Four Periods of Public Education as Reviewed in 1832, 1839, 1846, 1862* (London 1862), pp. 63-4.

[2] Cf. Chapter 1

[3] Cf. Chapter 4.

[4] W.A.C. Stewart and W.P. McCann, *The Educational Innovators 1750-1880* (London, 1967), p. 329.

[5] W. Jolly (ed.), *Education, its Principles and Practices, as Developed by George Combe* (London, 1879), p. 232.

[6] Ibid, pp. 225-45.

[7] F. Smith, *A History of English Elementary Education, 1760-1902* (London, 1931), pp. 160-3.

[8] Ibid.

[9] P.P. 1856 XLVI, p. 408.

[10] S.E. Maltby, *Manchester and the Movement for National Elementary Education* (Manchester, 1918), ch. VI.

[11] D.K. Jones, 'Lancashire, the American Common School, and the religious problem in British education in the nineteenth century', *British Journal of Educational Studies*, Vol. XV, No. 3 (October 1967).

[12] First Report of the Manchester Model Secular School (March 1855), p. 10.

[13] T.S. Ashton, *Economic and Social Investigations in Manchester* (London, 1934), p. 1.

[14] D.K. Jones, 'Working-class education in nineteenth-century Manchester: The Manchester Model Secular School', *The Vocational Aspect* (Spring 1967), Vol. XIX, No. 42, pp. 22-33.

[15] J.A. Newbold 'The case of the Manchester Free School no argument for universal free schools', *Manchester Tracts on Education*, No. 1 (Manchester, 1887).

[16] Second Report of the Manchester Model Secular School (August 1856), p. 37.

[17] Newbold, op. cit.

[18] P.P. 1861 XXI (I), Report of the Commissioners Appointed to Inquire into the State of Popular Education in England (Newcastle), pt. i, ch. i, p. 73.

[19] Letter in N.P.S.A. papers at M136/2/3/663 in Manchester Central Library.

[20] Ibid.

[21] Stewart and McCann, op. cit., p. 337.

[22] First Report, p. 6.

[23] For further information on this exhibition, cf. D. Layton, 'Science in the schools: the first wave − a study of the influence of Richard Dawes (1793-1867)', *British Journal of Educational Studies*, Vol. XX (February 1972), pp. 38-57.

[24] Schools Enquiry Commission, XXVIII (4), pp. 502-3.

[25] The Edinburgh Secular School was opened in 1848 by George Combe and James Simpson with the aid of £100 donated by William Ellis (Jolly, op. cit., p. 212).

[26] First Report, p. 7.

[27] Ibid., p. 11.

[28] Ibid.

[29] This figure probably exaggerates the number of families consisting of one child. In five cases it was not stated whether the boy had any siblings.

[30] Second Report, p. 23.

[31] Second Report, p. 7.

[32] First Report, p. 11.

[33] Second Report, p. 10.

[34] Ibid., p. 11.

[35] Second Report, p. 6.

[36] Nineteenth Report of the Manchester Free School.

[37] The letters are taken from the Second Report, p. 13. Of the nineteen boys, eleven had gone to work, nine out of sheer necessity to make ends meet, four had been kept at home in order to care for other members of the family, three had either no shoes or no suitable clothes, and one being a Roman Catholic, had withdrawn for religious reasons.

[38] Fifth Report of the Manchester Model Secular School (September 1860), p. 12.

[39] Sixth Report of the Manchester Model Secular School (September 1861), p. 5.

[40] Fifth Report, p. 9.

[41] Eighth Report of the Manchester Free School (1864), p. 6.

[42] Second Report, p. 12.

[43] First Report, p. 13.

[44] Cf. Chapter 4.

[45] Second Report, pp. 13-24.

[46] First Report, p. 8.

[47] Second Report, p. 13.

[48] First Report, p. 6.

[49] Ibid.

[50] W. Cobbett, *A Grammar of the English Language* (London, 1819), p. 15.

[51] First Report, p. 8.

[52] A Briggs, *Victorian Cities*, (Pelican Books, Harmondsworth, 1968), p. 91.

[53] Second Report, p. 15.

[54] Ibid.

[55] Ibid., p. 18.

[56] Quoted in E.P. Thompson, *The Making of the English Working Class*, (Pelican Books, Harmondsworth, 1968), p. 329.

[57] Letter to Templar, 2 May 1858, quoted by Jolly, op.. cit., p. 198.

[58] B. Templar, *The Importance of Teaching Social Economy in Elementary Schools* (Manchester, 1858).

[59] Third Report of the Manchester Model Secular School (September 1858), p. 26.

[60] Fifth Report, p. 7.

[61] The correspondence between the managers and the Committee of Council is recorded in P.P. 1856 XLVI, p. 405ff., and P.P. 1857-8 XLVI, p. 331ff.

[62] Third Report, p. 30.

[63] Newcastle Commission, Vol. I, pt. i, ch. ii, p. 127.

[64] Newcastle Commission, Vol. I, pt. i, ch. i, pp. 33-9.

[65] Stewart and McCann, op. cit., p. 330.

Chapter 6:

Ideology and the factory child: attitudes to half-time education
Harold Silver

—

The half-time system, foreshadowed in the early Factory Acts and effective from 1845, began as a strategy for combating excessive child labour and became, in the 1850s and 1860s, an educational theory. Its basis was described by one of the first factory inspectors as 'combining school education with an industrial education in a wages-yielding employment'.[1] It began as an instrument of the state for the protection of children in certain kinds of employment. The half-time system was attacked as an industrial measure when, especially in the last quarter of the century, opinion turned in favour of achieving compulsory education for all by other means. Discussion of the half-time system has been previously concerned primarily with the tactics of its early introduction and with the politics of its later decline and defeat.[2] Between the two, however, considerable interest was shown in the educational implications of the half-time process: evidence was accumulated, educational theories were elaborated, ideological positions were adopted. It is with these, and with the effects of the system on the children, that we are mainly concerned.

The principle of education for factory children was introduced in the 1802 Health and Morals of Apprentices Act, and that of a minimum age for factory employment was enacted in 1819: the first 'protected children, being apprentices, against their masters. The second protected all children against their parents'.[3] Neither was in any important sense successful. Under the Factories Act of 1833 children between the ages of nine and eleven (rising to thirteen over a two-year period) employed in the main textile industries were to receive two hours' schooling on six days a week. The factory inspectors appointed under the Act soon complained of the difficulties of implementing the law.[4]

The Factories Act of 1844 crystallized the half-time system emerging under the previous legislation. It lowered the age of employment to eight, but provided for half a day's (normally three hours) education, five days a week, for children employed in textiles, up to the age of thirteen (eleven in the case of silk mills). Firms could, if they preferred, provide five hours' education on alternate days. The early inspectors tried to enforce what one of them, Leonard Horner, more than once described as 'attendance within four walls of a room called a school', over the quality of which they had no control.[5] The Factory Acts were extended to cover children in other sectors – printworks in 1845 (children having to attend school for at least thirty days each half year), mining, bleaching and dyeing in 1860 and lace in 1861. In 1864 the potteries children were 'brought under discipline'.[6] In 1867 foundries, metal, tobacco and other industries were covered, as were workshops employing fifty or more workers. In 1870 printworks, dyeing and bleaching were assimilated into the Factory Acts. In 1874 the minimum age of employment was raised to ten, and children covered by the Factory Acts who had not attained a given standard of education by the age of thirteen were required to stay at school another year. The disparities and confusions produced by the mid-1870s were summarized by an inspector of schools, pointing out that industrial legislation required

> the attendance of children up to 13, the Mines Act, for some unaccountable reason, releasing them from all obligation to attend school at 12 years of age. The Workshops' Act, again, requires five hours a week less school attendance than the Factory Act; and they all differ from the requirements of school boards acting under the Education Act.[7]

The factory and workshops legislation was consolidated in 1878. The 1870 Education Act and the principle of compulsory attendance enacted in 1876 and 1880 resulted in stronger pressures to raise the minimum age of employment, and to ensure full-time schooling for all children, but the half-time system was to continue until 1918.

The provision of education for factory children was rare before the 1833 Act. Some mills did provide schooling for the children they employed or provided pre-employment education.[8] After 1833 some employers were anxious to comply with the Act. Horner, for example, met with a willing response among many cotton millowners, notably Henry McConnel, Manchester's largest cotton spinner, who established what Horner described as an 'excellent school', attending three hours a day to the children's 'religious and moral training and habits of order, good breeding, and cleanliness and attention to neatness in dress'.[9] Before 1833 the Strutts tried to employ only children who had received education in the firm's day school. Factory education often included a requirement to attend Sunday school and religious worship: in 1839 it was reported that young persons under sixteen at Strutts' had for several years been 'required to attend the Sunday school'.[10]

Even after 1833 progress was slow and sporadic. A visitor to Wood and Walker's school for their mill children at Bradford in 1841 reported on the generous school provisions which the schoolmaster 'evidently took a pleasure in showing me',[11] but such reports were rare. Horner's report on his district in 1839 contained both McConnel's 'excellent school', one where children were taught by the fireman, 'and there are many intermediate grades'.[12] Evidence of apathy and inefficiency was abundant in the early 1840s. From the 1844 Act employers were also faced with the question of whether to send the children to local schools or provide their own. Only gradually did the educational content of the half-time system become a matter of widespread interest. In the 1840s discussion about the half-time system was primarily concerned with its role in limiting and therefore humanizing child labour.

Discussion of the educational value of the system was a feature of the late 1850s and 1860s. It was discussed, for example, at an educational conference in London in 1857.[13] Between 1859 and 1865 its educational significance was analyzed at the National Association for the Promotion of Social Science by such well-known figures as Nassau and Edward Senior, Mary Carpenter, Edward Wilks – Secretary of the British and Foreign School Society – and former H.M.I. Seymour Tremenheere. The Newcastle Commission asked for opinions about the system in a questionnaire in 1860. Edwin Chadwick compiled some 75,000 words of evidence on the system which he submitted together with a commentary to Nassau Senior, a member of the Commission. Chadwick's interest had stemmed from an address he intended to give to the N.A.P.S.S. in 1859.[14] In 1861 Senior published the documents he had drafted for the Commission in *Suggestions on Popular Education*, in which the half-time system featured prominently. The ideas of this quasi-pressure group, together with reports by the factory inspectors, were used by Marx in drafting a document for the First International in 1864, and in the first volume of *Capital*, published in German in 1867. The same sources were used by J.M. Ludlow and Lloyd Jones in their book on the *Progress of the Working Class 1832-67*, published in the same year. The discussion of the half-time system across these ten or so years is the centre-piece of any analysis of the process of half-time education.

The half-time system was intended, in Chadwick's words, 'as a primary security against overwork; inasmuch as if we secured their presence in school for three hours, we prevented their presence for that time in the workshop'.[15] The system was rooted in the controversies and campaigns of the 1830s and 1840s over the factory system, and especially over working hours and child labour. Our concern here is with the range of arguments used in support of half-time education.

The early reports of the factory inspectors describe attempts to provide factory schools, and their conviction that the half-time system represented major progress. Even in the late 1850s and 1860s the view was being constantly expressed that half-time education was better than none. In 1861, for example, factory inspector Robert Baker stressed that in Lancashire and Cheshire 'but for the provisions of the Factory Act, the numbers of uneducated children . . . must be greatly increased'. Three years later he declared that 'the half-time Act is a godsend to the Potteries, it being the only opportunity whereby the poor children can gain any education'.[16] A correspondent told Chadwick that school masters and other witnesses in Rochdale agreed 'that the half-time system has given to the children of these districts an education which they most certainly would not have obtained if long school hours had been required'. H.M.I. Tufnell told him that 'the question with the parents frequently is, education on the half-time plan, or no education at all'.[17]

A second, increasingly explicit set of arguments related to the system's likely moral and social utility. Millowners were discovering what others had discovered before them – that education could be a useful, socially manipulative instrument. 'Many of the mill-owners', reported one of the factory inspectors in 1839, 'who now approve of education, were among those who formerly deemed the application of it almost impossible, and not likely to be in the least degree beneficial'.[18] Once its utility was realized the important questions became – how much education, and of what kind? When the factory inspectors reported on the effects of the 1833 education clauses they offered evidence that the prevailing answers to these questions were – as little as necessary, and of a kind to instil right moral attitudes. An extreme version was that expressed by a firm of cotton manufacturers in

Derbyshire: 'We are of opinion that it is more conducive to the welfare of our people to endeavour to make them enlightened Christians than wise in wordly knowledge; we do not want statesmen in our factories, but orderly subjects.' At a flax spinners in Westmorland education was said to have improved 'the conduct and habits of subordination of the factory hands generally, which is very observable in the disuse of bad language, their orderly behaviour, neat and cleanly appearance, and increased diligence in the attendance of places of worship'. Education counteracted bad home influences, inculcated desirable moral attitudes, and led to a 'thorough knowledge of the nature and sins of lying, stealing, swearing and the like'. At least one school was also seen as an instrument of punishment for behaviour *in the factory*: at a cotton spinners near Bury the conduct of the children in the factory was reported to the school, where necessary punishment was inflicted, and 'general conduct is improved thereby, and . . . the school discipline is acknowledged beyond the precincts of the school'.[19]

The importance of this second set of arguments lies in its precise and confident assertion of the long-standing effects of half-time education — in terms, for example, of punctuality, obedience and other virtues. Education would *make* enlightened Christians and orderly subjects, thereby protecting the industrial system, society itself. Edward Wilks offered such a perspective when he saw the need for the half-time principle to 'be defended on the grounds of common humanity, social progress, and public security'.[20] Such arguments were not, of course, confined to the half-time system. Social discipline and 'public security' were familiar touchstones in debates about industry and education. At the end of the 1860s even a prominent voice in the National Education League could talk about children at work 'learning lessons of order, obedience, and industry in a factory, shop, or office'.[21] Most nineteenth-century English educationists saw a continuum between questions of popular education and those of social order.

A third cluster of arguments in favour of the half-time system concerned its contribution to the future well-being of the workers. This was often a subsidiary to other arguments, but occasionally the welfare and even the social mobility of the factory child became a focus of discussion. Mobility related, for example, to opportunities that were mentioned for children to become pupil teachers. The basic argument, however, was the future role of the working-class child in industry, and incidentally the prosperity of the economy. Employers and school-masters testified to Chadwick, for example, that boys who began work early 'begat a greater aptitude and readiness in any employment they may be called to'. Farmers found that boys who had combined education with out-of-doors work were 'much better servants than the mere school-boy'. Mary Carpenter thought one of the chief problems was 'how best to prepare the young person for the future work of life', and Edward Senior explained that he and his fellow Poor Law Commissioners believed it to be of the greatest importance that 'children who have to live by their labour should be trained to labour early . . . boys should be accustomed to work at the earliest practicable age'.[22] Some factory children did graduate from half-time education to higher-status occupations: a Rochdale teacher reported, for instance that of his half-timers 'one is an Independent minister at Barlow-on-Humber, one a Baptist minister in America, another in the same country as an Independent; three clerks in one establishment, and several others in different country houses in the town'.[23] The numbers making such a transition must have been minute, but any such educational development in the nineteenth century caused unease somewhere that working-class children were being educated 'above their station'. The head of a half-time school in Manchester thought that a child's education 'must be adapted, as far as possible, to his probable future position in society', which meant that 'it should not be so extended as to make him vain and conceited'. H.M.I. Tufnell recorded that many people objected that children were being over-educated at half-time schools, 'but my reply has always been, that I never wished them to receive more education than is necessary to ensure that they shall never become paupers again'. Mary Carpenter, discussing working-class children, thought 'the study of languages and other branches of knowledge which require great length of time, is not necessary for this class'.[24] She told the N.A.P.S.S. in 1861 that in the education of such children 'there must be nothing to pamper self-indulgence, to raise the child in his own estimation above his natural position in society'.[25] Even the most eager supporters of the half-time system had a clear notion of the limits beyond which education should not go, limits related to the 'natural' structures of society.

Other declared reasons for support for the half-time system included important claims − to which we shall return − for combined manual and intellectual effort. Reasons for support were not always, however, clear or unambiguous. Few respondents to the Newcastle Commission's questionnaire were able to explain their attitude to the system. Of the fifty-nine published replies from educationists, headmasters, clergymen and others, only twenty-one can be construed as positively supporting the half-time system: thirty either failed to answer the question about it or declared their inability to do so. Those who expressed support did so generally with vague expressions of its being 'very valuable' or suited to manufacturing districts or worthy of trial.

Support for the system went together with a defence of its efficiency or effectiveness. Examples of efficient half-time schools, or of schools which effectively combined half-time and full-time education, were publicized by H.M.I.s, interested manufacturers and others in the 1850s.[26] The reputation of such schools, and of those which had operated since before 1844, began to increase confidence in the system. Fresh claims began to be made for it, particularly as, by the late 1850s and 1860s, it was widely held that the quality of available schools was improving.

Edward Wilks summarized the optimistic view in 1859 by declaring that results had 'proved the principle sound in theory, wise in legislation, and practical in working': schools were now more widespread and more efficient.[27] The Newcastle Commission commented that 'the difficulties of providing efficient education are not so great now as they were in 1833'.[28] Nassau Senior, as a member of the Newcastle Commission, criticized the quality of the education of most half-timers, but in the mid-1860s Tremenheere pointed to 'a very great improvement' in the schools since Senior's comments.[29] Chadwick's documents for the Newcastle Commission were designed to show that the half-time system was working efficiently. H.M.I.s and factory inspectors occasionally reported broadly to the same effect. In 1861 the secretary of the N.A.P.S.S. wrote that the half-time system would soon 'be established over the whole country. This is one of the subjects on which the quiet influence of the Association . . . has been productive of great benefit.'[30] A group within the N.A.P.S.S. had convinced it, mainly on the basis of Chadwick's evidence, that the system was being increasingly successful. Charles Kingsley, like others connected with the Association, considered the matter proven: the half-time system had been 'proved to work so well . . . by so many able judges, and especially by my friend . . . Mr Chadwick, in his letter to Mr Senior, of 1861'.[31]

Triumphant claims made for the half-time system and the evidence on which they rested concealed uncertainties. They also produced counter-claims. Although later in the century criticism of the system was to be directed primarily against its role in perpetuating child labour, in the 1850s and 1860s the most frequently expressed concern was about the system's inefficiency or failure. The main complaints were directed against the effect of the system on National and British schools. H.M.I.s reported that the attendance of factory children disrupted the work of the schools.[32] There was some support for the idea of isolating half-timers in separate schools, though there were practical difficulties.[33] Some schools refused to admit half-timers or made them unwelcome.[34] Evidence to the Cross Commission confirmed the complaint that 'the admixture of half-timers with the whole-time scholars injures the organization and working of the school'.[35]

Reservations about the system's effectiveness sometimes led to stronger statements. Wilks, in 1859, thought that 'the educational results have not been as satisfactory as might be desired'. Baker was frank about the system's deficiencies, whilst defending it against 'any who may speak ... of education in combination with labour as a failure'.[36] Voluntaryists who had since the 1843 bill opposed state involvement in education naturally attacked the half-time system. In 1856 the chairman of a voluntaryist meeting criticized laudatory comments by Lord John Russell about the system, on the grounds that half-timers 'were very indifferent to teaching, and came to school half asleep after their half-day's work, whilst they disregarded the institution also, because it was forced on them by law'.[37] Whatever welcome school inspectors gave to the educational clauses of the Factory Acts they were aware of the often crippling effects of the system on schools attended by half-time children, but also of its inadequacy for the half-timers themselves. In 1851 Morell found 'the most conflicting reports among schoolmasters' as to the possibility of communicating a 'satisfactory amount of mental culture to the children' once they had begun work in the factories: the results were 'very discouraging'. Education for factory children, he found, was 'far from what education ought to be, and far from giving any cause of congratulation as to the future history of the scholars now under instruction'. The tiredness of the children (especially when attending in the afternoons) was, said another H.M.I., one of the main 'hindrances to the progress of education'. A third felt 'unable to speak with the unhesitating confidence of some better authorities' and thought 'experience thus far affords little ground for an expectation that the half-time system will produce a working population fairly educated'.[38]

Such reservations about the adequacy and effectiveness of half-time education were being expressed from the 1850s. Factory inspector Redgrave concluded in 1857 that it possessed 'in the abstract, all the elements of success; but in practice it has entirely failed'. Neither employers nor parents had understood its purpose: 'it is not looked upon as a system of education, but as an adjunct to employment'.[39] Horner in 1857 was defending the system against those who had 'confidently stated on various occasions that the long-tried experiment in the factories has proved a failure',[40] and many of the respondents to the Newcastle Commission's enquiry thought the system of doubtful value. In the absence of legislation to improve the quality of schools, Chadwick himself was bound to admit that half-time education had by the end of the 1850s been 'extensively nominal and illusory, and often fraudulent. From officers who have seen only the failures, the majority of cases, you will get testimony that the half-school time is an utter failure.'[41] The campaign in support of half-time education had to reckon with its known drawbacks and with sustained doubts and criticisms.[42]

At the centre of discussion emerged a comparison of the relative effectiveness of full-time and half-time education. This involved a comparison not only of the standards reached, but also of such factors as attendance, since the enforced regular attendance of many half-timers could compensate for their lack of previous education. Given the problems of securing regular attendance at elementary schools generally, factory children may have had a better attendance record than full-timers. The discussion came to pivot, however, round the possibility that half-time education not only might be better than nothing, but might actually be more effective than full-time education. Attitudes to the education and culture to be transmitted to factory children were implied, and sometimes made explicit, in the discussions about the merits of half-time and full-time education.

From the beginning claims were made that half-timers fared educationally as well as, or even better than, full-timers. In 1839 factory inspector Saunders reported testimonies from two mills that half-time children often made 'as great progress' or 'very frequently as much progress as the others'.[43] The Newcastle Commission heard that schoolmasters thought 'half-time teaching is far more nearly equal to full-time than would be supposed. Some go so far as to assert that it is "very nearly as good".'[44] Chadwick's 'Communications' to the Commission contain repeated claims as to the 'relative superiority of the short-time school children', who were 'quite equal' to the full-timers, 'nearly equal' or 'fully equal in attainments', 'not quite up to the full-timers, but there is really very little difference', or made 'greater progress than

Plate IX *Half-timers leaving Haggas's Mill, Ingrow, Keighley*

the full-timers'. Half-timers are described as giving 'more fixed attention'. They 'come fresh from work to school, and they go fresh from school to work'. One witness calculates the ratio of attainment as 'about five to seven of the full-day scholars'.[45] Similar claims are echoed in the reports of the factory and school inspectors.[46] Chadwick himself believed that half-timers made greater progress than full-timers and developed a 'superior habit of mental activity'. He thought the evidence 'of all the best teachers . . . clear and decisive' on this score.[47]

These claims were contradicted − often in the same places as the ones we have quoted − though not as part of a coherent counter-campaign. While factory inspector Saunders was quoting positive evidence in 1839 his colleague T.J. Howell was reporting that 'in schools admitting Factory children together with other pupils, the latter, so far as my inquiries have extended, invariably outstrip the former'. One (though only one) of Chadwick's witnesses confessed that in his school the full-time scholars were 'certainly in advance of the half-time scholars, and get on faster' — and he accounted for this by reference to differences in the social backgrounds of the children.[48] The master of the Birkbeck secular school at Peckham told the Newcastle Commission that 'after you have done all that the half-time system will enable you to do, children are turned out much less efficient in school matters than they would be if they had the whole time' — a view which Nassau Senior rejected on the 'remarkably full and complete' evidence as to the equality of half-timers and full-timers in good schools.[49] The Newcastle Assistant Commissioner who reported positive views also attacked the extravagance of some claims for the system: teachers admitted universally, he stated, that 'under similar conditions of attendance, half-time teaching cannot, as some enthusiasts have said, produce as great a result as full-time'.[50] Inspector Baker quoted a witness whose views he thought deserved respect, and who talked of the opinion 'gaining ground that "half-timers are almost as proficient in their studies as day scholars;" in this opinion I cannot concur'. The opinion had, in the witness's view, 'taken possession of the minds of certain learned but not very practical men'. Baker quoted views on the factors which affected differences of attainment between full-timers and half-timers — different intellectual, moral and other powers among the two groups, their family backgrounds, visual and verbal abilities and memories.[51]

The school inspectors also provided evidence as to the relative backwardness of half-time children. J.G. Fitch, for example, in 1864 made a forthright 'protest against the extravagant claims which are sometimes made for the half-time system'. Factory children might often learn relatively more than full-timers, but 'that they learn absolutely more, or nearly as much, is, I think, a mischievous fallacy'.[52]

The Code regulations sharpened hostility to the half-time system among teachers from the early 1860s, because the same grant-earning standards were required of the half-time children.[53] The H.M.I.s' reports, particularly in the 1860s, and evidence later to the Cross Commission and in the pages of *The Schoolmaster*, show that teachers, resentful of payment by results, found the Code regulations for half-timers particularly unfair.[54]

The critics of exaggerated claims for the half-time system produced not a comprehensive explanation of the relative success of some half-timers, but occasional insights. Baker's reports show an awareness that half-timers from better homes performed better. Half-timers also had an advantage over full-timers in being older.[55] Since factory children tended to start school from a lower educational base line, they might be seen to be making comparatively rapid progress.[56] Their regular attendance was seen to be a factor. An argument pressed by *The Schoolmaster* from the 1880s was that half-timers only did comparatively well because full-timers did comparatively badly. Full-timers in Bradford, for instance, had 'no further advantage over half-timer than of getting the same lesson twice over. They are not carried forward to any new educational ground.' Full-timers in Oldham, similarly, were 'merely double half-timers', having 'no educational advantages beyond the iteration of the work which the others get at intervals'.[57] When a commentator in 1907 talked of the repetition of lessons and of day scholars having to 'mark time' for the half-timers,[58] he was describing what had always been true. Only the most perceptive witness would have seen the force of 'double half-timer' much before the 1880s.

Nevertheless, evidence accumulated to defend the half-time system was received relatively uncritically in earlier decades, when the Factory Acts needed to be shown to be working. Contrary evidence and critical views were, as we have seen, available.

Some of these considerations explain the appearance at the end of the 1850s of the group of half-time enthusiasts whom we have seen described as 'learned but not very practical men'.

Chadwick was the crucial figure. In 1861 Lord Brougham described Chadwick's collection of 'Communications' on the subject as 'an event in the history of education'.[59] Chadwick compiled this collection of interviews and statements to show, among other things, the number of hours he and his witnesses thought children could sustain attention, and to justify a preference for half-time over full-time education. Others joined him as campaigners, and Chadwick's 'Communications' was their campaign guide.

The witnesses questioned by Chadwick tended to agree that three hours a day was the maximum period for what a British schoolmaster called 'bright voluntary attention' on the part of the children. Most witnesses thought three hours was the number that would 'suffice', would secure 'concentrated and willing attention', and would not exhaust the children's 'capacity of attention'. Some witnesses suggested how the three hours might best be divided up or discussed the different spans of attention of children of different ages.[60] A factory schoolmaster spoke of the 'common opinion of school teachers that school time in such (full-time) schools is much wasted in the afternoons'.[61] Chadwick's own commentary underlined that full-time schooling was mentally and physically injurious.

Mary Carpenter, one of Victorian England's authorities on the education of the poor, made the social class basis of her psychology explicit: she told Chadwick that 'in the higher or more cultivated classes, where the organization is more adapted to mental exercise, and the culture of the intellectual powers is essential to after life, I do not think eight hours per diem too much to be employed in direct instruction'. On the other hand, she believed 'three hours per diem of good scholastic instruction would be amply sufficient for the children of the working classes, and of the neglected classes, if I may so call that class below them'. She told the N.A.P.S.S. that it had been 'proved that three hours daily of direct intellectual instruction is quite as profitable as a longer period, and even more so' – calling the witnesses of the Newcastle Commission to her support.[62] At the same meeting Edward Senior quoted the Chadwick evidence – and Mary Carpenter's – with especial enthusiasm, commenting that 'of the six hours' school, nearly two or three hours are real literary labour, and three or four enforced sedentary idleness'.[63] Leonard Horner thought that lengthening the school day for factory children would be 'an entire mistake' since the effect would be 'that their prolonged confinement and wearisome activity would render the school still more hateful to them'.[64] Nassau Senior told the N.A.P.S.S. in 1863 that – in full-time schools, for all social classes – 'we are employing labour on the part of our masters, and time, health and energy on the part of our children not only fruitlessly but absolutely mischievously'. Repeated assertions were often referred to as proof.[65]

The three-hour philosophy was not without its critics. Inspector Baker reported in full the critic who argued against the 'very able men' who favoured a maximum of three hours' mental effort. Children's minds were already taxed for only a small proportion of the day – in fact by scriptural knowledge and arithmetic, not by less demanding reading and writing. H.M.I. Fitch considered 'the opinion of some philanthropists that five hours at school per day, for five days a week, is too much for a healthy child' to be a 'wholly imaginary' evil.[66] The educational theory born of the half-time system drew, of course, on the pervasive opinion that popular education should reach out for only limited objectives. The question for Chadwick was not how long 'the children of the labouring classes may be kept in school', but 'in how short a time they may receive elementary instruction, and be freed from it'.[67] This is a profoundly important concept. Even more than was common in discussion of elementary education Chadwick was here postulating an educational optimum for working-class children: once it was attained, they could be 'freed' from education.

The argument for a 'sufficient' education was an interpretation of the class function of education. This was also expressed clearly in related support for drill as a school activity, particularly by Chadwick. Half-time began to be interpreted as any combination of mental and manual work (including, in some cases, needlework), or even of book learning and drill. Drawing especially on the experience of naval and military schools, Chadwick saw the half-time system as including a major component of drill.[68] The cultural and social intentions of the advocacy of drill were precise, typified by the witness who told Chadwick that it was an important way to 'maintain the attention, and insure decorum and promptitude'. Drilled boys were 'prompt, obedient, and punctual', and less inclined to mischief and insubordination. One vivid description of the effects of drill contrasted 'the loutish bearing of the Lancashire lad and the firm, erect respectful, and self-respecting carriage and behaviour of the same person after he had been thoroughly disciplined and polished by the military drill'.[69] Nassau Senior thought the effect of drill 'a remarkable educational phenomenon', and it began to be seen even as an alternative to industrial experience, and as a contribution to national defence.[70]

From the outset Horner and others had hinted at the educational soundness of combining mental and industrial activity. Much subsequent discussion underpinned such a theory, which was elaborated by factory inspectors, in contributions to the N.A.P.S.S., in evidence to the Newcastle Commission, by Chadwick, Mary Carpenter and Nassau Senior, and by Marx and Engels.

Marx and Engels' use of this theory was based partly on the evidence and views we have discussed, and partly on educational views given particular emphasis in early nineteenth-century Britain by Robert Owen. In his *Condition of the Working Class* (published in German in 1845) Engels criticized the failure adequately to implement the educational provisions of the 1844 Act: 'the attempt to introduce compulsory education for factory children has failed, since the Government did not provide good schools'.[71] This was almost exactly the standpoint that Horner had adopted after 1833. In *The Communist Manifesto* in 1848

Marx and Engels went further and called for 'public and free education for all children. Abolition of factory work for children in its present form. Education and material production to be combined.'[72] They had seen in the Factory Acts the herald of a future pattern of education. Marx was receptive to ideas and experience in this field, and in 1866 expressed the theory more firmly, considering 'the tendency of modern industry to make children and juvenile persons of both sexes co-operate in the great work of social production, as a progressive, sound and legitimate tendency'. This tendency had been 'distorted into an abomination' by capitalism, but in a rational state of society every child from the age of nine 'ought to become a productive labourer', though protected against excessive hours of labour. For Marx education now contained three elements – mental education, bodily education ('such as is given in schools of gymnastics, and by military exercise') and technological training ('which imparts the general principles of all processes of production'). Marx had adopted a great deal from the discussions of the half-time system in the early 1860s, and turned it into a conviction that 'the combination of paid productive labour, mental education, bodily exercise and polytechnic training, will raise the working class far above the level of the higher and middle classes'.[73]

Capital, published in German the following year, contained a similar discussion, quoting from inspector Baker and Nassau Senior. The 'paltry' education clauses of the Factory Act, said Marx, 'provided for the first time the possibility of combining education and gymnastics with manual labour'. The factory inspectors had discovered that 'the factory children, although receiving only one half the education of the regular day scholars, yet learnt quite as much and often more'. Senior had shown the mono-tony and uselessness of long school hours; Robert Owen had shown the factory system to contain 'the germ of an education that will, in the case of every child over a given age, combine productive labour with instruction and gymnastics, not only as one of the methods of adding to the efficiency of production, but as the only method of producing fully developed human beings'.[74] In 1875 Marx wrote that

> A general prohibition of child labour is incompatible with the exis-
> tence of large-scale industry . . . Its realization – if it were possible –
> would be reactionary, since, with a strict regulation of the working
> time according to the different age groups and other safety measures
> for the protection of children, an early combination of productive
> labour with education is one of the most potent means for the
> transformation of present day society.[75]

The objective no longer lay in the future. Ten years later Engels defended Marx's view, rejecting technical education in schools, opposing a view that it should replace gymnastics, and quoting *Capital* against what he considered a weaker programme of educational reform.[76]

A full discussion of the use that Marx in particular made of the theory of 'combined' education would require detailed discussion of the educational views of Owen and other early nineteenth-century radical educators, and of how far Marx, interpreting Owen, diverged from him. It would need to show that Owen was not concerned with — and in fact resisted — early paid employment, but with education as a preliminary to occupying a place in a changed society. It would need to show that Marx's 'early combination of productive labour with education' does not derive from the tradition he claimed for it.[77]

More important, Marx selected only positive statements from Senior and Baker, and used them uncritically. Marx claimed, quoting from Baker's 1865 report, that

> The factory inspectors soon found out by questioning the schoolmasters, that the factory children, although receiving only one half the education of the regular day scholars, yet learnt quite as much and often more. 'This can be accounted for by the simple fact that, with only being at school for one half of the day, they are always fresh ... The system on which they work, half manual labour, and half school, renders each employment a rest and a relief to the other ...'[78]

The quotation in this passage is not, in fact, from Baker, but from one witness quoted by Baker, in a report which contained opposite testimony from other teachers. Marx's view of what the factory inspectors had found out is also misleading, since — as we have seen — they reported conflicting evidence, and Baker himself had in other reports quoted critical attacks on the half-time system. Marx ignored the criticism and the critics, and gave the impression of impregnable support by the factory inspectors (which was certainly not true of Redgrave, for example), and he completely ignored the evidence of the school inspectors. It is true, as Baker points out, that in the early 1860s opinion was 'very strong in the direction, that wherever children are employed at all, education shall be combined with labour'.[79] Marx's use of Senior and Baker reflected this trend in public opinion, but his assertions that half-timers were 'always fresh' and experienced 'a rest and a relief' through the system did not reflect the disquiet that already

existed about such evidence even while Chadwick was collecting it.
H.M.I. Stokes reflected the basically contradictory and inconclusive
nature of the kind of evidence Marx accepted when he concluded in
1868 that 'the time seems opportune for some inquiry into the effects
of the half-time system upon the children themselves as well as upon
the schools which they frequent'.[80] Marx clung to the most optimistic
reading of his sources, as no doubt did the secretary of the Catholic
Poor School Committee, who justified the half-time system by
reference to the combination of agricultural labour and mental culti-
vation in the Benedictine and Cistercian monasteries.[81]

Plate X *Half-timers asleep at their desks*

By the 1880s the 'half manual labour, and half school' system was
being widely condemned, as having 'no intellectual advantage',[82] at the
Cross Commission, by socialist organizations,[83] and in *The Schoolmaster*.
In 1891, when the half-time system was presented as a combination of
school and technical education which 'sharpens the children's wits' –
an argument used from Horner in the 1830s to Marx in the 1860s – A.J.
Mundella called the theory 'one of the most preposterous fallacies ever
trotted out by an interested class to hoodwink the community'.[84]

Margaret McMillan described the half-timers' school in 1906 as, at best, 'a
place where Hope becomes so very moderate that Ambition dies'.[85] The
following year the half-timer was described as 'practically condemned

(unless unusually intelligent) to unskilled and low-paid labour for life'.[86] Both of these were true for the whole period during which the system operated. Half-timers were often said to be from the lowest, poorest strata of the working class. As early as 1846 an H.M.I. mentions that full-timers' parents sometimes removed their children from school, 'afraid of contact and contamination from their poorer school-fellows' who came as half-timers. The Newcastle Commission heard from Rochdale and Bradford that half-timers 'spring from a lower grade of society than the day scholars'. Factory inspectors reported teachers' comments that half-timers who had not previously attended school were 'generally of an inferior class, frequently depraved', or were 'the children of negligent or improvident parents, or orphans, and otherwise destitute'.[87] Mary Carpenter, as we have seen, distinguished between 'the children of the working classes, and of the neglected classes, if I may so call that class below them'. The reality for these children was summed up by the Bradford teacher who commented in 1884 — though it could have been said at any time during this period — on the meagre amount of learning acquired by the half-timer: he was 'inclined to think it will be sufficient to meet the wants of their case. It must not be forgotten what they are likely to remain, and the stations they will fill in life.'[88] The half-time system was an important means of cementing the hierarchy of stations of life.

Given the extreme poverty of most half-timers' parents, the half-timer acquired an early status as wage-earner, and developed a characteristic behaviour resulting from this sense of independence. In the 1860s there were references to the fact that early half-time employment induced insubordination not found among full-time pupils: half-timers 'bring into school rude manners and clothes; they are less amenable to discipline than others, as in fact they pay for themselves'.[89] The children were learning adult roles and behaviour in the factory, whilst at school — in many cases being attended for the first time — they were children. In necessitous families their wage-earning capacity resulted in prematurely adult behaviour. Fullest evidence is available from the 1880s, but again it is equally applicable to earlier decades.

The Schoolmaster quoted a report on the behaviour patterns of half-timers in Bradford:

I have watched children enter the mill for the first time, come to this school bright, happy, obedient, and with every desire to win the approbation of their teachers. This gradually gives place to feelings of indifference and carelessness, which rapidly degenerate into obstinacy and a disposition to resist any authority.[90]

Half-timers, the Cross Commission heard from one witness, 'already make their money, and they are inclined to insubordination'. Their factory-acquired 'sharpness', said another witness, made them 'more ambitious to baffle and defy the teacher than to make educational progress'. Mixing with older boys in the mill weakened 'their willingness to subject themselves to anything like school discipline'. The witness had seen parents cry 'because of the change in conduct of their children', resulting in 'heartless impudence', because children could remind their parents 'that they are earning their own living and ought to be their own masters'. The children became 'too worldly for their age'.[91] All of these must have been true of earlier decades, as was the comment in 1907 that half-timers 'become clever at repartee and in the use of "mannish" phrases ... . They lose their childish habits.'[92]

For these and other reasons the schools themselves aimed at rigidly defined patterns of social and cultural behaviour. The adequacy of three hours' education a day was expressed in terms of a very low cultural level at which schools for half-timers should aim. Good half-time teaching from nine to thirteen was 'abundantly sufficient to furnish a child of average capacity with a sound elementary education', said a Newcastle Assistant Commissioner. Half-time education should not concern itself with matters of 'taste', said a Bradford millowner. The problem was how quickly children 'may receive elementary education, and be freed from it', said Chadwick (adding that 'the convenience of the school teacher and of the school should at every stage be made subordinate to the fair demands of labour').[93]

All such arguments were aimed at securing an efficient education which would 'free' children as rapidly as possible, but which would in the process inculcate a necessary social discipline — something made particularly explicit in the case of factory children. One H.M.I. described the effects of the Factory Acts as being to make the children of the poor 'more accessible to Christian, literary, and all other ennobling influences'. Another thought its effects would reform 'the discipline of our humbler homes'.[94] All discussion of the half-time system was ultimately concerned with its social purposes, expressed primarily in terms of conduct and order. The factory inspectors were always anxious to demonstrate that education made the children more 'civil in their manners'. But learning to read and write was by itself unimportant, because unless the result of such training was to have the effect of correctly instructing a child in its relative duties, and inducing him to conduct himself in accordance with those instructions, it might in reality prove to be injurious, rather than beneficial.[95]

The permanent habits induced by half-time education would make a youth 'more likely to look to the Mechanics' Institute or the local night school for the employment of his leisure hours'.[96] Instruction in moral duties was fundamental. A works library was said to promote 'habits of sobriety and order'.[97] Drill produced habits of decorum and promptitude.[98] The half-time system helped to spread moral virtues and adherence to the Christian faith.[99]

Decency and cleanliness were commonly expressed objectives. 'The moral condition of the lower classes cannot be ameliorated', wrote a factory inspector, 'until their social habits are changed, until decency is introduced into their dwellings, until cleanliness is a system and no longer an exception.' Arguing for swimming and plunge baths, Mary Carpenter commented that 'the free application of cold water to the person of children is very important, both physically and morally'.[100] Schools were also seen as combating bad language, and promoting the right use of leisure. The latter, in the opinion of one commentator, would encourage the singing of 'something that would be worth hearing, instead of those filthy and obscene songs, so much in use in our factories at present', and the reading of 'publications which would do them good, instead of the infidel productions of Paine, Volney, &c.'[101] The half-time system was in general, said Wilks, 'a union between the classes of society', and 'that mutual interest which really exists between the employed and the employer'.[102]

Education would, therefore, contribute to the future well-being — defined in specific terms — of the half-timer. He would be adapted 'to his probable future position in society'.[103] At the heart of this perception of the half-timer was the knowledge of his low social status, and prevailing social difficulties and tensions. As one of inspector Baker's witnesses commented in 1865: 'besides being rough and seldom using "thank you", many scarcely knew there were such words as "Sir", or "Ma'am".'[104]

We have been concerned with features of the half-time system and with the interpretation of its purposes. Ideological positions are discernible in the discussion of its educational details from the middle of the nineteenth century. In the last quarter of the century teachers, socialists and others were concerned to show not only that half-time education was inefficient, but that the continued employment of young children was evil. In the conditions of the 1850s and 1860s those who, like the early factory inspectors, saw flaws in the existing system looked forward to improved schools, an educational test before admission to employment, and a higher age of exemption from education.[105] Some, like Nassau Senior, looked towards compulsory education.[106] Some, including H.M.I.s and factory owners, wished at least to extend the Factory Acts to agricultural and other employments.[107] In 1870 Lyon Playfair looked forward ambitiously to the conversion — under a system of compulsory education for all children — of half-time factory schools 'into useful secondary schools to teach the principles of science and art relating to the actual industries of the half-timers'.[108] By the 1860s there were demands for a wider system of national education and for further restrictions on child labour. Higher levels and ideals of education for working-class education were being canvassed than were embodied in the half-time system. Doubts, opposition, proposals for improvements were being voiced. Ideological capital was being made out of enthusiastic interpretations of what was possible and desirable in an industrial society. Those involved must be judged not by our ideologies but by close scrutiny of what they made of their own.

NOTES

[1] Quoted in P.P. 1861 XXI (I), Report of the Commissioners Appointed to Inquire into the State of Popular Education in England (Newcastle) p. 205.
[2] For the early period see Sanderson, 'Education and the factory in industrial Lancashire, 1780-1840', *Economic History Review*, 2nd ser., Vol. XX (1967), and Gertrude Ward, 'The education of factory child workers, 1833-1850', *Economic Journal Supplement* (February 1935). For a general account see A.H. Robson, *The Education of Children engaged in Industry in England 1833-1876* (London, 1931), and for the political discussions of the later period see Edmund and Ruth Frow, *A Survey of the Half-time System in Education* (Manchester, 1970).
[3] Newcastle Commission, I, p. 202.
[4] Cf. e.g. P.P. 1839 XLII, Reports by the Four Factory Inspectors on the Effects of the Educational Provisions of the Factories Act, p. 26.
[5] P.P. 1852-3 XXIV, Report from the Select Committee on Education (Manchester and Salford, etc.), p. 193; see also Nassau W. Senior, *Suggestions on Popular Education* (London, 1861), p. 179.

[6] P.P. 1866 XXIV, Reports of the Inspectors of Factories for the Half Year ending 31 October 1865 (Baker), p. 115.

[7] Report of the Committee of Council on Education 1876-7 (Sandford) (London, 1877), p. 553.

[8] CF. e.g. Frances Collier, *Family Economy of the Working Classes in the Cotton Industry 1784-1839* (Manchester, 1965), p. 45, for education at the Gregs' Styal mill.

[9] K.M. Lyell (ed.), *Memoir of Leonard Horner* (London, 1890), Vol. I, p. 329; Reports by the Four Factory Inspectors (1839), pp. 5-6. For McConnel's see also W.C.R. Hicks, 'The education of the half-timer: as shown particularly in the case of Messrs McConnel and Co. of Manchester', *Economic History* (February 1939).

[10] Reports by the Four Factory Inspectors (1839), pp. 38-9.

[11] W. Dodd, *The Factory System Illustrated in a Series of Letters to the Right Hon. Lord Ashley* (London, 1842; 1968 edition), p. 41.

[12] Reports by the Four Factory Inspectors (1839), p. 6.

[13] Cf. A. Hill (ed.), *Essays upon Educational Subjects read at the Educational Conference of June 1857* (London, 1857; 1971 edition), particularly contributions by E. Akroyd, C.H. Bromby and A. Redgrave.

[14] P.P. 1862 XLIII, E. Chadwick, Letter to N.W. Senior, Esq. . . . explanatory of Communications and of Evidence on Half School Time Teaching . . . , p. 2. The evidence was submitted under the title, Communications from Edwin Chadwick, Esq., C.B., respecting Half-Time and Military and Naval Drill, and on the Time and Cost of Popular Education on a Large and on a Small Scale.

[15] Chadwick, Letter to Senior, p. 4; see also R. Bray, *Boy Labour and Apprenticeship* (London, 1911), p. 78.

[16] P.P. 1862 XXII, Reports of the Inspectors of Factories for the Half Year ending 31 October 1861 (Baker, p. 37; Reports . . . 1865, p. 124.

[17] Chadwick, Communications, pp. 12, 74.

[18] Reports by the Four Factory Inspectors (1839), p. 29.

[19] Ibid., pp. 11, 15, 28, 41, 47.

[20] E.D.J. Wilks, 'On the educational clauses of the Factory Acts, their practical Working and the possible extension of their Principle', *Transactions of the National Association for the Promotion of Social Science, 1859* (London, 1860), p. 363.

[21] G. Melly, *The Children of Liverpool, and the Rival Schemes of National Education* (Liverpool, 1869), p. 11.

[22] Chadwick, Communications, pp. 9-10, 41; E. Senior, 'The Half-time system and agricultural schools', *Transactions of the N.A.P.S.S., 1861* (London, 1862), pp. 326-7.

[23] Chadwick, Communications, p. 9.

[24] Ibid., pp. 28, 45, 74.

[25] M. Carpenter, 'The application of the principles of education to schools for the lower classes of society', *Transactions of the N.A.P.S.S., 1861* (London, 1862), p. 348.

26 Cf. e.g. Minutes of the Committee of Council on Education 1855-6 (Morell), pp. 465-9; Matthew Arnold's report for 1856 in F. Sandford (ed.), *Reports on Elementary Schools 1852-1882* (London, 1889), pp. 58-9; Akroyd, in Hill, *Essays upon Educational Subjects*, pp. 266-73, and in *Transactions of the N.A.P.S.S., 1864*, pp. 479-80.
27 Wilks, *Transactions of the N.A.P.S.S., 1859*, pp. 363-4.
28 Newcastle Commission, Vol. I, p. 208.
29 H.S. Tremenheere, 'The extension of the Factory Acts', *Transactions of the N.A.P.S.S. 1865* (London, 1866), p. 291.
30 [G.W. Hastings] Introduction, *Transactions of the N.A.P.S.S., 1861*, p. xxxi.
31 C. Kingsley, *The Address on Education read before the National Association for the Promotion of Social Science ... 1869* (London, 1869), p. 3.
32 Cf. e.g. Minutes of the Committee of Council, 1846, Vol. I, p. 439; Minutes of the Committee of Council, 1848-49-50, Vol. II, p. 190.
33 Some such schools were created, for example by Leicester School Board. See Report of the Committee of Council, 1878-9, p. 470.
34 Cf. Reports of the Inspectors of Factories . . . 1861 (Baker, p. 34; Newcastle Commission, Vol. II, p. 231; Report of the Committee of Council, 1868-9 (Stokes), p. 317.
35 P.P. 1888 XXXV, Royal Commission appointed to Inquire into the Working of the Elementary Education Acts, England and Wales (Cross Commission), Final Report, p. 161. The Commission heard many witnesses attacking and urging the abolition of the system; see, for example, Second Report (1887), pp. 18, 26, 34, 41, 196, 208.
36 Wilks, *Transactions of the N.A.P.S.S., 1859*, p. 364; Reports of the Inspectors of Factories, 1865 (Baker), p. 127.
37 *Illustrated London News*, Vol. XXVIII, No. 792, 5 April 1856, p. 343.
38 Minutes of the Committee of Council, 1851-2 (Morell), pp. 565, 569; Report of the Committee of Council, 1868-9 (Pickard), p. 159, (Stokes) p. 318. For similar comments see Report of the Committee of Council 1876-7 (Stokes), pp. 580-1; Report of the Committee of Council 1879-80 (Pennethorne), p. 360.
39 Hill, *Essays upon Educational Subjects*, p. 219.
40 Newcastle Commission, Vol. I, p. 204.
41 Chadwick, Letter to Senior, p. 4.
42 The most detailed commentaries, applicable to the earlier period also, were in *The Schoolmaster*. See especially a series of articles entitled 'In Clog-Land: the Troubles of the Half-Timer', 20 December 1884, 27 December 1884, 3 January 1885, and a special supplement on 'The Half-Timer', 9 February 1895.
43 Reports by the Four Factory Inspectors (1839), pp. 45, 51.
44 Newcastle Commission, Vol. II, p. 232; see also Bromby, in Hill, *Essays upon Educational Subjects*, pp. 260-1, and Senior, *Transactions of the N.A.P.S.S., 1861*, p. 327.
45 Chadwick, Communications, pp. 8-12, 14, 26, 32, 38, 41.

[46] Cf. e.g. Reports of the Inspectors of Factories . . . 1865 (Baker, p. 119; Report of the Committee of Council, 1868-69 (Steele), p. 221.

[47] Chadwick, Letter to Senior, pp. 11, 33, 35; for similar later claims see Swire Smith, *Night Schools and Technical Education* (Leeds, 1886), p. 14, dubiously using Keighley statistics; A.J. Evans, 'A History of Education in Bradford during the period of the Bradford School Board (1870-1904)', Leeds M.A. thesis, 1947, p. 146, quoting Bradford employers, 1891.

[48] Reports by the Four Factory Inspectors (1839), p. 20; Chadwick, Communications, p. 11.

[49] Senior, *Suggestions*, pp. 267-8, 289.

[50] Newcastle Commission, Vol. II, p. 232.

[51] Reports of the Inspectors of Factories . . . 1861 (Baker, pp. 31-3; Reports of the Inspectors of Factories . . . 1865, pp. 117-23.

[52] Report of the Committee of Council, 1864-65 (Fitch), p. 179; cf. also Minutes of the Committee of Council, 1851-52, Vol. II (Morell), pp. 565-9.

[53] For comments cf. Report of the Committee of Council, 1866-67 (Routledge), pp. 175-7; Report of the Committee of Council 1868-69 (Capel), p. 60.

[54] Cf. e.g. *The Schoolmaster*, 8 January 1881, p. 41, and 1 June 1889, p. 763. Cf. also Cross Commission, Second Report, pp. 18, 20, for examples of evidence; Final Report, p. 160 for managers' hostility.

[55] Cf. Reports of the Inspectors of Factories . . . 1861 (Baker), p. 35; Chadwick, Letter to Senior, p. 33.

[56] Cf. discussion by Alexander Redgrave quoted in Robson, *The Education of Children Engaged in Industry*, pp. 91-3.

[57] *The Schoolmaster*, 20 December 1884, p. 924, 27 December 1884, p. 956.

[58] Peter Sandiford, 'The half-time system in the textile trades', in M.E. Sadler (ed.), *Continuation Schools in England and Elsewhere* (Manchester, 1907), pp. 334-5.

[59] Quoted by Nassau Senior in 'Address on Education', *Transactions of the N.A.P.S.S., 1863* (London, 1864), p. 68.

[60] Chadwick, Communications, 3-5, 7, 10-12, 34.

[61] Ibid., p. 8; see also pp. 19, 39.

[62] Ibid., pp. 44-5; Carpenter, *Transactions of the N.A.P.S.S., 1861*, p. 348. She made similar comments in answer to the Newcastle Commission's enquiry; see Newcastle Commission, Vol. V, p. 111.

[63] E. Senior, *Transactions of the N.A.P.S.S., 1861*, pp. 326, 330-1.

[64] Newcastle Commission, Vol. I, p. 205.

[65] N. Senior, *Transactions of the N.A.P.S.S., 1863*, p. 71. See also a later contribution to the N.A.P.S.S., by Chadwick: report of a paper 'On the rise and progress of the half-school-time system of mixed physical and mental training', *Transactions of the N.A.P.S.S., 1880*, p. 501.

[66] Reports of the Inspectors of Factories . . . 1861 (Baker), p. 32; Report of the Committee of Council, 1864-65 (Fitch), p. 179.

[67] Chadwick, Letter to Senior, p. 39.

[68] By 1880, drill had for Chadwick replaced the role of factory employment (see note 65 above).

[69] Chadwick, Communications, pp. 8, 10, 13, 16, 19, 25, 33, 75.

[70] N. Senior, *Transactions of the N.A.P.S.S., 1863*, p. 68. For a comment on the national implications see Report of the Committee of Council, 1868-9 (Sandford), p. 210. Chadwick interested Matthew Arnold in the subject: see Sandford, *Reports . . . by Matthew Arnold*, p. 242. Cf. also Chapter 7.

[71] F. Engels, *The Condition of the Working Class in England* (1845, first published in English 1887; 1958 Oxford edition), p. 195.

[72] D. Ryazanoff (ed.), *The Communist Manifesto of Karl Marx and Friedrich Engels* (London, 1930), p. 10. The *Manifesto* was published in German in 1848 and in English in 1850.

[73] *Documents of the First International, 1864-1866*, Vol. I (Moscow, n.d.), pp. 343-6. The document is Marx's 'Instructions for the Delegates of the Provisional General Council'.

[74] K. Marx, *Capital* (1867, first published in English 1887; 1954 Moscow edition), pp. 299n., 482-4, 488.

[75] K. Marx, 'Critique of the Gotha Program', in K. Marx and F. Engels, *Selected Works* (Moscow, 1949), Vol. II, pp. 33-4.

[76] F. Engels, *Anti-Dühring* (1878, first published in English 1934; London edition, n.d.), pp. 352-3.

[77] Cf. e.g. Owen's 'Report to the County of Lanark' (1820), in H. Silver (ed.) *Robert Owen on Education* (Cambridge, 1969), pp. 183-6; Owen's 'Six Lectures delivered in Manchester' (1837), in ibid., pp. 205-8.

[78] Marx, *Capital*, p. 483; see Reports of the Inspectors of Factories . . . 1865 (Baker), pp. 118-20.

[79] Reports of the Inspectors of Factories . . . 1861, pp. 31-3, 36.

[80] Report of the Committee of Council, 1868-69, p. 317.

[81] Newcastle Commission, Vol. V, pp. 28-9.

[82] Cross Commission, Second Report, p. 29.

[83] See Frow, *A Survey of the Half-Time System*, chs. III-V.

[84] Quoted in *The Schoolmaster*, 9 February 1895, p. 255; see also F. Keeling, *Child Labour in the United Kingdom* (London, 1914), pp. xxiv-xxv.

[85] M. McMillan, *Child Labour and the Half-Time System* (London, 1896), p. 3.

[86] Sandiford, in Sadler, *Continuation Schools*, p. 337.

[87] Minutes of the Committee of Council, 1846, Vol. I, p. 440; Newcastle Commission, Vol. II, p. 231; Reports of the Inspectors of Factories . . . 1861 (Baker), pp. 33-7. See also Baker's 1865 report, pp. 119, 123, and Report of the Committee of Council, 1868-69 (Steele), p. 221.

[88] *The Schoolmaster*, 20 December 1884, p. 925.

[89] Report of the Committee of Council, 1868-69 (Stokes), pp. 317-18.

[90] *The Schoolmaster*, 20 December 1884, p. 925.

[91] Cross Commission, Second Report, pp. 18, 21, 26, 29, 379.

[92] Quoted by Sandiford, in Sadler, *Continuation Schools*, p. 334.

[93] Newcastle Commission, Vol V, pp. 446-7; Chadwick, Letter to Senior, p. 39.

[94] Report of the Committee of Council, 1864-65 (Fitch), p. 179; Report of the Committee of Council, 1876-77 (Steele), p. 578.

[95] Reports by the Four Factory Inspectors (1839), p. 21.

[96] Bromby, in Hill, *Essays upon Educational Subjects*, pp. 250-1, 263-4.

[97] T. Tooke *et al.*, *The Physical and Moral Condition of the Children and Young Persons employed in Mines and Manufactures* (London, 1843), p. 235.

[98] Chadwick, Communications, pp. 8, 16, 25, 75; see also Chadwick, *Transactions of the N.A.P.S.S., 1880*, p. 503.

[99] See Bromby, in Hill, *Essays upon Educational Subjects*, pp. 263-4, and Akroyd in ibid., p. 269; also Horner in Reports by the Four Factory Inspectors (1839), p. 195.

[100] Redgrave, in Hill, *Essays upon Educational Subjects*, p. 220; Chadwick, Communications, p. 45. See also, Carpenter, *Transactions of the N.A.P.S.S., 1861*, p. 348.

[101] Dodd, *The Factory System*, pp. 55-6, 118, 156.

[102] Wilks, *Transactions of the N.A.P.S.S., 1859*, p. 364.

[103] Chadwick, Communications, p. 16.

[104] Reports of the Inspectors of Factories . . . 1865 (Baker), p. 121.

[105] Cf. e.g. Reports by the Four Factory Inspectors (1839), pp. 15, 30, 49-50.

[106] Cf. Senior, *Suggestions*, p. 241.

[107] Cf. Kingsley, *Address on Education*, p. 3; Report of the Committee of Council, 1868-69, pp. 69, 96, 184; Akroyd's reported comments in *Transactions of the N.A.P.S.S., 1864*, p. 479.

[108] L. Playfair, 'Address on education', *Transactions of the N.A.P.S.S., 1870* (London, 1871), p. 59.

Chapter 7:

Drill, discipline and
the elementary school ethos
J. S. Hurt

Sir Thomas Elyot's treatise, *The Governour* (1531), provides the first discussion to be written in English of the value and place of physical education.[1] Just over a hundred years later, during the disturbed conditions that followed the outbreak of the English Civil War, John Milton took up the theme of physical prowess in his pamphlet, *On Education* (1644). Neither writer was concerned with the education of the mass of the people. Elyot's readership was drawn mainly from the new Tudor aristocracy. Milton had designed an education for the privileged few who commanded sufficient leisure and social standing to speak in the councils of the nation in peacetime and to 'come out of a long war . . . perfect commander[s] in the service of their country.'[2] Similarly Herbert Spencer, two centuries later, had mainly the problems of middle-class education in mind when he published *Education: Intellectual, Moral, and Physical* in 1861. The genteel ladies' academies that he condemned because they forbade any form of vigorous physical activity were far removed, both socially and economically, from the public elementary schools attended by their less fortunate sisters.

By the 1850s, when Spencer's treatise was appearing in its original form as a series of articles in the review journals of the day, the debate on education was no longer confined to a discussion of the attributed needs of a privileged minority. The growth and concentration of manufacturing industry in England, together with the associated social changes that accompanied it, had raised the historically novel problem of defining the nature of the education that was to be given to an urban wage-earning proletariat. The migration of an expanding population to the towns provided visible and disturbing evidence of the extent to which pauperism, vagrancy and unemployment existed. A problem that traditional society normally had been able to contain now had to be tackled if the stability and economic viability of an expanding society were to be safeguarded.

Although the sheer number of children made the problem appear to take on a novel aspect, the solutions adopted were traditional. The linking of industrial training with moral education, urged by almost all interested parties in the nineteenth century, had its roots in the apprenticeship system of an earlier age. Similarly, reliance was put on the age-old virtues of submission and obedience. An early nineteenth-century manual provides an example:

> Word of Command by Teachers:
> 'Out': They step nimbly over the form, and stand behind it, keeping their eyes on their teacher. The boys place their hands behind them; the girls hold theirs before them.
> 'Go': They walk away rapidly, but quietly, under the conduct of their teacher.[3]

Robert Owen, socialist, philanthropist, and capitalist, was amongst the first of the new industrialists to give serious attention to the problem of training and educating a young labour force. In 1816 he described his methods to the Select Committee on the Education of the Lower Orders in the Metropolis. He thought the monitorial system practised by the two religious societies, the National Society and the British and Foreign School Society, had one great drawback. The speed with which the children acquired the rudiments of learning did not allow sufficient time 'for the proper formation of their dispositions and habits'. He accordingly provided at New Lanark 'healthy and useful amusements for an hour or two every day' so that his pupils could 'acquire an education which prepares them for any of the ordinary activities of life'.[4]

A generation later, the idea that children destined to spend their lives amongst the ranks of the labouring poor should receive both physical and vocational training received official endorsement. Dr James Kay, the first secretary of the newly-created Committee of the Privy Council on Education, instructed his inspectors 'to ascertain whether any ground, and to what extent, is to be appropriated to the recreation of the children, how it will be enclosed, and whether it is intended to furnish it with the means of exercise and recreation; and whenever his [the inspector's] advice is sought he will encourage the adoption of such arrangements.' As for vocational training, the inspector was to enquire whether the girls would be instructed in household management and 'whether the instruction of the boys will have a practical relation to their probable employment'.[5]

Dr James Kay, E. Carleton Tufnell, and Edwin Chadwick, disciples of the Utilitarian school and sometime .colleagues at the Poor Law Commission, saw education as the great engine of social regeneration. The class that most needed moral redemption was the pauper whose alleged taint of hereditary pauperism they attributed, not to functional unemployment in an underdeveloped economy, but to inherited and inbred moral shortcomings. If the state was to avoid the expense of keeping the future pauper adult in a workhouse or prison for the whole of his life, he had to be taught the habits of industry in his youth. 'If workhouse children', Kay wrote, 'grew up educated in reading, writing, and arithmetic only, they would be unfitted, for earning their livelihood by "the sweat of their brow".'[6] The Poor Law District Schools, made possible under the Poor Law Amendment Act, 1844, the drafting of which *The Times* attributed to Chadwick,[7] provided the institutional instrument. Drill provided the educational instrument.

The six District Pauper Schools, erected by 1860 under the pro-visions of the 1844 Act, replaced many of the former privately owned 'farm' schools for pauper children. With the exception of Mr Aubin's establishment at Norwood which became a model whose standards the poor law guardians were encouraged to emulate, most of the pauper schools in private hands had been badly run. After the death of nearly two hundred children at Druet's establishment near Tooting from cholera in 1849, nearly all the large ones were closed down. Aubin's was taken over by the Central London School District, the first London school district to be formed, with the former proprietor retained in a salaried capacity.[8] On an early visit Dr Kay found that the equipment included a mast for training the boys in seamen's duties together with four- and six-pounder guns on which a seaman-gunner provided instruction. Drill exercises were given to the inmates 'to introduce regularity into the movement of so large a body of children, to secure prompt obedience to the direction of the teacher, and to maintain personal cleanliness and propriety.' Kay noted with approval: 'The moral training pervades every hour of the day, from the period when the children are marched from their bedrooms to the washhouse in the morning, to that when they march back to their bedrooms at night.' Drill was the means whereby Aubin sought 'To procure a punctual observance of the hours allotted to rising and going to bed . . .

[and] to preserve uninterrupted decorum in attitude, expression, and manner during the meals and religious services.'[9]

Up to the late 1850s two main arguments for the inclusion of military drill in the curriculum of the workhouse schools held sway. Firstly, it was conducive to the maintenance of order. The sudden bringing together of two or three hundred children who had known little or no formal restraint in the past was a hazardous undertaking. At the North Surrey School a riot within the first month of opening had cost £100 in damaged property. The first intake into the Manchester School had tried to set fire to the buildings. It generally happened, Tufnell told the Newcastle Commissioners during their enquiry into the state of elementary education in England, that there was a riot on the opening of a District School. It was little wonder that those in authority saw the payment of the drill master's salary as a form of premium on an insurance policy against fire.[10] Moreover, masters of the Union Schools were convinced that the consequences of losing a drill master were dire. When this had happened at the Stepney Union School, Alfred Mosely the superintendent found that: 'all the smartness of the boys entirely went; they were slovenly in their dress; there was no neatness or pride in themselves in any way whatever.' William Smith, the principal of the North Surrey District School, experienced a general breakdown of discipline on the dismissal of the drill master as an economy measure that was not restored until the appointment of another.[11]

The second main reason advanced for teaching drill was that it was beneficial to the health of the children. This consideration weighed especially heavily with Chadwick whose experiences at the Board of Health had given him first-hand experience of the living conditions of the poor. It was held that physical training would increase a man's productivity either as an individual or as a member of a team. 'In all engineering and building trades men are frequently required to use their strength in concert, lifting, carrying, and drawing; men, to use their joint strength not only effectively but safely, must have confidence in each other. Two trained men will lift and carry more, easily and safely, than four untrained men. . . . Drill and training would probably double the effective human power of any establishment, especially if numbers are instructed in joint feats of strength. That which is taught to youth is never forgotten in after life.' [12]

In the late 1850s a third consideration, the military needs of the nation, was advanced following the establishment of the Volunteer Rifle Club Movement in 1859. British suspicions about the underlying

motives of Napoleon III's involvement in the cause of Italian unifica-
tion had brought her growing concern about her defence needs to a
head. A series of crises in the 1850s had revealed the extent to which
British forces were stretched during an emergency. 'The Crimean War
had given the public a real shock, and the revolt of the mercenary
troops in Bengal had followed as a staggering blow. Not only had the
War Department been found wanting, but the whole administration of
India had proved to be utterly rotten.' Although the earlier Bantu up-
rising of 1850-2 has been overshadowed by these later events, one
military historian has described it as 'a menace nearly as formidable,
on its own scale, as [the 1857 mutiny] in India'. At times the army had
had difficulty in meeting its manpower requirements. For instance, the
troops who behaved with exemplary courage when their ship, *The
Birkenhead*, foundered were part of a draft of young and inexperienced
recruits on their way to the front as reinforcements. The situation
during the Crimean War seems to have been worse. In a debate in the
House of Commons in 1858 it was alleged that commissions had been
offered to young men without purchase if they raised men for the
colours. The going rate was held to have been a thousand men for a
Lieutenant-Colonelcy and a hundred for an Ensigncy.[13]

Thus the inclusion of military drill in the curriculum of the schools,
at first the Poor Law schools and later the voluntary ones, was in
accord with the views held by the classical economists and utilitarians
on education. Since drill seemed to the outward eye to teach habits
of obedience and discipline, it helped to preserve law and order and
diminish crime. It provided an investment in human beings by raising
their productivity and giving them an opportunity of enhancing their
earnings. Most important of all, it helped to eradicate pauperism. Some
saw this as drill's greatest service not only to society as a whole but to
the paupers themselves. The lot of the pauper children was thought to
be so wretched that one advocate of their education declared it could
be said 'without profanity, that it would be better that millstones were
hanged about their necks and they were cast into the sea, than that
they should grow up as they are doing, cankering the very core of the
society that neglects them.'[14] In this rescue operation, drill assisted in
two ways. It taught the 'habits of industry', thereby ridding children of
their 'hereditary taint'. By providing them with vocational training it
gave them the passport to a career in the army or the Royal or
mercantile Navy. In a few cases the children were remarkably successful. For instance 521 had joined the army from the North Surrey

District School at Anerley, near Penge, of whom six had reached commissioned rank by 1869.[15]

At the other end of the social and educational spectrum such regimentation was both unnecessary and impracticable. E. Warre, an assistant classics master at Eton College, told the Clarendon Commission on the Public Schools why drill could not be made compulsory there. At Eton, he said, 'the spirit of liberty is too strong in the place to admit of that'. Moreover, drill was 'rather against human nature, especially with boys'. The boys of the leading public schools, 'the chief nurseries of our statesmen', unlike the children of the labouring classes had a vested interest in the maintenance of the existing *status quo*. In their schools they acquired 'their capacity to govern others and control themselves, their aptitude for combining freedom with order, their public spirit, their vigour and manliness of character, their strong but not slavish respect for public opinion, their love of healthy sports and exercise'. In this last process it was the cricket and football fields, not the barrack square, that helped 'to form some of the most valuable social qualities and manly virtues, and they held', continued the Commissioners, 'like the class-room and the boarding-house, a distinct and important place in public-school education'.[16]

In contrast, in the elementary schools much of the initiative in popularizing drill came from Edwin Chadwick who worked through the aegis of the Society of Arts. The activities of the Society in 1869 reflect the concern that contemporaries felt about national defence in the face of Prussian success on the continent. In February 1869 Henry Cole, Secretary of the Science and Art Department, South Kensington, read a paper entitled 'On the Efficiency and Economy of a National Army, in connection with the Industry and Education of the People'. In it Cole advocated the use of retired soldiers to teach drill in every boys' school in the country.[17] Another speaker, G.C.T. Bartley, lectured to the same Society on 'The Training and Education of Pauper Children'. He outlined a system of compulsory education that would fit boys for service in the army or navy where they would be removed, he claimed, from pauper influence and idle associates. He quoted from E. Carleton Tufnell's *Report on Union Schools* in the *Twentieth Report of the Poor Law Board* to argue the needs of the merchant service. 'The deficiency of sailors is well known; many ships go to sea half manned, supplied with Lascars and foreigners, who often do not speak English, and generally fail in an emergency.' Tufnell, who inspected Poor Law Schools in the Metropolitan area, wanted every pauper boy either to be a musician for the army and navy bands, or to be a sailor for the Royal Navy or merchant service. Bartley wanted to send the 'cream of the boys, and at an early age' into one of the armed services. Pauper girls would become household servants. Those boys and girls whom the attentions of the drill master failed to redeem, 'the idle and unemployed and those returned to the workhouse', were to be shipped off to the colonies. Chadwick, the chairman of the meeting addressed by Bartley, argued that the outcome of the recent Austro-Prussian War showed the need for a trained reserve. The Prussian army, augmented by its trained reservists drawn from civilian life, had defeated Austria's standing army. 'The trained men, enervated by the dissipation and idleness of the cantonments and camps of Austria went down before the strong high-waged men, called immediately from the forge or the plough into the ranks of the popular army of Prussia at Sadowa.'[18]

In furtherance of his campaign to introduce drill into schools, Chadwick arranged a visit to the North Surrey District School at Anerley. Amongst those who went were four members of the peerage, Henry Cole, Professor Thomas Huxley, Bernhard Samuelson, Bartley and H.M.I.s Tufnell and J.G. Fitch. The distinguished company went 'to see the value of the half-time system of mental and physical and industrial training carried on in the Poor Law Union Schools'. Chadwick claimed that such a system would reduce the cost of elementary education by two or three million pounds a year if it were applied to the country as a whole and replaced full-time schooling. The money thus saved on elementary education could be applied to secondary education. In addition, 'hereditary mendicancy would be suppressed, and the great bulk of the male population might be constructed into an inexpensive reserve force for military purposes'. Lastly a further economy would be effected because 'military training and exercises would be carried out during the non-productive and school stages of life, instead of during the adult productive ones'.

After the march past of the children, Chadwick and Tufnell enlarged on the difficulties that the drill instructors had had to overcome. The children were of such stunted growth, Chadwick explained, that even after a military training only a small proportion were found to reach the standards required by the army. However, since the passage of Lord Shaftesbury's Act, 1851, regulating conditions in common lodging houses 'the proportion of the decrepit has diminished . . . the children are of a less repulsive type, and of an improved physical and mental standard'. Tufnell was even more unflattering to the young performers. 'All who are admitted here come from the lowest class, generally born amid filth and squalor, and under the worst moral and physical conditions. You will see proofs of their origins in their countenances. They are all of stunted growth . . . in fact their low stature and physical defects are the chief obstacles we have to overcome in preparing them for the business of life.'[19] The Society of Arts then arranged a review of the boys from the Poor Law District Schools near London together with others from the Royal Military Asylum at Chelsea and the Royal Naval School, Greenwich, to be held before Prince Arthur of Connaught. Although this function had to be postponed, a second display was held at Anerley later the same month, July 1869.[20]

Plate XI   *Drill review held before the Prince and Princess of Wales on 25 July 1872, at the Royal Horticultural Gardens, now the site of Imperial College, London*

The following autumn the Society of Arts appointed a committee to consider how drill could be introduced into all the schools throughout the United Kingdom. Ten of the sixteen members were either serving or retired officers from the army and navy. The Committee arranged a review of nearly 3,000 boys drawn from seventeen schools to be held in the presence of His Serene Highness Prince Teck, the husband of Princess Mary of Cambridge, a cousin of Queen Victoria. A report in *The Times* drew attention to two disquietening features. 'There were some of the smallest boys seen out of cradles among the parish schools, and the "uniform" of some was not in taste, being of the old degrading workhouse character.' The attitude seems to have been that children should start drill at as early an age as was possible. Two years later, the *Illustrated London News* reported that the children in another review were aged from six years and upwards. Chadwick thought this early start good educational practice. 'Drill corporals find they can begin with children at five and a half or six and that by ten they have imparted to them a very advanced drill and practice with light rifles.'[21]

The Society of Arts held further reviews under its supervision in 1873 and 1875. During this period it spent £944 from which it recouped £400 by the sale of tickets. Concern over this rate of expenditure induced the Society to seek the co-operation of the recently established London School Board. As an inducement the Society offered 'a handsome set of colours' to be competed for by the schools and an annual prize of £20 for the boys of the successful school. In 1876 nearly 10,000 boys paraded in Regent's Park where Lord Alfred Churchill, an uncle of Lord Randolph Churchill, presented the banner to Sir Charles Reed, the chairman of the London School Board, on behalf of the Society.[22]

The design of the banner, woven by the School of Art Needlework at a cost of nearly £100, was based on a submission made by Sir Henry Cole in November 1875. Although his original design seems to have undergone some modification, the nationalistic and anticipatory jingoistic motif of his first specification remained. After stipulating that it should be thirteen feet in length, Cole indicated:

1 It should have the Cross of St George indicative of nationality.
2 The inscription setting forth the object of the work on a tablet resting on a golden field crossed by branches of laurel both expressive of glory.
3 The field parted into blue and red, emblematic of the naval and military services to be entered in after life by the boys: these divisions to be filled by the arms of the London School Board, the emblems of the Society of Arts, the feathers of the Prince of Wales, its president, whilst the Imperial crown surmounts the staff.[23]

The 1877 parade, which like that of the previous year involved nearly 10,000 boys, was the last of the great reviews. The London School Board, finding these monster functions a strain on its resources, instructed its drill organizer, Regimental-Major William Sheffield, to select the forty best boys from each of the ten best schools. The first of these smaller functions was held in the grounds of Lambeth Palace in 1879. The regular use of this venue from 1879 onwards, with the permission of the Archbishop of Canterbury, brought the Church militant and the London School Board under the same banner. In March 1887 the London School Board threw the drill competition open to the voluntary schools in its area.[24]

By the late 1880s drill had become an established part of the curriculum in both voluntary and board schools. School inspectors saw drill as the linchpin in an educational system that had as one of its aims the teaching of social discipline to the children of the labouring poor. Just how well 'disciplined' were the elementary schools of mid- and late-Victorian England is a question that is as hard to answer as the same enquiry about today's schools. Opinions and experiences of individuals differed then as now.

In a general criticism made in 1864, C.H. Alderson thought that the standard of discipline in the British schools he inspected over a wide area of eastern England was poor. He complained that teachers attached more importance to imparting knowledge than they did to securing good order. He saw this as putting the cart before the horse. 'If half the pains and ingenuity expended on methods of instruction were devoted to the attainment of good discipline, the results achieved by popular education would be far greater.' Teachers were too ready, Alderson felt, to accept low standards. 'When they [the teachers] have suppressed the turbulent elements to the point of a chronic simmer they are content. . . . They even have a definite theory. . . . So many boys *must* make so much noise.' The reading on the decibel scale was a function of the size of the school. A school of a hundred boys was expected to be twice as noisy as one of fifty. Alderson's advice was: 'It is better for the teacher to assume that there need be no noise at all.' The teacher who did not act on this dictum came to accept noise as the norm. 'His ear has become blunted to the noise that reigns around, and in the midst of which day after day is passed.' Alderson thought that good discipline began in the infants' school where the mistress's task was 'to break in the children, as it were to a sense of order and the necessity of obedience'. He suggested that she should split up the morning's work with short intervals of recreation for 'the value of frequent drill as a means of bringing their bodies into something like subjection is obvious'.[25]

The experience of an individual inspector could vary considerably. The Rev. N. Gream, an inspector of Anglican schools in Lancashire, had visited one consisting of more than 500 boys where 'a pin's fall might be heard. Not a word was spoken until work commenced, and then only so much talking as the work required.' Gream had been to much smaller schools 'where every child has been talking, and I have been repeatedly obliged to stop and request the teacher to enforce silence'. At times Gream even had had to step in and obtain order. 'When banging the desk, and whistling, and other means have been used in vain by the teacher to invoke silence, I have stood up in the school and said to the children that I wished to hear the clock tick.'[26] Mrs Fielden's school at Todmorden provides a further contrast. Here E.A.G. Holmes, writing ten years after Gream, found: 'Silence, if it be enforced, is absolute. Places are changed so quietly that not a sound comes from wooden clogs moving over a tiled floor.'[27]

Given the central position occupied by religious education, one would expect to find that on the day of the inspector's visit all was well. Yet the Rev. F. Watkins witnessed scenes in schools in the West Riding of Yorkshire that were almost as astonishing as anything Gream saw. 'The school prayers, in several schools', he wrote, 'are not devotional, indeed, are hardly decent. Neither the masters nor the teachers kneel down. The prayer is either a rapid gabble or a coarse intonation. A hymn is shouted, and the day's devotions are at an end.'[28] Similarly, the Rev. G. Steele found it 'no uncommon thing [in Lancashire schools] to hear the most sacred names, and topics, shouted before a class of little children, without any approach to propriety of manner, or reverence.'[29] Yet the Rev. G. French was more fortunate in the North and East Ridings of Yorkshire where, in contrast to Watkins in the West Riding, he found teachers who 'with scarcely an exception [are] careful and anxious to instil into the minds of their scholars those principles of true religion, which may be profitable to them, come weal, come woe'.[30]

However the introduction of the Revised Code with its requirement that the individual child be examined, made inspectors acutely aware of the problem of classroom discipline. If the new method of assessing a school's grant were to work satisfactorily, inspectors had to ensure that children did not copy or talk during their examination. Their early comments suggest that all was not well in the classroom. H.M.I.s C.H. Alderson, W.W. Howard, J.G. Fitch, H. Waddington, E.H. Brodie and P. Le Page Renouf complained about or took steps to prevent copying.[31] In contrast, the Rev. B.J. Binns found that in the Anglican schools of South Wales 'The new system of examination [the Revised Code] . . . has checked prompting, copying, and uneasy shifting from place to place, and it has inculcated habits of truthfulness, self-reliance, and upright dealing to an extent beyond what could have been foreseen.'[32]

Concern over the standard of school discipline, belief in the school as an agent of social control, and the growth of the Volunteer Movement gave Chadwick allies both inside and outside the Education Department. Shortly before the creation of the Volunteers, W. Ewart, M.P. for Dumfries, had asked Robert Lowe to include drill in the work of the schools. Lowe, at a time of attempted financial retrenchment, refused. 'The business of the Council was education. In his opinion they should confine themselves to that, and not be led aside in the promotion of any other object, however desirable it might be.'[33] Two years later Lord Elcho, inspired by a visit to the Limehouse District School 'in which children of the very lowest and most criminal class, many of them stunted in growth and naturally scrofulous, were being educated' found it 'really astonishing to see what tidy, obedient, orderly, and respectable boys the military training to which they were subjected made them'. Although he duly rehearsed the utilitarian arguments, Lowe stonewalled again, repudiating the 'idea that it was the duty of the Privy Council to devise means in addition to the existing grant to promote the teaching of anything because it might be deemed useful'. Lowe saw a tied grant, such as Elcho suggested, as a dangerous principle that might be applied 'to music, shoemaking, or any other branch of trade'.[34]

Within the Education Department a number of inspectors commented favourably on the value of drill and urged its merits. H.M.I. the Rev. H.M. Capel, an inspector of schools in Leicestershire and Warwickshire, complained in 1865 that there were few schools where it was taught well. This omission he deplored since 'drill made the children ready, attentive, and simultaneous in their movements'.[35] A.V. Hadley shared Capel's enthusiasm for simultaneous movements. 'The rapid distribution of books, slates, pencils and etc, [is] executed in the better schools [of Lancashire] at the command of the teacher with the precision of a regiment of soldiers under drill.' He thought 'this methodical order' as being of 'unmixed advantage. The school is thus effectively controlled and the mechanical arrangements expeditiously made, while the children instinctively learn habits of submission, of order, and of neatness.'[36] The Rev. H.W. Bellairs anticipated the publication of the 1871 Revised Code by writing: 'The drill in our schools is generally bad; I should like to see a regular system of military drill introduced, with marching tunes and, where practicable, with drum and fife bands. Arrangements with the adjutants of the militia and volunteers for providing the necessary teaching might easily be made, and the expense of it by employing drill serjeants would not be great.'[37] German military success prompted H.M.I. the Rev. H. Sandford to extol the virtues of 'the educational training to which, especially in Protestant Germany, the mass of the youthful population is subjected'. As a consequence the Germans had shown themselves superior to the French 'in regard to discipline, and . . . the habit of self-control and the power of acting in concert in obedience to orders, which discipline gives'.[38]

Against the background of successive German victories the Gladstone administration 'fully aware of the advantages of drill to the children themselves, apart from any possible ulterior advantages to the country'[39] introduced military drill into the 1871 Code. This allowed a maximum of forty hours' drill a year, taught under a competent instructor, to count as school attendance for grant-earning purposes. Schools could either employ an instructor from a nearby detachment of Volunteers, at the rate of sixpence a day plus a penny a mile marching money, or a schoolmaster who had passed his serjeant's examination before an adjutant of the Volunteers. To remove all possible ambiguity, the 1875 Code specified drill as military drill. The same Code offered an additional grant of a shilling a head to schools whose managers satisfied the inspectors that they took all reasonable care 'to bring up the children in habits of punctuality, of good manners and language, of cleanliness and neatness, and also to impress upon the children the importance of cheerful obedience to duty, of consideration and respect for others, and of honour and truthfulness in word and act'.

It has been said of the Volunteer movement that 'Only those whose memories went back fifteen years could understand the change of sentiment which made the arming of the volunteers in '59 possible.'[40] The same is equally true of Chadwick's campaign for drill in the elementary schools and its eventual inclusion in the Revised Code. In the 1830s and 1840s the elementary school with its 'regulation of the thoughts and habits of the children by the doctrine and precepts of revealed religion' had been seen as a means of combatting the current social unrest. Similarly the schoolmaster's training was designed to encourage him to accept the beliefs and values of the propertied classes and reject the tenets of Chartism. Yet by the 1870s, the children of the labouring classes were being drilled by a schoolmaster who had probably been a member of his training college's Volunteer Corps and whom the government was encouraging to take his serjeant's examination.

Two inspectors in the industrial north, where Chartists had once illegally drilled, now saw the innovations in the Code as offering a defence against a working class discontented with its allotted role in a deferential society. E.A.G. Holmes, in the West Riding of Yorkshire, wanted military drill taught in every school. In such a district as his, 'Where "one man is as good as another", the drill serjeant's influence is wholly for good, even if he do no more than teach strict discipline and prompt obedience'.[41] The views of H.E. Oakley in the Manchester area were more forthright:

> The habit of obedience to authority, of immediate obedience to commands, may tend to teach the working classes a lesson which many so sadly need in the north of England, that immediate obedience and submission to authority, deference to others, courtesy to equals, respect to superiors — these are the real marks of a manly self-respect and independence, and not the vulgar and pernicious doctrine that one man is as good as another, and that courtesy or deference is the property of a servile nature.[42]

The Rev. D.J. Stewart was one of the few inspectors to sound a dissenting note and question the belief that the blind obedience of the barrack square was synonymous with good discipline. 'I see, in fact,' he protested, 'a great deal of drill and too little discipline. Drill . . . often degenerates into harshness . . . there are too many schools in which everything is done with a roughness of language and manner which is out of place and mischievous in its effects.' His idea of a well-disciplined school was one 'where the daily business of the school proceeded without any apparent effort on the part of the teacher and a bond of sympathy existed between the two parties.'[43]

Manuals of teaching method published during the last three decades of the nineteenth century offer further evidence of the standard of discipline expected in elementary schools. J.J. Prince's *School*

Management and Method, which was first published in 1879 and reached its sixth edition by 1894, re-echoes the sentiments of the 1875 Code. 'The object of an elementary school is to provide efficient instruction and education for children of mechanics, artisans, and the poorer classes and to train them in habits of punctuality, cheerful obedience to duty, good manners and language, and of honour and truthfulness in word and act.'[44] In a section on good manners and language, Prince commendably expected children to be polite to all. 'They must rise at the entrance of any of the humbler class, just the same as at the entrance of any lady or gentleman.' Special deference was to be shown to teachers. 'In many schools it is the custom for each child, on being handed a slate, book, pencil, or anything else by his teacher, to make a bow when thanking him for it, and also for the pupil to salute his teachers when meeting them in the street or elsewhere.'[45]

Prince also gave the young teacher advice on order and discipline. He defined discipline as 'the training to order, attention, diligence, obedience, and other habits which will prepare children for the reception of moral and religious instruction so that it shall be permanently beneficial to them'. To secure good order, the first point to be attended to in any school, the general movements of the scholars had to be performed with promptitude, regularity, and precision.[47]

Other handbooks of method furnish similar advice. As late as 1896 one writer stated: 'The class at drill should be a mere machine, actuated only by the will, and at the word, of the teacher.' He further advised: 'Every order should be given smartly; and its execution with unhesitating promptitude should invariably be as rigorously demanded.'[47] Further extracts show how the class, the mere machine, was taught to distribute books and set about its work.

Let the children take their orders from the teacher, as 'Pass rulers'; let each use one hand only, and without speaking.[48]
In both distributing and collecting it should be insisted upon that material should not be accumulated in the hand of one child – the rules should be 'use one hand', and 'one thing only in the hand at the time'.[49]

The handing out of copy-books, like ordering arms on parade, was carried out to numbers.

The copy-books should be placed ready at the end of each desk,

or group of desks, and should be distributed to numbers thus:—
One. Books passed till the right child is reached; then placed un-
opened in front of the child.
Two. The left hand is placed on the book ready to open it.
Three. The proper copy is found, and the hands are placed behind
it.[50]

When the children had been marched into their places, the disciplining of their bodies was reinforced by the disciplining of their
minds. The integrity of Clio was breached for the sake of social order.

It [history] furnishes excellent material for teaching moral lessons.
What could better assist in promoting contentment and thankful-
ness among the people than comparing the condition of the working
classes at the present day with that of their fore-fathers, or even
with that of our foreign neighbours? What can assist more in promoting habits of industry than *tracing the improvement in the
condition of the people?*[51]
It [history] calls forth feelings of patriotism. It stimulates the
national pride, promotes a love of virtue, gives powerful object
lessons against vice, and tends, rightly taught, to make good
citizens.[52]

Thus the aim of a lesson on the 'Invincible Armada' was 'to show how
love of country united a brave people in defence of hearth and
home'.[53]

A geography lesson provided similar opportunities for the inculcation of patriotism. Thus the object of a lesson on the Suez Canal was
'to show the Imperial and Commercial importance of this highway to
the East'.[54] The justification for a lesson on British trade and commerce was 'England is the greatest manufacturing and commercial
nation of the world. If this supremacy is to be maintained, the productive districts and the chief markets, actual and potential, should
be known.' Similarly, a lesson on emigration was justified on the
grounds that 'Fields for emigration are essential to relieve the surplus
population and to carry out the advisable and beneficent planting
of the earth by the English people.'[55]

To take the strictures of the inspectors, the provisions of the Revised
Code and the advice given in books on teaching method at their face
value is to conjure up a picture of well-disciplined children conforming
to the norms of the Victorian middle classes. In reality the situation

was somewhat different. For instance there is evidence that children failed to meet one of the basic demands of school discipline, that of punctual attendance. Since religious instruction was given at the start of the morning's work after 1870 the diocesan inspectors, who took over the task of inspecting religious instruction in the Anglican schools, frequently complained about the late arrival of pupils. Sometimes the teachers themselves set a bad example. The Rev. J. Wycliffe Gedge, a diocesan inspector in the archdeaconry of Surrey and the Channel Isles, often found schools shut at 9 a.m. 'the professed hour for beginning school', as late as 1877.[56] The inspectors of the Education Department found similar grounds for complaint. H.M.I. W. Warburton found: 'Even on the day of the examination when, if ever, children might be supposed to be on good behaviour, the inspection, if it begins at 9 o'clock, is constantly interrupted by children straggling into their places for the first hour, and this appears to create no impression of surprise and to cause but little concern on the part of the teachers or managers of the school.'[57]

Children, like their parents before them, were slow to learn the discipline of the clock.[58] The poorest working-class families, as the practice of knocking-up which persisted into the 1930s reminds us, would have found even a cheap clock an unattainable luxury. Similarly the managers of those schools without clocks regarded them as unnecessary luxuries. Even if a school possessed a clock it did not always work. In 1877 Steele found that 'in half the schools at least [in the Preston area] the clocks are wrong, or standing, providing a ready-made plea if the timetable is not strictly observed'. C.W. Collins complained on surprise visits to schools in the agricultural Midlands that he found the registers unmarked and the school clock stopped.[59]

Poverty created two obstacles to punctuality. Not only could many working-class families not afford clocks, they could also not afford to dispense with the income a child's casual earnings brought into the home. For instance the London School Board was so concerned about the problem of late attendance that it set up a sub-committee in March 1882 to 'consider how regularity and punctuality at schools might be improved'. The committee resolved to alter the existing regulations under which the school gates were closed *an hour* after school began and to ban all children from admission who were more than fifteen minutes late unless they produced a special pass. Before giving effect to these decisions they sought the opinions of the superintendents of the Board's sub-districts. The consensus of their opinion was that the committee's plan would make the existing situation still worse. Children would be only too glad to be shut out of school and to be provided with a ready-made excuse not to attend. The superintendents of Lambeth and Westminster drew attention to 'the real family necessities' that caused unpunctuality because of the children's early-morning employment. Their Greenwich colleague thought that '[a] great outbreak of feeling amongst the honest poor would result, [the] thriftless and indifferent would have another opportunity of neglect'. The Lambeth official predicted that any increase in the number of prosecutions for non-attendance would alienate public sympathy. A 'revolt against such action would result and have public sympathy as well as magisterial'. Despite these warnings the committee decided to close the school gates at a number of selected schools for a trial period of six months. Although the results of their efforts to secure punctuality are not known, the evidence of this particular incident shows how the economic plight of the poor prevented them from meeting the aspirations of their social superiors.[60]

A politically articulate section of the working class provided a further restraint as they refused to accept the form of social discipline wished upon them by the middle-class disciples of Utilitarianism. Benjamin Lucraft, the sole representative of working-class opinion to be elected to the London School Board in 1870, and the Rev. G.M. Murphy, a nonconformist minister, moved a resolution at a meeting of the London School Board in July 1875 condemning the drill reviews held by the Board. In a resolution reflecting the hostility traditionally felt by the respectable working classes to the army, Lucraft and Murphy condemned drill as creating 'a passion for what is called "glory", [and which is] pernicious in its consequences to thousands by diverting their thoughts and aspirations from honourable and useful employment to a life of idleness and all its terrible concomitants, dreaded as a plague by their [the children's] parents'.[61]

A few months later the same two members introduced a deputation of protest from the Council of the Workmen's Peace Association and the St Pancras Working Men's Club. Randal Cremer headed the delegation. Cremer, together with Odger, Potter, Lucraft and other labour leaders, had helped to found the International Working Men's Association in 1865. Cremer and Lucraft had been amongst those who had represented the London Trades Council at the first conference of the International held the following year at Geneva. After Garibaldi's visit to London in 1865 the same two men had been founder members of the Reform League which had pressed for the extension of the franchise at a number of public meetings including the demonstration in Hyde Park on 23 July 1866 and the more peaceful one in Trafalgar Square on the same day. In 1870 Cremer, together with a number of his former associates in the Reform League, had formed a Workmen's Peace Committee to gain working-class support for neutrality in the Franco-Prussian War. A year later, the Committee became the Workmen's Peace Association with Cremer as its secretary until his death in 1908. Its offices at 9 Buckingham Street, Strand, were part of a Radical centre that also housed the Land Tenure Reform Association under the presidency of John Stuart Mill whose step-daughter, Helen Taylor, became an ally of Lucraft on the London School Board after her election in 1876.

Cremer informed the Board that he opposed the teaching of military drill because it gave children a love of war, which 'tended to collisions amongst nations' thus paving the way for conscription. He thought that children could be taught to behave in school without recourse to drill. In his day, he stated, children had been told to toe the line and this had proved sufficient to keep them in order. At the same meeting the Board received a petition from a number of the ratepayers of the Metropolis who protested that military drill was a waste of time which led children away from the pursuit of honourable and useful industry to a life of military idleness. The Women's Peace and Arbitration Auxiliary rounded off the proceedings by presenting yet another protest.[62] Despite the unsympathetic response of the Board to these remonstrances, Lucraft made further efforts to stop the teaching of drill later the same month and again in July 1878. A year later, thirty-two members of the Workmen's Education Committee re-opened the issue when they branded the principal promoters of drill as advocates of conscription, a method of recruitment which they abhorred since it had 'wrought such terrible evils in Continental nations'.[63]

A resolution passed at the T.U.C. Conference held at Stockport in 1885 seems to have provided the immediate impulse to the last organized remonstrances against the teaching of drill in London's schools. The resolution, passed by a large majority, accused a number of School Boards of forming cadet corps with the help of the War Office who were said to be providing rifles and uniforms. After describing this move as a step-by-step preparation for the pernicious Continental system of conscription, Congress entreated 'the working-class representatives to use every effort to frustrate the designs of the promoters, and confine School Boards to the task for which they were designed, viz to develop the intellectual and moral faculties of the children committed to their care'.[64] In London the Workmen's Peace Association and the Hackney Radical Federation of combined political clubs responded to the call. A fortnight later, on 22 October, the Rev. G.M. Murphy and Miss Taylor introduced a delegation from the Women's Peace and Arbitration Association.[65]

The action of the T.U.C. produced a rejoinder from Chadwick who argued that if trade unionists visited the schools in which drill was taught, they would find that it brought about 'the better promotion of the health, strength and working ability, and the advance of the earnings of their children'. Chadwick, who at times showed a singular lack of awareness of the ridiculous, went on to argue that working men would save on their bootmakers' and tailors' bills.[66] Children, who were taught to tread more evenly, saved shoe leather. School teachers, he averred, found that they saved one pair of boots a year by treading evenly. Moreover, 'the even tread saves trousers by throwing up less mud on them'. In two respects, however, Chadwick's writings at this time point to an improvement in the lot of the pauper and near-pauper boy during the last twenty-five years. Their employment prospects were brighter. He had gone down to Anerley that year to obtain volunteers for the army but without success. Boys now found they could earn 12*s.* a week on leaving school and 24*s.* a week as they grew older and stronger. He also noted an improvement in the appearance of the children at that year's drill parade. 'At the former early exercises, the boys presented only a sorry appearance, their countenances were pallid, and generally of a tallowy aspect, and their dress, in the large proportion, poverty-stricken.'[67]

Although the anti-drill group lost every tactical encounter, the citadel eventually fell sapped by forces from within. In 1894 a committee of mayors, representative of the boroughs within the area of the London School Board, demanded the ending of the annual competitions. Their suggestion was that the Society of Arts' trophies — a second had been given for Swedish drill in girls' schools in 1887 and a third for vocal music in 1889 — should be awarded on the merit of the whole school and not on the performance of a chosen group of pupils. In addition they wanted the competitions replaced by a display given by the best schools. Their views were eventually heeded.[68] In 1897 the Board informed the Society of Arts that it was abandoning the drill competitions.

From the start the London School Board had taken an active part in the provision of physical education for the pupils in its schools. In June 1871 Professor Huxley's committee on curriculum reported that it regarded drill as an essential subject for all children. The appointment of Sheffield the following year as drill master made possible the training of most of the Board's masters as qualified instructors of drill by 1874. Physical exercises for girls and the training of mistresses to take the classes began two years later. Three years later the Board engaged a Swedish teacher, Miss Concordia Lofving, to train the mistresses and introduce Swedish exercises into the girls' and infants' schools. By 1892 a comparable advance had been made with the development of boys' physical education. Masters now had to obtain the Board's certificate in the 'English combined system' of drill and physical exercises. Lastly the Board began to equip the schools with dumb-bells, Indian clubs and ropes.[69]

Thus by the end of the century a much more imaginative programme of physical exercises had replaced the earlier unimaginative and mechanical military drill. The Board which earlier had rejected demands for the abolition of military drill now, rightly proud of its achievements, refused demands for its reinstatement. On 12 July 1900, while the Boer War which had revealed an unexpected degree of military incompetence was still being waged, the Board discussed a letter from the Earl of Meath, the founder president of the Lads' Drill Association. The chief aim of this Society, the Earl indicated, was to inculcate the teaching of military drill and exercises in the elementary schools. The London School Board, standing firmly by its revised syllabus, replied that many military exercises were not suitable for boys. 'The poor physique of many of the half-million underfed London children', the Board stated, 'makes it very difficult to insist on any exercises which demand continuous and severe muscular strain.' The 'English combined system' achieved the desired result far more effectively. 'Habits of discipline, obedience, quickness to hear and obey, . . . , and all the qualities that military drill is supposed to teach, are, in the opinion of the School Board for London, taught a great deal better under the system of physical exercises adopted for their schools.'[70]

Meanwhile, the School Boards of Birmingham, Liverpool, Bristol and other large towns had followed London's example of replacing military drill with a more liberal programme of physical training. In 1890 the Education Department recognized physical education as an alternative to drill for purposes of school attendance. The 1895 Code

Plate XII *Physical Education in 1906*

took the process a stage further by making the higher grant eligible only to those schools that provided for 'Swedish or other drill or suitable physical exercises'. Thus although drill was still linked to discipline, greater flexibility was being allowed. Finally in 1900 the newly formed Board of Education permitted organized games as a substitute for Swedish drill or physical exercises.[71]

Alarm over British military weaknesses at the turn of the century brought, as it had forty years earlier, concern for the physical education and well-being of the nation's children. In the 1860s unwillingness to spend public money, combined with a lack of suitable school playgrounds and playing fields, had been instrumental in restricting physical education to drill. The rejection of 40 per cent of those who volunteered for the army in the South African War showed the long-term dangers of leaving the country's children too ill-fed to undertake exercises 'which demand continuous and severe muscular strain'. The Education (Provision of Meals) Act, 1906, the institution of medical inspection the following year and of grants for the necessary medical treatment in 1912 helped to make it possible for children to profit from the liberalized physical education being developed in the schools. Thus by 1914 children could find their physical education and games lessons far more enjoyable and profitable than their fathers had believed possible.

NOTES

[1] W.H.G. Armytage, 'The first English work on physical education: Sir Thomas Elyot's *The Governour*,' *Physical Education*, Vol. 44 (1952), pp. 122–3.

[2] L.E. Lockwood (ed.), *Of Education, Areopagitica, The Commonwealth by John Milton* (London, 1912) p. 9.

[3] Quoted from J. Poole, *The Village School Improved* (1813) by P.H.J.H. Gosden, *How They Were Taught* (Oxford, 1969), p. 5.

[4] P.P. 1816 IV, Report from the Select Committee on the Education of Lower Orders in the Metropolis, Robert Owen's Evidence, pp. 239–40.

[5] P.P. 1840 XL, Instructions to Inspectors, 8 August 1840, p. 13.

[6] P.P. 1838 XXVIII, Fourth Annual Report of the Poor Law Commissioners, 'Report on the Training of Pauper Children by J.P. Kay', Appendix B (3), p. 146 (294).

[7] S.E. Finer, *The Life and Times of Sir Edwin Chadwick* (London and New York, 1970), p. 244.

[8] I. Pinchbeck and M. Hewitt, *Children in English Society* (London, 2 vols., 1973), Vol. II, p. 508.

[9] J.P. Kay and E. Carleton Tufnell, Reports on the Training of Pauper Children (1839), 'Report from Dr Kay', pp. 1014.

[10] P.P. 1861 XXI, Report of the Royal Commission on the State of Popular Education in England and Wales [The Newcastle Report], 'E. Carleton-Tufnell's evidence', p. 3164.

[11] Ibid., 'Mosely's evidence', p. 4501; N.W. Senior, *Suggestions on Popular Education* (London, 1861), pp. 310–12.

[12] Senior, op. cit., pp. 315–16.

[13] D. Beales, *England and Italy, 1859–60* (London, 1961), pp. 65–6; J.W. Fortescue, *A History of the British Army* (1889–1930), Vol. XII, pp. 549–50; Vol. XIII, p. 520; Parl. Deb. (Third Series), Vol. 149, 12 March 1858, 137–8.

[14] *Journal of the Society of Arts*, Vol. XVII, 1868–9, p. 190. (Hereafter *J.S.A.*).

[15] *J.S.A.*, Vol. XVII, 1868–9, p. 666.

[16] P.P. 1864 XXI, Report of the Commissioners on the Revenues and Management of Certain Schools and Colleges [Clarendon Report], 'E. Warre's evidence', pp. 5375, 5378; ibid. P.P. 1864 XX, pp. 56, 41.

[17] *J.S.A.*, Vol. XVII, 1868–9, pp. 206–16.

[18] *J.S.A.*, Vol. XVII, 1868–9, pp. 188–94, 224.

[19] *J.S.A.*, Vol. XVII, pp. 665–70, 694–5.

[20] Ibid., pp. 699, 711, 727–30.

[21] *J.S.A.*, Vol. XVIII, 1869–70, pp. 343–4; Minutes of Committees of the Society of Arts, 1869–70, folio 303; *Illustrated London News*, 2 August 1872; *J.S.A.*, Vol. XVII, 1868–9, p. 225.

[22] *J.S.A.*, Vol. XXIV, 1875–6, p. 859.

[23] Minutes of Committees of the Society of Arts, 1874–6, Meeting of 19 November 1875, folios 305–7.

[24] D. Hudson and K.W. Luckhurst, *The Royal Society of Arts, 1754–1954* (London, 1954), pp. 241–2; Minutes of the School Board for London, 3 March 1887.

[25] P.P. 1864 XLV, C.H. Alderson's Report, pp. 179–80.

[26] P.P. 1865 XLIII, N. Gream's Report, p. 83 (177).

[27] P.P. 1878–9 XXIII, E.A.G. Holmes's Report, p. 594.

[28] P.P. 1867–8 XX, F. Watkins's Report, p. 223.

[29] P.P. 1868–9 XX, G. Steele's Report, p. 223.

[30] P.P. 1867 XXII, G. French's Report, p. 68.

[31] See the relevant reports at P.P. 1864 XLV, pp. 179–80; P.P. 1865 XLIII, pp. 94 (188), 170 (264), 196 (290); P.P. 1866 XXVII, pp. 251, 275–6.

[32] P.P. 1866 XXVII, B.J. Binns's Report, p. 64.

[33] Parl. Deb. (Third Series), Vol. 156, 16 February 1860, 1131–2.

[34] Parl. Deb. (Third Series), Vol. 168, 8 July 1862, 23–8.

[35] P.P. 1865 XLII, H.M. Capel's Report, p. 43 (137).

[36] P.P. 1867 XXII, A.V. Hadley's Report, pp. 89–90.

[37] P.P. 1871 XXII, H.W. Bellairs's Report, p. 26.

[38] P.P. 1871 XXII, H. Sandford's Report, p. 177.

[39] Par. Deb. (Third Series), Vol. 204, 8 March 1871, 1559.

[40] G.M. Young, *Portrait of An Age* (Oxford 1964), p. 81.

[41] P.P. 1878-9 XXIII, E.A.G. Holmes's Report, p. 604.

[42] P.P. 1880 XXII, H.E. Oakley's Report, p. 351.

[43] P.P. 1871 XXII, D.J. Stewart's Report, p. 205.

[44] J.J. Prince, *School Management and Method* (London, 1879), p. 12.

[45] Ibid., p. 46.

[46] Ibid., p. 39.

[47] F.W. Hackwood, *Practical Method of Class Management: A Ready Guide of Useful Hints to Young Teachers* (London, 1896), pp. 19-20.

[48] Ibid., p. 16.

[49] Ibid., p. 17.

[50] T.A. Cox and R.F. Macdonald, *The Suggestive Handbook of Practical School Method* (London, 1896), p. 151.

[51] Prince, op. cit., p. 158.

[52] A.H. Garlick, *A New Manual of Method* (London, 1897), p. 258.

[53] Cox and Macdonald, op. cit., p. 368.

[54] Ibid., p. 398.

[55] Ibid., p. 217.

[56] J. Wycliffe Gedge, Fifth Annual Report (1877), p. 5.

[57] P.P. 1870 XXII, W. Warburton's Report, p. 248.

[58] E.P. Thompson, 'Time, work-discipline and industrial capitalism', *Past and Present*, No. 38. (December 1967), pp. 56-97.

[59] P.P. 1877 XXIX, G. Steele's Report, p. 580; P.P. 1878 XXVIII, C.W. Collins's Report, pp. 433-4.

[60] Greater London Council Record Office, S.B.L. 790, folios 43-4, 60-1.

[61] Minutes of the School Board for London, 14 July 1875 (hereafter L.S.B. Minutes).

[62] H. Evans, *Sir Randal Cremer; His Life and Work* (London and Leipsig, 1909), pp. 31, 36, 40-4, 82-4; *The Times*, 2 March 1876; L.S.B. Minutes, 1 March 1876, 15 March 1876, 3 July 1878.

[63] L.S.B. Minutes, 6 August 1879.

[64] *The Times*, 14 September 1885.

[65] L.S.B. Minutes, 8 and 22 October 1885.

[66] For another example see Finer, op. cit., p. 507.

[67] *J.S.A.*, 1884-5, pp. 925-6, 1070-2.

[68] L.S.B. Minutes, 3 May 1894, 2 July 1896.

[69] Final Report of the School Board for London (London, 1903), pp. 114-15.

[70] L.S.B. Minutes, 12 July 1900.

[71] P.C. McIntosh, *Physical Education in England since 1800* (London, 1952), pp. 111-17.

Chapter 8:

Social environment, school attendance and educational achievement in a Merseyside town 1870-1900

W. E. Marsden

'... excellence of attendance and efficiency seemingly go hand in hand ... the base of the pyramid is lowest both in attendance and in proficiency.'[1]

Bootle in the late nineteenth century

Environment and population growth

During the third quarter of the nineteenth century Bootle became an integral part, geographically if not administratively, of the growing Merseyside conurbation. In addition to the original inland agricultural village, a separate resort and residential area developed along the Mersey shore in the first half of the century. The northward encroachment of Liverpool's dockland reached the Bootle boundary in mid-century. The resort and residential functions were displaced northwards, to be replaced in Bootle by a marked intensification of land use, dominated by warehouses, factories and railway sidings, interspersed with working-class terraced housing.

The population grew steadily in the first half of the century and thereafter by leaps and bounds.

Table 1 *Population growth of Bootle, 1801–1901*

1801	500	1871	16,200
1841	2,000	1881	27,400
1851	4,000	1891	49,200
1861	6,400	1901	58,600

The environmental impact of this growth is illustrated by the 'bird's eye view' of 1881 (Plate XIII) and by maps (1 and 2) showing, among

Plate XIII *Bootle in the early 1880s*

other things, the spread of the built-up area. The town was roughly divided, both physically and socially, by the Leeds and Liverpool Canal and the Liverpool-Southport railway line. A middle-class enclave grew on the inland side of the railway, its axis running along Merton Road and into Breeze Hill (Map 1). By contrast, a sea of working-class dwellings dominated the urban landscape between the canal and the

BOOTLE IN 1874

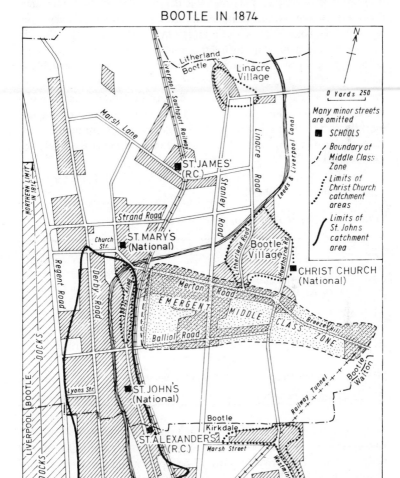

Map 1.

docks, forming the most disadvantaged social area of the town. The main thoroughfare of this 'ghetto' was Derby Road, frequented by 'few who wear cloth and silk'.[2] Working-class zones later spread east of the railway and northwards to the Seaforth boundary (Map 2).

Social condition

The urban landscape to a considerable degree reflected the broad social divides of Bootle. But to differentiate these on a straight middle-class/working-class basis is obviously a gross over-simplification of reality. In relation to the main purpose of this study, the exploration of the relationship between social condition and elementary school achievement, a more detailed social classification is needed. It seems particularly desirable, for example, to distinguish 'white-collar' workers from manual on the one hand; and skilled or semi-skilled manual workers (who might see in education a means of upward mobility for their children) from unskilled workers (who were much less likely to) on the other.

The full socio-economic grouping (SEG) adopted includes five categories shown in Table 2.

Table 2 *Classification of socio-economic groupings*

SEG	including	Broad class division
I	Managerial and higher professional (legal, medical and C. of E. clergy)	Upper middle
II	Lower professional (teachers, other clergy, larger local employers)	Lower middle ↑
III	Shopkeepers and assistants, clerks, small employers (up to five men)	↓
IV	Skilled and semi-skilled manual workers	Upper working
V	Unskilled labourers	Lower working

Among the many problems implicit in such a classification, and particularly in separating the broad categories on the right of the table, is that of identifying 'critical' occupational cases at the discontinuities. Hence the lower middle class is here taken to include teachers, office workers and shop assistants, even though such occupations did not necessarily command higher earnings than those of skilled manual workers.[3] A related problem is the picking out of internal distinctions within each major category. The number of servants in the household ranks among the criteria for sub-classifying the middle class, for example.[4] For the unskilled labouring group, Booth's sub-divisions are suggestive of some heterogeneity, ranging from 'occasional labourers, loafers and semi-criminals – the elements of disorder' (Class A); through 'very poor – casual labourers, hand to mouth existence, chronic want' (Class B); to 'poor – standard poverty – small earnings either through irregularity (Class C) or low rate of pay (Class D)'.[5]

Accounts 'from the field' confirm a detailed hierarchical structure within the Victorian working-class community. Hence Roberts writes of Salford at the turn of the century: '. . . each street had the usual social rating: one side or one end of the street might be classed higher than another. . . . Every family, too, had a tacit rank, and even individual members within it.'[6]

The level of earnings to some extent reflects a class differential, as revealed in Table 3 below.

Table 3 *Earnings in Bootle (1885–1900 period)*[7]

SEG	Selected occupations	Earnings
I	Town Clerk	£800 – £1000 p.a.
II	Borough surveyor and accountant; Clerk to School Board; heads of board schools	£200 – £400 p.a.
III	Clerks in Town Hall departments; assistant schoolteachers	£40 – £100 p.a.
IV	Foremen – Borough Surveyors' Department Bricklayers	56s. per week 36s. per week
V	Dock labouring 'élite' e.g. coal heavers and stevedores Casual dock labourers Scavengers	35 – 40s. + 15 – 20s. per week 19 – 22s. per week

The main break therefore comes between those defined as lower middle class and upper middle class; rather than between non-manual and manual workers.

Although national earnings rose between 1880 and 1900,[8] a trend reflected in middle-class earnings in Bootle, wage rates on Merseyside as a whole remained relatively stagnant.[9] The dock labourers, the most numerous element in Bootle's work force, also suffered from notoriously unreliable earnings. The casual labour force was kept at a high enough level to be able to meet the needs of the port at the busiest times. The chance movement of shipping, bad weather, strikes and fluctuations in the trade cycle could have dire effects on the earnings of thousands.

Hence a critical feature of earnings, which in general distinguished the unskilled from the skilled worker, was their excessive fluctuation. This had consequences for the life style of the group. Irregular earnings accustomed families to privation in bad weeks, yet incited indulgent spending in good ones. Rathbone stresses also that even among the 'regular' dock labour aristocracy the amount given to the wife for housekeeping reflected the earning levels of the 'irregular' casual labourer, and that the standard of family life was fixed by the amounts brought home during slack periods.[10]

The percentage of earnings spent on drink was an undoubted factor in depressing standards of living and health. It was estimated that in Bootle expenditure of 3s.6d. to 4s.6d. per week on drink was normal in many poor labouring families. This represented more or less the weekly cost of renting a terraced house in the dock area. Drink was seen by the churches, the Town Council and the School Board as a key social problem, a prime cause of degradation, crime and truancy. Temperance lectures became a pointed component of the social control function of the school during this period.

Overcrowded and insanitary living conditions, and rampant child neglect were reflected in appalling rates of mortality among the under fives. Infantile mortality in Bootle in 1879 accounted for 55 per cent of the total deaths, and rose during epidemics of infantile diarrhoea to over 70 per cent.[11] Present-day figures are less than 3 per cent. Infectious diseases reached epidemic proportions quickly and frequently, with catastrophic effects on school attendance. As one head teacher ruminated: 'Premonitory indications harbingering a near epidemic of measles are so apparent as to give cause for anxiety.'[12]

Linking home and school:

Catchment areas

An inevitable consequence of Bootle's rapid population growth was an increase in the numbers requiring school accommodation. The first school to be built in the town was St Mary's, in 1835. Thirty years later, further Church of England schools were established, at Christ Church (Plate XIV) and St John's, serving respectively the old Bootle village and other outlying areas, and the south-west dockland area of the town. The Catholics also provided schools in the 1860s, at St

Alexander's, for south Bootle and adjoining parts of Kirkdale, and St James's, for north Bootle (Map 1).

Plate XIV   *Christ Church School, Bootle*

The rapid population growth outlasted the stamina of the voluntary bodies, which became less and less able after 1870 to furnish the necessary school accommodation. Increased public funding of education was required to fill the gaps. Bootle School Board had been formed as early as 1871, but for a long time made a priority of safeguarding the interests of the ratepayers. It was only after prolonged stalling that the Board was forced to succumb to Whitehall pressure to provide additional schools. Two large and expensive board schools were finally brought into operation in 1885, Bedford Road (Plate XV) serving south, and Salisbury Road (Map 2) north Bootle. Even these could not cope with the northward surge of people, and further schools had to be provided in the 1890s, at Hawthorne Road and Gray Street (Map 2).

Links between homes and schools can be highlighted by mapping and analysing catchment areas, from data contained in schools' admissions registers. The catchment areas of three Bootle schools are plotted on Maps 1 and 2.

In the 1870s the St John's catchment area was compact and socially homogeneous, covering a part of Bootle which had developed as a working-class zone over the previous twenty years. By the 1890s (Map 2) it had expanded to the east of the railway line into districts not built up in the 1870s. Here it infiltrated the sphere of influence of Bedford Road. The Bedford Road catchment area was remarkably

Plate XV   *Bedford Road School, Bootle, about the turn of the century. Note the bell tower, a means of summoning children to school*

compact, reflecting the increasingly bureaucratic policy of the School Board which, in response to pressure on accommodation, and to discourage unnecessary flitting from school to school, zoned the town fairly rigidly for board school purposes.

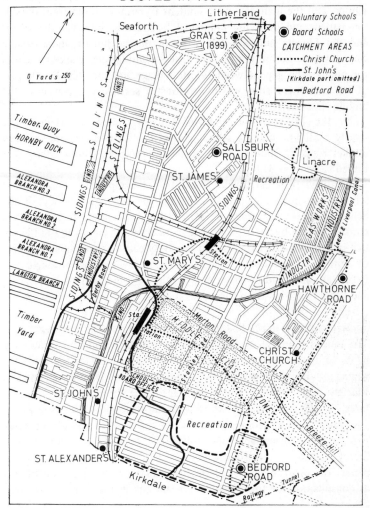

Map 2.

The catchment zone of Christ Church in the 1870s was much more
diffuse than that of St John's, and encompassed more differentiated
social areas. The contrast in size and shape was a consequence of the
nature of the growth of the built-up area. At this time, Christ Church
lay at the inland limit of housing and on the margin of the middle-class

zone. Bootle Village itself could not provide enough pupils to fill the school, and the managers were content to enrol children from outside the parish, and even the municipal boundaries. Between the village and the Linacre and Kirkdale parts of the catchment, there existed clear-cut gaps in the built-up area, representing long walks to school for pupils. The gap between Bootle Village and the west Bootle part of the catchment zone was by contrast a social one, made up of the middle-class enclave.

By the 1890s, however, Christ Church's immediate vicinity was largely built up, and the school could be filled with a more localized intake. Kirkdale children were no longer accepted (though they continued to be so at St John's).

Although their catchment areas are not mapped, the two Catholic schools are interesting in anticipating the restrictive policy of the School Board as a means of combatting 'capricious migration',[13] a stratagem used by some parents to avoid domestic creditors and the notice of school board officers, and relatively easy to accomplish in an era of rented accommodation. The managers divided the borough into two. Catholic children from the north were directed to St James's, and those from the south to St Alexander's.

Social conditions in the St John's/St Alexander's catchment areas

The most striking social area in Bootle was the squalid dockland slum in its south-western corner, which did much to earn for the town the stigma of 'Brutal Bootle'. Here a trio of streets, Dundas, Lyons and Raleigh, seem to have constituted the most 'troublesome thoroughfares' in the borough, in which the sub-stratum of its society was concentrated. Courtroom accounts of the 'ruffianism' of the menfolk and the formidable bellicosity of the womenfolk (the 'Lyons Street Viragoes') consistently enlivened the pages of the local newspaper. The Medical Officer of Health regularly branded the inhabitants as conspicuous for their lack of precautions in the face of infectious disease.

Overcrowding was endemic. The census enumerators' returns of 1871 show that over 850 people occupied the tiny living space of Lyons Street (Map 3), of whom 140 were lodgers. A breakdown of the social make-up indicates that 32 per cent of the heads of households were in SEG IV,[14] and 68 per cent in SEG V. A Bootle School Board investigation of a group of seven streets in this zone in March 1872 counted 332 houses, 421 families and 817 children under 13, of whom 158 between the ages of five and thirteen were not attending school.

The two schools bearing the brunt of the social problems prevalent in this part of Bootle were St John's and St Alexander's. In an 1870s sample of St John's pupils (to be discussed later), 46 per cent of the children were in SEG IV and 40 per cent in SEG V, giving 86 per cent as the proportion of children of manual workers in the school. Nearly 60 per cent of the children lived in the dockland zone south of Miller's Bridge (Map 4). In the early 1890s the percentage in SEG V was about the same (see Table 12). This was a relatively small proportion, however, compared with St Alexander's where, at the turn of the century, 80 per cent of the children came into this group. The evidence is clear that the Catholic element was dominant in the casual labouring population of the area.

It is interesting to compare these figures with the London elementary schools Booth identified at about the same period as being of 'special difficulty'[15] though the comparison can only be a rough one because our SEG IV overlaps with Booth's poor working class *and* 'working class comfort' categories. In Booth's lowest grade of school, well over 85 per cent of the children derived from poor or very poor groups; in his middle grade 60–75 per cent; and in his upper grade from less than 10 per cent to over 30 per cent. St Alexander's would probably have qualified in these terms as a 'special difficulty' school, and St John's as one of the poorer middle grade. Booth's figures also show over 70 per cent in the 'poor' group and below in Catholic elementary schools, higher than the figure for the board schools (60 per cent) and much higher than for the non-Catholic voluntary schools (about 25 per cent).

The headteachers and managers of St John's and St Alexander's, in conjunction with their respective churches and other voluntary agencies, played a prominent part in social welfare activity. The poor children of St Alexander's were regularly supplied in the winter with second-hand clogs and clothing. In the severe winter of 1885 a 'free dinner' experiment was conducted at St John's for children whose parents were in receipt of fees from the poor law guardians.[16] The headmaster of the school testified to the improved physical appearance and increased capacity for school work which had resulted from this provision. The order of priority of needs is clear.

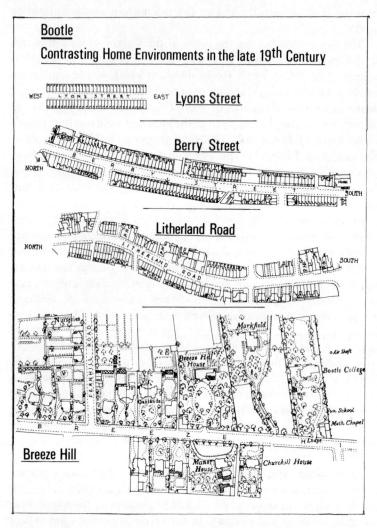

Map 3. (based on 25" O.S. maps, 2nd edition, 1890s)

The vicinity of Christ Church School

At the other social extreme lay the Merton Road–Breeze Hill axis, of which Breeze Hill is shown on Map 3. Whereas rents for a house in the Lyons Street area would amount to £9.10s. per annum, those in the best middle-class areas might rise to as high as £90. In Merton Road, a large double-fronted semi-detached villa with five bedrooms could cost between £775 and £800. The contrast in living space between the two extremes is stark. In terms of 'area on the ground', the 857 people of Lyons Street in 1871 were fitted into a space not quite as large as the grounds of Bootle College (Map 3), which developed in the 1880s as the town's only serious middle-class boys' private school. The population of Breeze Hill and Merton Road in 1871 totalled 393, with 62 households, containing 92 servants. 44 per cent of the heads of households were in SEG I; 24 per cent in each of II and III; and only 8 per cent in IV and V together.

One of the few points of contact between the Merton Road and Lyons Street areas lay in the fact that many members of the Bootle School Board were drawn from the former (Map 4) and sat on the committee which summoned the parents of the latter for not sending their children to school. There was virtually no contact through schooling for the children of these social extremes, for the children of the middle classes were not submitted to popular education. In later years a few exceptions occurred, however, a small number of upper middle-class children being found on the registers of the relatively élite Christ Church 'higher grade' school.

As Map 1 reveals, the core of the Christ Church catchment area lay round the old Bootle village, from which the longest street to emerge was Litherland Road (Map 3). This was a less homogeneous street in social terms than either Lyons Street or Breeze Hill, largely because a social divide crossed it. Medium sized semi-detached houses were concentrated at the southern end, joining on to Merton Road, and were rented at about £30 per annum. Elsewhere the houses were terraced, with front doors opening on to the street, and rents dropped as low as £10 per annum.

A breakdown of the social make-up from the 1871 census returns shows 2 per cent of households in SEG I; 12 per cent in II; 24 per cent in III; 38 per cent in IV and 24 per cent in V, with 93 households and a total population of 493.[17] This well-balanced mix of social groups is reflected in the 1870s sample for Christ Church in which, of the twenty-three children who lived in Litherland Road, five belonged to category III, eleven to IV and seven to V.

Berry Street: a 'fringe zone'
Like Litherland Road, Berry Street (Maps 1 and 3) had a varied occupational mix, with no representatives of SEG I, but 17 per cent in II;

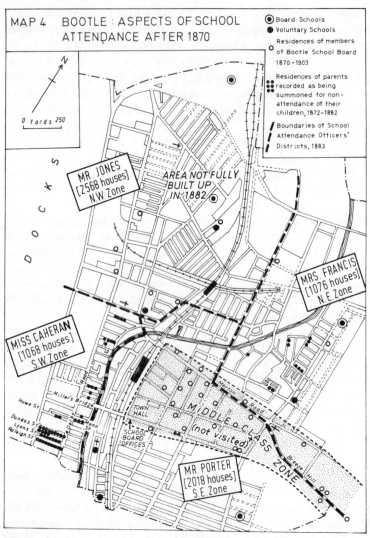

Map 4.

47 per cent in III; 25 per cent in IV and 11 per cent in V. For the small terraced houses opening directly on to the main street, rents of £14 to £17 were the norm. But for those set that little way back from the street, with embayed front windows, rentals up to £25 per annum could be achieved. Berry Street was very much the dwelling place of

mariners — ship's masters, chief officers, engineers, and stewards — a difficult group to classify in socio-economic terms and placed, according to rank, in either SEG II or III.

Berry Street is a particularly interesting one in the educational context. It was very much in a fringe zone between the three catchment areas of Christ Church, St Mary's and St John's. Complicating the issue, however, was the presence of a considerable number of private adventure schools within the area. There were five on Berry Street alone in 1876, of which the smallest had eight and the largest fifty-five pupils.[18] In the previous year, a School Board check had revealed seventy-six children in three rooms of one house, where the teaching was said to be 'of a superior character', but the crowding necessarily 'injurious to health'. Another of the schools was very much a 'dame's school', with the lady not regarded as 'suited to teach'.[19]

It seems that parents in this area were in an ambiguous social position, and one in which choice of school could be exercised. In the St John's sample for the 1870s, seven children from Berry Street are recorded, all in SEG II or III, suggesting that this was one of the more desirable streets in that school's catchment. Of these children five had come up through the infant's department, and one each had previously attended St Mary's and a private school. In the thirteen from Berry Street in the Christ Church sample, however, six were in SEG II, five in SEG III, and two in SEG IV, and of these no less than seven had previously attended private schools, two St Mary's, while only one had come up through the infants' department. It might be speculated that certain Berry Street parents had tried private schools, found them wanting, and then decided to send their children not to St John's or St Mary's, but to the relatively distant, and probably socially more desirable, Christ Church school.

There is no doubt that parents with aspirations for their children were rating schools according to rough academic and social criteria. In consequence, a hierarchy of elementary schools grew, as Booth's categories imply.[20] By the 1890s Christ Church was clearly an élite establishment of its type, 'a wonderful school for its time', according to an ex-teacher.[21] To some extent, this status reflected the school catchment area. But to build such a reputation, examination results had also to be good, and the lowest class of children excluded. To send away children arriving at the school barefooted was regarded by the headmaster of Christ Church as a 'reasonable excuse' for non-admission.[22] Difficult children were offloaded on to the board schools as they were built. The headmaster of Salisbury Road Board School referred to the well-known weeding process of the voluntary schools. 'The children admitted at the present here consist wholly of outcasts from other schools.'[23] Similarly, in justifying to the Education Department the opening of a new Select School, in a quite different location from the main schools, the priest of St James's explained that 'our shopkeeping class wish to have their children educated in separate schools from the poorer children'.[24]

Social attitudes towards popular education:
The evidence of school attendance
        'Several renowned truants have put in an appearance.'[25]

Obliging children to attend school is a social phenomenon of compelling interest not least because the reactions to it of the providers and consumers of educational facilities shed light on their attitudes to popular education in general. On the side of the consumer it has been suggested that 'patterns of school attendance may be redefined as the record of family decisions about formal education'.[26] On the side of the promoter the building of a school could only be justified on the grounds of some social or political principle (such as expediency) and in practice if sufficient children were available and attracted to fill it.[27]

The problem is a complex one, however, for expressed motives cannot always be taken at their face value on the one hand, while on the other so much of the evidence is circumstantial. Several interlocking questions can be asked. Did the attitudes of both groups change intrinsically over the last thirty years of the nineteenth century? Was the manifest improvement in the attendance figures a consequence of more effective policing or of a genuinely enhanced awareness of the 'potential benefits' of education? If there was such an improvement in attitude, did it vary between different social groups (which might be evidenced by differential attendance records at schools with socially distinct catchment areas)?

The motive of the voluntary bodies and the state in providing popular schooling is generally interpreted as a means of exercising social control over a potentially hostile working-class population. Such a view is reflected in a memorial from the Bootle School Board to Whitehall in 1877, in which the veiled threat is contained that 'your Memorialists do not look for any sensible diminution in the number of criminals until the children of the lowest class are taught to read and write well'.[28]

The temper of this memorial is radically different from the optimistic pronouncements of the early days of the Board, however, when parents were exhorted to send their children to the voluntary school of their choice, and thus obviate the necessity of expending ratepayers' money on procedures to compel attendance. 'In making this appeal the members of the Board are actuated by the best motives — they would rather see by the voluntary effort of the parents that they appreciate the inestimable advantages of education — provided by the wisdom of the legislature for their children, than that by the apathy and indifference of parents occasion should arise for enforcing the compulsory powers which the Board possess. . . .'[29]

Yet by 1872 the Board were under no illusions as to the size of the task confronting them. The number and distribution of the parents claiming fees provides a clue as to the scope of the problem (Map 5). The appointment of school attendance officers became inevitable, first one, then two, then four and eventually six. As Map 4 indicates, each officer enjoyed a distinct sphere of influence, with the middle-class enclave excluded territory. The abuse heaped on the officers in the Derby Road area, and their lack of welcome in Merton Road, could be taken as symptomatic of the ambivalent social position in which they found themselves.[30] Criticisms of their efforts by the headteachers of the voluntary schools and in the local press may have been a consequence of personal failings, but were more likely to have reflected their scapegoat role, condemned for the sin of their masters in taking so much money from the ratepayers. It was suggested, in the days when there was only one visitor, that he preferred the agreeable part of his duties (i.e. the office work) to the disagreeable . . . 'it may be asked whether there are not some streets in Bootle which Mr Porter would rather not visit'.[31] The headteachers of the voluntary schools publicized the feeble efforts of the School Board in compelling attendance, complaining, among other things, that the visitors were satisfied with attendance records of eight out of ten appearances per week.[32]

The Board's zeal unquestionably improved over time. Between 1879 and 1891 nearly 10,000 irregularities were dealt with, as a result of which nearly 3,000 parents were brought before the magistrates, and over 200 children committed to industrial or truant schools. Bootle built its own day industrial school in 1895 but the conduct of its affairs, if not its *raison d'être*, was viewed with suspicion. In providing free meals and bathing facilities it was held to be too attractive to some parents, who were criticized as evading their responsibilities.

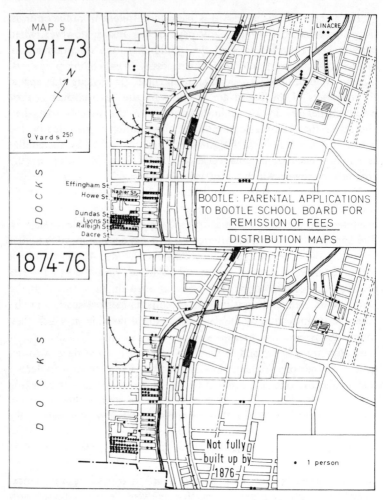

Map 5.

'A child must be incorrigible before an order can be made, and it is not infrequent that a burly father, six feet in height, appears before the Bench and complains that he has no control over a puny piece of humanity.'[33]

However well intentioned their public statements, the Board faced a built-in logistical dilemma for, in its early years particularly, an over-zealous enforcement of school attendance would have strained accommodation well beyond the breaking point. Even the building of board schools did not solve this problem. As late as 1895 all three board schools had more pupils on their rolls than they could provide accommodation for, and at Salisbury Road the accommodation was insufficient even to meet the average attendance.

Despite disquiet over increased spending on schools (and the School Board precept approximately trebled between 1880 and 1890, and more than doubled between 1890 and 1900), the attitudes of ratepayers over the years seem to have softened, or at least become resigned, to the increased demands on their purse. Over the years the *Bootle Times* had frequently levelled the charge of extravagance at the School Board. By the turn of the century it had become almost reconciled to its expenditure. 'So long as the School Board can show a good educational return (in the shape of good inspectors' reports) for their outlay, they need not fear any unreasonable objection to their keeping pace with the requirements of the borough.'[34]

There is much less direct documentation of the attitudes of the consumers. Circumstantial evidence can be sought in attendance records. The difficult nature of Bootle's social problems might have been expected to have been demonstrated in poorer than average overall attendance records. In fact in 1881 the local H.M.I. compared Bootle's 62 per cent average unfavourably with, among others, Southport's (almost 70 per cent). He did not attribute it to social problems, however, but considered it 'to excite some doubt whether sufficiently efficacious measures are taken to remedy it by the School Board there'.[35]

Bootle did not accept this figure, nor the rebuke. Records put out by the local authority show a continual improvement over the years. Provision of board schools in the 1880s was matched by more rigorous enforcement of the by-laws, and a striking improvement took place from the mid-1880s (Table 4).

The fact that the Bootle figures from the 1880s were better than the national average was periodically used by the Board to silence its critics. Clearly the national figures are brought down by the poor performance of many rural boards. Better figures in the towns may merely reflect the greater resolve and efficiency of the attendance enforcement agencies. But they may also denote that Katz's notion of a persistent 'estrangement between the school and the working class

community'[36], related to an American context, is too sweeping to be
applicable to this group in general in this country.

Table 4 *Average attendance figures in Bootle elementary schools*
(expressed as a percentage of those on rolls)

School	1870	1877	1883	1888	1896*	1900*[37]
St James's	33	70	54	79	83	81
St Alexander's	42	59	72	79	85	83
St John's	66	66	67	79	86	81
Christ Church	71	63	68	82	85	89
St Mary's	66	63	69	82	89	81
Bedford Road	–	–	–	80	89	87
Salisbury Road	–	–	–	87	86	89
Hawthorne Road	–	–	–	–	87	91
Gray Street	–	–	–	–	–	89
Overall	64	63	67	82	85	86
National	68	68	73	77	82	82

Admittedly the regular transference of bodies to school is not proof
that hearts and minds were in the right place. Enforcement became
coercive enough to impress all but the hard-liners, while incentives
designed to promote good attendance were openly ulterior. Having
tried lock-outs, corporal and other forms of punishment without much
success, both voluntary and board school authorities turned to more
positive inducements, including presents of sweets, geese, plum cakes,
toys and clothing for Christmas; raffles for prizes, and even interesting
'object lessons' on Friday afternoons, a bad time for attendance. Public
accolades of medals and certificates were bestowed at annual prize
distributions, at one of which a reporter wrote of the 'bright and happy
appearance of the children, many of whom were evidently "veterans"
from the number of medals they displayed'.[38]

Large numbers of children were clearly attending very regularly
indeed. But were these mostly the children of the lower middle class
and those 'in working class comfort'? If this were so, it would be likely
that the schools of special difficulty would have the most serious
attendance problems. Table 4 provides little evidence to support such
an interpretation. While the earlier figures are suspect and included
only to show the manifest improvement over time, there is no overall
evidence of variation spatially between social areas. It is strange, in fact,
that the board schools, which were purported to take the more difficult
children in some parts of the town, had better records than the voluntary

schools, with averages at the end of the School Board's tenure of 89 per cent and 85 per cent respectively.[39] The figures for St John's and St Alexander's, on the face of it the schools most at risk, seem to have kept up remarkably well. At St Alexander's for example, with over 80 per cent of its children in SEG V, averages of over 80 per cent were maintained during the 1890s. The intractable problem seems to have been concentrated in *part* of the casual labouring group (see Booth's sub-divisions) and was not spread over that group as a whole.

There seems little doubt that education came to be valued not only by the shopkeeping and clerical groups (SEG III), but also by increasing numbers of the working class (SEG IV) as well, as a means of upward mobility by way of improved occupational opportunity. Though the data is admittedly thin, there are log book references as early as 1872 of boys reaching Standard IV going on to work in offices,[40] while in 1887 Standard VII is mentioned in this context.[41] There may conceivably be in this a hint of improving standards and rising expectations of employers.

There is also evidence of a clear-cut but limited parental concept of the purpose of schooling. Basic literacy and numeracy were valued above all.[42] One Bootle headmistress noted difficulty in getting her children to draw maps, rated by at least two of her parents as 'a useless piece of education for a girl'.[43] This instrumental view was no mere working-class phenomenon. It seems to have been shared by the middle-class parents of boys at Bootle College, not to mention Liverpool Collegiate and Institute schools.[44] At an annual prize distribution at Bootle College, for example, reference was made by a guest speaker to 'an unfortunate inclination, fostered by the business customs of Liverpool, to shorten a lad's education'. Parents were advised 'to set their faces against the habit too common in this part of the world of taking children away from school too soon'.[45]

That elementary education was seen to be effective in fostering mobility is evident in a statement of a local newspaper columnist, concerned about the social impact of the board schools, and lamenting that the children's minds were being 'tortured':

'. . . the spark of false pride is fanned into a flame, until the bosom of the youth is scorched with a sense of degradation at the idea of earning his living by means of his father's trade. . . and meets his father's request to "buckle to" with the question: "Did you educate me only to make a labourer of me?" And he chooses, rather than a laborious craft, the mahogany desk, the high stool, and 20s. per week.'[46]

The realistic prospect of upward mobility seems to have been confined largely to the respectable working class, however. The children of the 'low poor' left early to become errand boys or casual labourers in the docks. At Salisbury Road, considered by its head to tap a very poor neighbourhood at the northern end of the town, 'Standard V is the fence over which comparatively few will leap'.[47] In Bootle the proportion of children of casual labourers was clearly larger than the average. On the one hand this made more difficult the task of the attendance officers though, as we have noted, the impact on school attendance averages was not catastrophic. On the other, the group continued into the following century as a stumbling block to the educational reformer, with a life condition that made it quite impracticable to view schooling as a priority or as a ray of hope.

Home background and school achievement

'Every lesson is now a species of examination.'[48]

The way in which academic achievement is related to social condition is an important dimension of the school's function as a socializing agency. In recent times large amounts of energy have been expended in demonstrating the nature of the relationship. The data can readily be collected. For the late nineteenth century appropriate information is much harder to come by, but is by no means non-existent.

This final section of the Bootle study makes use of information on 'standard reached' from schools' admissions registers as an index of achievement. It attempts to correlate such achievement with other variables such as age of entry to the school, length of stay at the school, and previous school attended. Information on these can also be derived from admissions registers. More particularly, correlation is sought between achievement and socio-economic grouping. The richest source of information for this variable are the census enumerator's returns, currently available up to 1871. Data can also be found in some admissions registers, and to a certain extent in local directories. The basis of the method used was to note addresses in admissions registers, from which cross-referencing of social and educational data between the returns and the registers could be effected. This process of matching entries requires care and a number of problems are liable to be encountered.

In this case, the first constraint was the shortage of admissions registers dating back as far as the late 1860s and early 1870s. Two registers, for the boys' departments of Christ Church and St John's schools, were found. It was apparent, however, that for the first two or three years at least, the registers were not fully entered. On the basis of other evidence, it is certain that there were more scholars enrolled at this period than the registers suggested.

A more general problem was the mobile state of the population at this time, with people moving from address to address fairly quickly. Hence to obtain a reasonably large sample of names which could be matched between admissions registers and census returns, register entries up to the mid-1870s had to be consulted. Of the 454 names entered in the Christ Church admissions register between 1868 and 1876, only 104 could be traced in the census enumerators' returns with any certainty and of these, owing to inadequate completion of the registers, only 97 could be included in the analysis. At St John's, of 581 names entered between the same dates, 120 were traced in the census returns, of which 112 could be used in the analysis. Hence the samples were 'imposed' ones.

It was also apparent that these imposed samples could hardly be taken as representative of the population as a whole. The presence of people living in the same house between the date of their entry in registers and returns would suggest that they might represent a more stable element in the population than the norm. A rough numerical comparison (not a statistical analysis) was therefore made between the figures for 'length of stay' (an index of stability) for both the imposed samples and for consecutive entries respectively for the two schools.[49]

Table 5 *Comparison of 'imposed samples' and consecutive entries, Christ Church and St John's, 1870s*

1870s	Christ Church		St John's	
Length of stay	Imposed sample	Consecutive entry	Imposed sample	Consecutive entry
Under 2 years	26	27	26	28
2–5 years	41	46	25	41
Over 5 years	33	27	49	31

It is clear that the difference between the imposed sample and the consecutive entry is more marked at St John's, where the imposed sample contains a much larger percentage of children staying on over five years. It is probable therefore that the St John's sample is less representative of its consecutive entry than is the case with Christ Church.

In addition, it is likely in any case that the total school entries, particularly at this early period, were not representative of the whole population for, as we have seen, large numbers of children were not sent to school. Hence children of the 'low poor' were probably under-represented in these imposed samples. At the other extreme, children from the highest social group (SEG I) would not be present, and relatively few from SEG II.

For the 1890s period, of course, no census enumerators' returns were available. It was fortunate that admissions registers were found for St John's boys' and Bedford Road girls' departments which contained the vital data on both standards of achievement and occupations of parents. The information was not wholly complete, however, and only entries in which both sets of data were included could be used, again giving an imposed sample. As far as possible, the entries analysed were taken consecutively over periods of time, for 1891–3 in the case of St John's (a sample of 112); and 1892 and 1894 for Bedford Road (a sample of 98). These were the years for which the data were most comprehensive. But the relative lack of vigour of some heads in completing admissions registers' sections on standard reached must occasion cautious interpretation.

Further caution is needed in interpreting 'standard reached' as an index of achievement. To promote the functioning of the payment-by-results system, a clear-cut means of assessment had to be evolved, which entailed spelling out objectives in a way which we might refer to today as 'operational'. The objectives presupposed little more than the achievement of basic levels of literacy and numeracy. But the system was taken very seriously by teachers and by many parents and employers. The results are also reasonably comparable from school to school, for the Education Department laid down strict regulations for inspection. The same inspector (with assistants) covered all the schools in his particular area. Not least, this information is the only measure of elementary school achievement we have.

As part of the statistical analysis a chi-squared technique (see Appendix 2) was used to investigate possible relationships between 'standard reached' (the index of achievement) and the variables of 'age at entry', 'length of stay',[50] 'previous school attended' and, most important of all for the purposes of this study, 'socio-economic grouping'. This test showed whether the correlation for each of these variables was significant (Appendix 1) *school by school*. A further test was applied to see whether *differences between schools* for each variable were significant, by means of an analysis of the significance of the differences between the percentage figures of pairs of schools.[51]

1) *Age at entry/standard reached* (Christ Church and St John's)

The chi-squared test indicated no significant relationship between these variables for Christ Church (1870s only), but a significant relationship (*) for St John's both for the 1870s and the 1890s samples.[52] The suggestion embodied in this comparison is that children coming up through the infants' department of a particular school, thus entering the main school at the earliest possible age, might achieve higher standards than those entering at a later age. This proved to be the case at St John's at both dates.

Table 6 *Significance of differences in percentages entering at different ages: Christ Church and St John's, 1870s samples*

Age at Entry	CC	%	SJ	Relationship
Under 8	60		77	**
8 – 10	28		15	*
Over 10	12		8	N.S.

Comparing the two schools (Table 6) in the early 1870s, a significantly higher percentage of St John's than of Christ Church's intake entered the school under the age of eight. This could be interpreted as meaning that more of the Christ Church children had previously attended other schools, and particularly private adventure schools (rather than not attending school at all), thus seeking entry at a later age. The significance of this comparison may not, however, be entirely a valid one, for the caveat that St John's imposed sample was less representative of its consecutive entry than Christ Church's must be followed up. This is done in Table 7.

Table 7 *As Table 6, but using 1870s consecutive entries*

Age at Entry	CC	%	SJ	Relationship
Under 8	60		68	N.S.
8 – 10	24		21	N.S.
Over 10	16		11	N.S.

Thus in the comparison of two entries that *can* be taken as reasonably representative, there is *no* significant difference between the two schools in terms of this particular variable.

Table 8 *Significance of differences in percentage entering at different ages, St John's 1870s and 1890s (consecutive entries)*[53]

Age at Entry	SJ ('70s)	%	SJ ('90s)	Relationship
Under 8	68		49	**
8 – 10	21		19	N.S.
Over 10	11		32	**

The finding that a significantly larger percentage of boys was entering this predominantly working-class school at a later age in the 1890s than in the 1870s is a most interesting one. It contains the hint, if no more, that the population of its dockland catchment area was in a more fluid state at the later date, with more people moving in and out, and in consequence more children entering the school at a later age.

2) *Length of stay/standard reached* (Christ Church and St John's)
The chi-squared test showed that the relationship between length of stay and standard reached at Christ Church and at St John's at both dates was in all cases highly significant (**).[54] It might be argued that this is merely a more precise way of stating the obvious: that the longer the children stay in school the higher the standard they tend to reach. Yet the confirmation of this fact is of more significance than merely the statistical in suggesting that even in the socially disadvantaged circumstances of St John's, so long as the children stayed on in school they were likely to achieve the standards the system set for them. Again we must bear in mind that the results for the imposed sample for St John's might be flattering. Even so, there were 86 per cent 'manual working-class' children in this sample. Hence the perception of the time that length of stay, combined with good attendance, were crucial variables in school achievement, appears to be supported by these figures.

An analysis of the 'percentages for different lengths of stay' shows no significant difference between Christ Church and St John's in the 1870s. This is not the case, however, for St John's at the two different periods, using consecutive entry figures (Table 9).

The fact that so many more children were staying at school for less than two years in the 1890s tends to confirm the previous indication

Table 9

Length of Stay	SJ ('70s)	%	SJ ('90s)	Relationship
Under 2 years	28		60	**
2 – 5 years	21		19	N.S.
Over 5 years	31		18	**

that the population in the St John's catchment area was in a more mobile state in the later than in the earlier period.

3) *Previous school/standard reached* (all three schools)

The three categories of 'previous school' considered were the 'feeder' infants' departments; other elementary schools; and private schools. For this variable, Bedford Road was added to the other two schools but only at St John's in the 1870s was it significant (*).[55] Hence the children attending St John's who had come up through its infants' department achieved better results than those who entered from other schools. A very tentative explanation might be that the children who came in from other schools included a proportion from the dame schools which abounded in this neighbourhood. They arrived at the elementary school in a lamentably backward state, and were likely to be unable to catch up on the other children to reach equivalent standards. It is difficult, however, to interpret the probable effect of the nature of the imposed sample for this particular variable, which contained a lower proportion of children from other schools than the consecutive entry.

Between the schools the following differences proved to be significant.

(a) A larger proportion of the 1870s intake at St John's came up from the infants' department than in the 1890s (**), and a larger proportion of the 1890s intake entered from other elementary schools (**), thus reinforcing the earlier evidence of greater residential mobility in this area in the 1890s.

(b) A larger proportion of children had previously attended private schools in the case of Christ Church (1870s) than Bedford Road (1890s) (**), a confirmation of the widely held contemporary opinion that the establishment of board schools sounded the death-knell of the private adventure school sector.

(c) A larger proportion of the children at Christ Church had previously attended private schools than at St John's in the 1870s (*).

It is likely that the private school element of the Christ Church sample was less backward than that of St John's, however, as no significant difference was shown for the group in terms of standard reached in the former case, though the school log books do contain complaints about the quality of this intake.

4) *Socio-economic grouping/standard reached* (all three schools)
This was regarded as the 'key correlation' of this study. The five major socio-economic categories (page 196) were collapsed into three for the purposes of the chi-squared test (see Appendix 2). The first category subsumed SEGs I–III (in effect II and III, i.e. lower professional and white-collar workers); the second was equivalent to SEG IV (skilled and semi-skilled); the third to SEG V (unskilled manual workers).

The test indicated no significant relationship between socio-economic category and academic achievement except at Bedford Road (*)[56], perhaps a surprising result in view of the reasonably well-favoured location of that school, certainly as compared with St John's. Or might it conceivably have reflected the well-known off-loading of less desirable children on to the board school?

This result relates to the outcome of a general three-fold correlation. Further information was gained by breaking this down into two-fold divisions.[57] Such an analysis of the Bedford Road data showed that while children of manual workers did not achieve such high standards as those of the white-collar groups (*), there was *no* significant intra-working-class difference between the skilled and unskilled manual groups.

The Bedford Road situation is of course atypical in representing a girls' department, but whether the result can be taken to reflect a sex differential must be speculative. It would be tempting but improvident to postulate a differential expectation on the part of working-class parents towards their daughters as compared with white-collar parents, resulting in a lower standard of achievement of girls from the former group.

For St John's in the 1870s the correlation between socio-economic grouping and standard reached comes close to significance. This is worth mentioning because the sample used is the imposed one, i.e. the more 'stable' social group. It may be conjectured, for reasons given, that had the consecutive entry been matchable in the census enumerators' returns for information on socio-economic background, a significant result might have emerged. The breakdown of the three-fold correlation for St John's reveals significantly lower achievement (*) on the part of children of unskilled manual workers than of skilled workers, in a school which we have seen had a relatively homogeneous intake from an area of high social disadvantage.

In general terms it may at first sight seem surprising that more relationship has not been demonstrated between social class and educational achievement. The Victorian working class was widely perceived as 'apathetic' or 'indifferent' towards education. A causal relationship between the two variables is widely accepted today.

By way of explanation, two technical points must be made. To begin with, the samples used were necessarily socially attenuated, containing virtually no children from the upper middle classes, and probably a less than representative sample from the 'low poor'. In addition, the children were, if need be, given more than one opportunity to sit for each standard. Indeed, each standard was prerequisite for the next. There are many examples in the registers of children repeating the same standard, though rarely more than once. Hence a slower child could achieve higher standards by extending his length of stay.

There are also two more general factors. It is well known that the payment-by-results system encouraged rote learning, which must have lowered the power of the examination to discriminate. Discrimination was not in any case its purpose. In these circumstances, the frailer aptitudes of the socially disadvantaged children would be less than clearly exposed. The innate ability and imagination of brighter children would constitute a kind of overkill for which there was no tangible reward in the shape of better results.[58]

Perhaps more important, there is evidence of positive discrimination in the schools on behalf of the slower children. As the headmaster of Christ Church revealed: 'The teachers have been examining one another's classes during the week (a tactic designed to simulate the inspector's visit, accustoming the children to 'a variety of voice and manner'). There is of course a backward division in each standard, upon which they are bestowing great pains. . . .'[59] Government grant depended as much on the results achieved by less able as more able children. Far from considering that less able pupils merited less able teachers, a head might well find it expedient to put an experienced teacher in charge of a small group of slower children, leaving pupil teachers to attend to the rest, and particularly in the critical period after Christmas which in Bootle led up to the annual examination.

Expectation of success must needs be the same for all but a small minority of children, who were excluded from the examination on grounds of excessive ill-health and/or absence, or extreme 'dullness'.

Further information emerged from the comparison of different schools in terms of these two key variables.

(a) Table 10 *Significance of % differences for socio-economic grouping at Christ Church and St John's (1870s)*[60]

SEG	CC	%	SJ	Relationship
I–III	36		14	**
IV	43		46	N.S.
V	21		40	**

The better balance of the social mix at Christ Church is clear, the figures reinforcing the earlier discussion of the social interaction of catchment area with the school: Christ Church in a middle-class fringe area, and St John's in the heart of dockland.

(b) Table 11 *Significance of % differences for standard reached at Christ Church and St John's (1970s)*[61]

Standard	CC	%	SJ	Relationship
0 – II	35		56	**
III – IV	45		28	**
V and over	20		16	N.S.
III and over	65		44	**

The standards reached were thus significantly higher at Christ Church than at St John's. We have already noted evidence of variation in achievement *inside* the two schools, in that at the socially well-mixed Christ Church there was no significant difference between the socio-economic groups, while at St John's there was a significant difference between SEG V and the rest. The fact that *between the schools* there was a significant difference in favour of Christ Church might be taken as further testimony to its more advantageous social setting.

On the other hand, the difference might equally be attributable to differences in the quality of teaching, a variable which cannot be held as constant between the schools. Log books and inspectors' reports might be used to throw light on teacher effectiveness, but it cannot be quantified, and is not investigated here.

(c) Comparisons between the two 'inland' schools, Christ Church

(1870s) and Bedford Road (1890s), show no significant differences in terms of the social make-up of the children, but in the context of 'standard reached' a significantly higher percentage (*) achieved Standard V or better at Bedford Road. This almost certainly would have been the case had the data existed to compare Christ Church's own results at the two dates. There is general evidence that children were staying on for longer and achieving higher standards by the 1890s.

(d) Table 12 *Significance of % differences for socio-economic grouping at St John's in the 1870s and 1890s*

SEG	SJ ('70s)	%	SJ('90s)	Relationship
I–III	14		26	*
IV	46		32	*
V	40		42	N.S.

Caution must be exercised in interpreting these differences in view of the less than representative nature of the 1870s sample. We have already seen that the St John's catchment areas was in a more volatile state in the 1890s, and it seems surprising to find a significant upward social mobility. Explanation can in part be found in the spatial expansion of the St John's catchment area at this later date (compare Maps 1 and 2), when it took in the socially more desirable areas to the east of the railway.

(e) Table 13 *Significance of % differences for standard reached at St John's in the 1870s and 1890s*

Standard	SJ ('70s)	%	SJ ('90s)	Relationship
0–II	46 (56)		40	N.S. (**)
III–IV	31 (28)		34	N.S. (N.S.)
V and over	23 (16)		26	N.S. (**)

In this table the 1870s figures include both the imposed sample and the consecutive entry, the latter being given in brackets. The more reliable comparison is with this consecutive entry. The figures reveal a significant improvement in standard achieved between the two dates, a result in line with earlier findings.

(f) Table 14   *Significance of % differences for socio-economic grouping
at St John's and Bedford Road (1890s)*

SEG	SJ	%	BR	Relationship
I–III	26		47	**
IV	32		34	N.S.
V	42		19	**

Again the difference in social terms between schools on 'either side
of the railway tracks' is marked. The overlap in the catchment zones
of the two schools has already been described (Map 2). It seems clear
that St John's at this time drew many of its children of higher social
groups from east of the railway. But this still represented a relatively
small percentage of its intake as compared with Bedford Road, all of
whose catchment zone lay east of the railway.

(g) There is in the strict sense no significant difference in terms of
'standard reached' between the 1890s results for St John's and Bedford
Road. This contrasts with the position in the 1870s where the children
of the 'inland' school, Christ Church, were shown to have achieved
significantly higher standards than the dockland school. It is possible
that standards were somewhat higher at Bedford Road, however, in
that consistent differences appear at the $p < 0.10$ level (over 10 per
cent probability of the differences being due to chance), which denotes a strong trend towards significance. It is dangerous to attempt to
interpret this difference in terms of differential social status, however,
for here the added variable of Bedford Road being a girls' school has
to be considered, not to mention possible variations in the effectiveness
of teaching.

Conclusions

This study has sought to bring into focus relationships between environment, social attitudes, and educational provision and achievement at
the grassroots level in a late nineteenth-century urban setting. These
relationships have been investigated by means of a range of methodo-
logies now available for interpreting the variety of source materials
which have emerged from a rich and complex scene. It is hoped that
the study has demonstrated that the intricacies of those relationships
need to be explored through numbers of such local case studies, and
lent weight to Katz's assertion that 'the close examination of one

[case] will yield more insight than an overview of many'.[62]

On the basis of so localized a survey it would be unwise to make grand extrapolations. An investigation of this sort obviously requires widespread replication before really firm conclusions can be reached. However, while the study does not establish, it would support with varying degrees of strength, the following general statements.

(1) Marked spatial variations existed in relationships between home and school in the late nineteenth-century urban milieu, a reflection of the gradual emergence of distinctive social areas. This was a key factor in the development of an incipient hierarchy within the elementary school system, the élite elementary school coming to compare favourably in esteem with all but the best private adventure schools.

(2) Variations existed in attitudes regarding the desirability of providing for popular education. The views of the promoters of education, prognosticating it as a general cure for social ills in the early stages of the period, became increasingly realistic in their later diagnoses. Nevertheless, evidence of increasingly positive attitudes towards popular education is indicated by the reconciliation of ratepayers, by the end of the century major providers of educational facilities, to the need to meet the cost of expanding educational demands, albeit conditionally and reluctantly.

(3) Among the consumers, the most marked discontinuities in attitudes seem to have been, on the one hand, between the upper and lower middle classes and, on the other, the 'respectable' working class and the 'low poor'; rather than between the 'respectable' working class and the lower middle class. The aspirations of these two latter groups seem to have grown over time, with the late 1880s and 1890s an important take-off period, no doubt made possible by the increased demand for white-collar workers at that time.

(4) These two groups seem to have been as one in their wish to protect their children from contamination by the offspring of the 'low poor', as more and more of that group entered the elementary school system.

(5) There was a certain harmony of perception between aspiring parents and the promoters of education as to the function of elementary schooling. In both cases the viewpoint was a limited and instrumental one, the object being to enhance the chances of children becoming white-collar workers. The office stool functioned as a symbol of upward mobility.

(6) *Within* schools, however, the social condition of the child was

not of necessity an arbiter of school achievement, though there is evidence of differential achievement *between* socially favoured and less favoured schools.

(7) A more significant factor in achievement was regular and con-tinuing attendance (not to speak of good health), though these in turn reflected social condition. So that indirectly it could be said that social class was a strong determinent of school achievement, to the extent that aspiring parents saw to it that the attendance criterion was observed.

(8) Even within the apparently homogeneous unskilled labouring group, there were clearly differences in attitude towards educational provision. It would be unsafe to generalize that there was widespread, conscious 'promotion of truancy' across the group. The gravity of life condition and chosen life style seem to have been important influences. In terms of the former, unfavourable attitudes towards education might well be redefined as getting priorities right. Survival had to come first.

(9) The fatalistic outlook of parents conditioned to wildly irregular earnings crucially handicapped the advancement of their children. Their outlook might be interpreted as realistic in the sense that their life style and social norms were at odds with the bourgeois ethos which underpinned the running of the elementary school. By contrast this was easily accepted, even eagerly swallowed, by the respectable working class. Hence elementary education as an agency of social mobility was a reality only for the more favoured segment of the working class, and probably only for those of that group who made conscious and pur-posive use of it.

Appendix 1 Statistical significance

The term 'significant' is used in its technical sense, meaning the degree of probability that a given difference could have arisen by chance. Arbitrary but rigorous standards, or *levels of significance*, have been designated to separate significant from non-significant differences, and are usually expressed as $p < 0.01$ *(marked in the text as **)*, which refers to a high degree of significance (i.e. that there is less than one chance in a hundred that the relationship or difference could have occurred by chance); or $p < 0.05$ *(marked as *)*, which is also an index of significance (less than one chance in twenty). Levels below this are regarded as *not significant (N.S.)*, though a sequence of results at the $p < 0.10$ (one chance in ten) might tentatively be regarded as suggesting a trend towards significance. Clearly common-sense criteria have to be borne in mind as well. A statistically significant relationship might also be a nonsensical one.

Appendix 2 The Chi-squared tests

As indicated in the text (page 217 ff), the variables were collapsed into sub-categories to make up the three by three matrices used in the chi-squared correlations. An example is shown below. Technically not more than one of the nine cells should contain a total of less than five. When this occurred, the matrices were further collapsed into three by two or two by three arrangements to check whether failure to meet the condition in the three by three matrix affected the final result. The three by two (or two by three) result was accepted as the more valid, as in the case which follows, though here neither result was significant.

Christ Church (1870s) : standard reached

		1	2	3	Row Totals		1	2/3
Age at	3	6	4	1	11	3	6	5
Entry	2	8	12	6	26	2	8	18
Column	1	18	27	15	60	1	18	42
Totals		52	43	22	97			

Chi-squared = 2.61 (N.S.)

Chi-squared = 2.97 (N.S.)

Acknowledgements

Thanks are particularly due to my colleague, Mr R.R. Stewart, for the considerable time and care he expended in advising on and assisting with the statistical processing; to the headteachers of many Bootle primary schools and to the vicar of Christ Church for access to records and for supplying the photograph of the school; and to the staff of Bootle Reference Library for supplying the other photographs and for their unfailing co-operation.

NOTES

[1] Entry in Salisbury Road Board School (Bootle) Log Book, 5 October 1888.

[2] *Bootle Times,* 18 October 1890.

[3] For definitions of 'lower middle class' see Departmental Committee on the Pupil Teacher System, Vol. 2, 'Minutes of Evidence' (London, H.M.S.O., 1898), Minutes 2691–3; A.L. Bowley, *The Change in the Distribution of the National Income, 1880–1913* (Oxford, 1920), p. 26; A.L. Bowley, *Wages and Income since 1860* (Cambridge, 1937), p. 93.

[4] C. Booth (ed.), *Labour and Life of the People in London,* Vol. II (London, 1892), pp. 40–1.

[5] Ibid., p. 40.

[6] R. Roberts, *The Classic Slum: Salford Life in the First Quarter of the Century* (Manchester, 1971), p. 4.

[7] Useful sources are the minutes of Town Council and constituent committee meetings, in which deliberations over appropriate earnings for particular groups may be recorded.

[8] Bowley, op. cit., p. 18.

[9] E.F. Rathbone, Report of an Inquiry into the Conditions of Dock Labour at the Liverpool Docks (Liverpool, 1904), p. 11.

[10] Ibid., pp. 43–4.

[11] Bootle's first Medical Officer of Health was appointed in 1873, and his reports are a mine of information on social conditions. An account may be found in M. Regan, *Children of Bootle* (Bootle, 1968).

[12] Salisbury Road (Boys) Log Book, 15 February 1889.

[13] See D. Rubinstein, *School Attendance in London, 1870–1904: A Social History* (Hull, 1969), p. 64.

[14] The SEG IV figure is likely to be an exaggeration, for those describing themselves as, for example, carpenters, could well be of a low-level, casual variety, with a status and social condition more akin to SEG V.

[15] Booth, (ed.), op. cit., Vol. III, pp. 196–9.

[16] *Bootle Times,* 21 February 1885.

[17] The streets on Map 3 are shown in their built-up state in the 1890s, when it is clear there were more households in Litherland Road than in 1871. The maps do, however, give a reasonable approximation to the situation in 1871.

[18] Bootle School Board Minutes, 7 April 1876.

[19] Bootle School Board Minutes, 12 November 1875.

[20] Booth (ed.), op. cit., Vol. III, pp. 197–9.

[21] C.F. Nathan, *A Schoolmaster Glances Back* (Liverpool, 1946), p. 79.

[22] Christ Church (Boys) Log Book, 9 February 1877.

[23] Salisbury Road (Boys) Log Book, 12 April 1877.

[24] Public Record Office, Education File 21/9080.

[25] Entry in St Alexander's (Boys) Log Book, 6 October 1886.

[26] M.B. Katz, 'Who went to school?', *History of Education Quarterly*, Vol. 12 (1972), p. 433.

[27] See N. Ball, 'Elementary school attendance and voluntary effort before 1870', *History of Education*, Vol. 2 (1973), p. 32.

[28] Bootle School Board Minutes, 14 December 1877.

[29] Bootle School Board Minutes, 16 March 1871.

[30] Rubinstein, op. cit., p. 45.

[31] *Bootle Times*, 29 March 1879.

[32] St Mary's (Girls) Log Book, 21 August 1891.

[33] *Bootle Times*, 3 April 1897.

[34] *Bootle Times*, 7 April 1900.

[35] Report of the Committee on Council of Education, 1881–2, p. 244.

[36] M.B. Katz, *The Irony of Early School Reform* (Havard, 1968), p. 112.

[37] *Figures for separate schools refer to one months only. While anomalies are therefore to be expected, a check of other monthly figures shows that they are reasonably typical. *Sources*: Bootle School Board Minutes; Reports of the Committee of Council; and Cross Commission (1886), Appendix C, pp. 522–3.

[38] *Bootle Times*, 4 May 1895.

[39] Bootle School Board Minutes, Triennial Report, 1903.

[40] St James (Boys) Log Books, 17 and 27 March 1872.

[41] Salisbury Road (Boys) Log Books, 27 May and 29 July 1887.

[42] See Newcastle Commission, Vol. 2 (1861), pp. 195–7.

[43] St Mary's (Girls) Log Books, 10 and 12 October 1887.

[44] See M.E. Sadler, Report on Secondary Education in Liverpool (London, 1904), pp. 19, 66.

[45] *Bootle Times*, 27 December 1890.

[46] *Bootle Times*, 2 May 1891.

[47] Salisbury Road (Boys) Log Book, 27 April 1888.

[48] Entry in Christ Church (Boys) Log Book, 7 January 1881.

[49] This comparison must itself be viewed with great caution for the presence of children from the imposed sample in the consecutive entry contaminates the result. But common sense suggests that the distinction is worth making and pursuing.

[50] The 'age of entry' and 'length of stay' variables were excluded in the case of Bedford Road, whose figures were not strictly comparable in these terms with the other schools, because it was organized with an intermediate department between the infants and the so-called 'senior' departments, resulting in later ages of entry and shorter lengths of stay than were characteristic elsewhere.

[51] See H.E. Garrett, *Statistics in Psychology and Education* (New York, 4th ed., 1955), pp. 236–7.

[52] Chi-squares: Christ Church 2.61; St John's (1870s) 7.94; St John's (1890s) 10.36.

[53] As was noted earlier, the samples for St John's and Bedford Road in the 1890s were almost consecutive ones.

[54] Chi-squares: Christ Church 34.12; St John's (1870s) 57.65; St John's (1890s) 27.64.

[55] Chi-squares: Christ Church 6.49; St John's (1870s) 12.13; Bedford Road 1.59; St John's (1890s) 1.96.

[56] Chi-squares: Christ Church 1.83; St John's (1870s) 9.47; Bedford Road 13.22; St John's (1890s) 4.75.

[57] See the 'three by two' and 'two by three' matrices of the chi-squared tests in the Appendix (2).

[58] This is making what is possibly a false premise: that the less able children were concentrated in the lower social groups. The statements of contemporary headteachers would seem to indicate, however, that they saw it this way.

[59] Christ Church (Boys) Log Book, 7 January 1881.

[60] As SEG data was derived from the census enumerators' returns, the figures represent the imposed samples, somewhat suspect for St John's. However, the consecutive entry would be likely to intensify the significance of this result rather than the reverse.

[61] The St John's figures represent the consecutive entry.

[62] M.B. Katz, 'The emergence of bureaucracy in urban education, the Boston Case, 1850–1884', *History of Education Quarterly*, Vol. 8 (1968), p. 157.

Chapter 9:

Socialization and the London School Board 1870–1904: aims, methods and public opinion[1]

David Rubinstein

'No equally powerful body will exist in England outside Parliament, if power be measured by influence for good or evil over masses of human beings.' Thus *The Times* on 29 November 1870,[2] discussing that day's election of the first School Board for London. Certainly the impact of the London School Board, to use its more common name, was very great. Sidney Webb, by no means a friend, commented at the end of its life that it deserved a good deal of the credit for 'one of the most remarkable chapters of social history', namely 'the transformation effected in the course of three-quarters of a century in the manners and morals of the London manual working class'. Webb continued:

> Not until the establishment. . .of the London School Board, was there any systematic attempt to rescue the whole of the children of London. . . .The voluntary schools stand, numerically, almost precisely where they did in 1870. It is the School Board which has provided the buildings for the half a million additional scholars brought under the wonderful discipline of the public elementary school. These five hundred new public buildings [occupy] 600 acres of valuable land. . . .And improvement in quality has kept pace with increase in quantity. It is, in the main, to the School Board that London owes the transformation which has, in these thirty-three years, come over its elementary schools – the change from frowsy, dark, and insanitary rooms, practically destitute of apparatus or playgrounds, in which teachers, themselves mostly untrained, mechanically ground a minimum of the three R's required by the wooden old code into the heads of their scanty pupils, to the well-lighted and admirably decorated school buildings of the present day, with ample educational equipment, with pianos, school libraries, extensive playgrounds, etc., served by a staff of trained professional teachers. . . .[3]

Webb's praise was exaggerated, but there is no doubt that the London School Board achieved a great deal in its short life. Before 1870 schools in London varied enormously in quality. Some were of reasonably high standard but others were abominable. School places were in pitifully short supply. Conditions were discussed in reports made to the Newcastle Commission on 'popular education' in 1861[4] and in the survey undertaken by the Education Department after the passing of the Education Act in 1870. The Department's calculations showed that about 319,000 children attended London elementary schools in 1871, but only about 230,000 of them attended schools judged to be 'efficient'. Complicated estimates suggested that between 250,000 and 300,000 additional places were needed, although at first the London School Board tried to convince itself that it need provide as few as 100,000 places.[5] The Board itself, in another calculation published at the end of its life, estimated that efficient voluntary schools had had 221,401 pupils on their rolls in 1871. In 1903 the number had dropped to 213,297, but in the same period the number of pupils on the Board's rolls had risen from 1,117 to 549,677.[6] Even after making allowances for an increase in London's school-age population of well over a third and for the inhibiting effects on the voluntary schools of the growth of the Board, the achievement is impressive.[7]

Exercising optional powers under the Education Act of 1870, the London School Board instituted a compulsory minimum leaving age of ten in December 1871. Compulsion to ten was made universal by Parliament in 1880; further Acts raised the minimum age to eleven in 1893 and (except for children employed in agriculture) to twelve in 1899. The Board's by-laws ensured that, by the beginning of the new century, almost all London children stayed at school full-time until they were 14.[8]

The creation of a framework of compulsory school involved much more than schools themselves. From 1872 the Board established a system of school attendance officers, whom it rather delicately termed 'visitors'. These men (and a tiny scattering of women), themselves normally of working-class origin, provided the first systematic information about the lives of the urban poor to be made available to local and national government authorities. Prior to their appointment there had been slum doctors, priests and charitable workers, as well as enquiring journalists, but there had been no permanent, standardized system to be tapped whenever necessary. Visitors were widely used for extra-educational purposes. As early as 1875 they were asked to prepare a census of wife desertion in London discovered during the course of their normal duties. Of the 110 witnesses before the Royal Commission on Housing in 1884-5, sixteen were London visitors. Their work was widely recognized. The Housing Committee of the new London County Council asked in May 1889 for the assistance of the School Board visitors in determining 'insanitary areas'. Charles Booth paid ample tribute to the London visitors in the first volume of his great study of London, saying that without their assistance 'nothing could have been done'. In their spare time some at least of the London visitors engaged in social work, assisting in the provision of charitable food and clothes. One of them, John Reeves, wrote in his memoirs: 'For nearly fifty years the whole of my leisure time has been given to objects in the interest and help of my poorer fellows.'[9]

The information provided by the visitors, by Her Majesty's Inspectors (H.M.I.s), School Board Inspectors and others such as Booth, led to a slow shift of public opinion towards more sympathetic treatment of the 'condition of the people' question. Towards the end of the century attention was concentrated on children and their social problems, resulting in the formation of a host of societies and agencies involved in feeding and caring for children. This public attention was to bear fruit in the legislation of the Liberal Government of 1906, a considerable portion of which was concerned with the condition of children. Some of the concern was caused by an infant mortality rate which stubbornly refused to decline until after the turn of the century, and some was caused by early reverses in the South African War of 1899-1902 and the resultant alarm about the physical condition of the working classes. But some too came from the schools and the condition of the children. Surveys published by the London School Board in 1889, 1895 and 1899 suggested that about one child in every eight in average attendance came to school hungry. An independent survey estimated in 1903 that 122,000 pupils, nearly one sixth of the elementary school population, received meals from charitable agencies. The work of the Board's medical officer, appointed in 1890, also showed the enormous amount of ill-health which school children suffered as the direct result of poverty.[10] Giving evidence in 1903 to the Inter-Departmental Committee on Physical Deterioration, Dr Alfred Eichholz, an H.M.I. with medical qualifications and duties, said that compulsory school attendance, more adequate enumeration of the elementary school population and the abolition of school fees had 'swept into the schools an annually increasing proportion of children during the last thirty years. These circumstances', Eichholz asserted, were 'largely responsible for focussing public notice on the severer cases of physical impairment', just as at an earlier stage the problems of blind, deaf, feeble-minded and crippled children had been brought to public notice. Eichholz also attributed in part to the work of the schools the disappearance of what he called the 'savage type. . .wild, unkempt, loosely built, ragged, barefoot children, who look like savages and not like human beings'.[11]

Educating the working classes was complicated by the divisions within their ranks. It is a convenient and not unduly misleading simplification to consider them in two main groups. Pressure from the skilled, relatively prosperous working men was partly responsible for the passage of the Education Act of 1870.[12] On the other hand, W.E. Forster, the minister responsible for the Act, asserted that those working men who wantèd universal compulsory education were 'among the most intelligent and upright of their class, but they formed only a small minority of the working men in the country'.[13] The division was widely recognized by working people themselves. Robert Applegarth, the leader of the skilled carpenters who was a strong advocate of the Education Act, said in a speech in 1869:

> No one knows better than the men themselves that there are amongst the working people two classes. There is the careless and indifferent man, who has been so long neglected and degraded that he does not understand the value of education; and him the other class, the better class of working men, have to carry on their backs. Those men who do not understand the value of education must be made to understand it.[14]

Thomas Wright, who wrote prolifically as 'The Journeyman Engineer' and who seems to have become a long-serving London School Board visitor, commented in 1871 that the working classes

> are practically and plurally *classes*, distinct classes, classes between which there are as decisively marked differences as there are between any one of them and the upper or middle classes. . . .There is an educated and really intelligent section, and an uneducated and ignorant section; a political section. . .and a non-political section. . . .No one has so impatient a contempt for the uneducated working man as has the educated working man.[15]

Nearly twenty years later Thomas Powell, a London School Board visitor, expressed a similar view in giving evidence to the Royal Commission on the Elementary Education Acts (the Cross Commission). Powell, who was also the secretary of a London trade union of skilled bookbinders, told the Commission that the district which he visited for the Board was very poor, 'not at all a district known to us by trade unionism'. Trade unionists, he added, were too 'self respectful' to keep their children away from school, and his operations against them were 'almost nil'. Such prejudice against compulsory education as existed was to be found 'amongst the very poor and unlearned'.[16]

It can, then, be accepted that most skilled workers in London were prepared and even eager to send their children to school. It was the poor, the unskilled, the casual, found in London in huge numbers, who were hostile or apathetic. Every kind of underpaid labour was found in London, dependants of the service trades, victims of sweating, providers of luxuries to the rich. Female labour, foreign labour, child labour were all in demand. Educating the enormous mass of their children was a problem larger than that facing any other school board.[17]

Why were the London poor, whom Charles Booth estimated in 1891 to total 1,292,737; 30.7 per cent of the population,[18] resistant to education of their children? There were three principal reasons. First, the London School Board took their homes. The Board necessarily built its schools where population was thickest. This meant dislodging the poor, and although the Board sometimes gave *ex gratia* compensation to those dislodged, they were not compelled to rehouse the tenants until an Act of 1899 required rehousing where twenty or more working-class houses were destroyed in any one parish. As early as 13 May 1872 the Board was authorized by the Education Department to acquire sixteen sites with 295 occupiers (in most cases, presumably, heads of families) for school building; at the end of its life, late in 1903, it announced plans to acquire compulsorily forty-six sites for school building or enlargement in eighteen Metropolitan boroughs. In the same year the Board agreed to pay the London County Council over £10,000 to rehouse 1,030 persons whom it had evicted, and negotiations to rehouse between 200 and 300 more soon followed. People who lost their homes, mean and inadequate as they might be, for school building, were unlikely to be very cheerful about the benefits of elementary education.[19]

Second, the London poor, like those elsewhere, needed the tiny wages which their children could earn to supplement the family income. London was the home of small workshops and domestic labour, and many types of process made ample use of agile and cheap fingers. The superintendent of visitors for the Hackney division pointed out early in 1879 that parents had been accustomed 'to make capital out of their children as soon as the little hands could make a match-box, or paint a toy, and naturally resented any interference with their supposed rights'. When the Board began its work, he added, half the children were at work in some parts of his division.[20] Factory inspectors could not hope to cover the enormous numbers of small workshops and work done in homes, even where they were legally allowed to do so. 'How can two or three inspectors keep in check the multitude of sweating dens of East London?' asked John Burnett, labour correspondent of the Board of Trade in 1887.[21] In 1893 Lady Dilke reported a comment by a mother amongst the matchbox makers of Shoreditch: 'Of course, we cheat the School Board. . . .It's hard on the little ones, but then their fingers is so quick – they that has the most of 'em is the best off.'[22]

By the 1890s regular child labour in school hours was largely a thing of the past, though the opportunities for it remained so great that it could not be wiped out entirely. It was replaced by work before and after school, which might extend to over forty hours a week. One London School Board visitor told a government committee in 1902 that the wages for such work, which might involve the sale of news-papers, running errands or doing housework, were no more than a halfpenny an hour.[23] But whether work was done in or out of school hours, their desperate poverty and desperate need of the financial assistance of their children did not endear the London School Board, its spying visitors, its prosecutions and fines, to the London poor.

Finally, to people situated as were the London poor in the late nineteenth century, elementary education must in many cases have seemed a monstrous irrelevancy. As early as 1854 Horace Mann put the problem in classic form. In his commentary on the schools census of 1851 Mann discussed the apathy of parents towards their children's education. He pointed out that for generations the working classes had been urged 'not to look *beyond their station*' and that as a result parents saw no practical value in advanced instruction, since children would inevitably follow their parents' occupations. He went on to ask:

> Must it not be, though reluctantly, allowed that they have only too much reason for their apathy? 'Of what avail' – they may, and not

unreasonably, ask — 'can education be to those who must, of sad necessity, reside in these impure and miserable homes, from which, if it were possible, ourselves would be the first to flee? Or what delight can education yield to those who, on emerging from the school, where taste has been acquired and appetite excited, find that both the treasures and the sweets of literature are far beyond their reach?' Such, really if not in words, are the much-too-reasonable questions by which parents, of the humbler ranks excuse their inattention to their children's education: they imagine they are doing just enough to fit them for their future and unalterable lot, and that all beyond would be at best but superfluity.[24]

Numerous observers of the time wrote of the social advantages of board schools. An H.M.I. observed in 1882: 'Every new Board school erected in the midst of the crowded and joyless streets of Walworth or Peckham is eagerly welcomed by the parents, and becomes a new centre of civilization and intelligence.'[25] Charles Booth wrote with simple eloquence in 1889: 'Each school stands up from its playground like a church in God's acre ringing its bell.'[26] Arthur Conan Doyle made Sherlock Holmes tell Watson in 1893 that the board schools were: 'Lighthouses, my boy! Beacons of the future! Capsules, with hundreds of bright little seeds in each, out of which will spring the wiser, better England of the future.'[27]

In the long run, even the middle run, this is what the board schools were; a signal of hope for the future. But, especially in the early years, they must have seemed, as another observer put it, 'like planting a fort in an enemy's country. . .the symbol of tyranny and oppression'.[28] Even in the later years poverty and lack of education fed upon each other to make Horace Mann's words of 1854 still valid. The managers of the Johanna Street School, Lambeth, wrote in September, 1898: 'The always prevailing poverty and the parents' utter lack of appreciation of educational work, intended for the elevation and mental benefit of their offspring, form great barriers in the path of progress. Most are so poor or possess such scanty powers of intellect that they have but one aim, viz., to get their children away from School at the earliest possible moment.'[29]

The problems of combining poverty and education were discussed in 1883 by T. Marchant Williams, a London School Board inspector who soon afterwards published the first reliable figures regarding overcrowding in a large part of London.[30] Williams wrote in his annual

LANT ST. BOARD SCHOOL (SOUTHWARK), 1875.

LANT ST. BOARD SCHOOL (SOUTHWARK), 1902.

Plate XVI   *Social progress over thirty years*

report about three schools in the Finsbury division in which 58, 82 and 85 per cent of the children's families lived in homes of one room. He continued in a passage which memorably summed up the difficulties involved in the education of the London poor:

> How is it possible, I ask, for the best Teachers to cope with the overwhelming difficulties which are implied by such facts as these,

which, by the way, are typical of a large number of the Schools of the London School Board? The Teachers of the Tower-street School work with all the energy and ability they can command, and they are materially aided by a careful and judicious Visitor; but they cannot house or feed the little children, nor can they clothe them; all they seem to be able to do is to attract a handful of them to School in time to learn (but not to understand) a few texts and a few facts from the Bible, and about 70 per cent. of them (on an average) to learn imperfectly the subjects prescribed for them in the Code. To many of the half-starved children of Seven Dials, St Luke's, Lisson-grove and Saffron-hill, the forty days' fasting in the wilderness and the miraculous feeding of 'five thousand men, besides women and children', with five loaves and two fishes, appear too commonplace, I should say, to excite much astonishment. It is really most difficult for the Inspector to know what results to expect from a year's teaching of these ill-housed, ill-clad, and ill-fed little children. . . .To teach in these Schools now is tantamount to sowing seed by the wayside, upon stony places, and among thorns.[31]

The London School Board consisted of men and of an unusually high proportion of women,[32] largely of the wealthier classes, elected to provide elementary education for the working classes. This situation was unavoidable in the social context of the time, but the fact that their children were compelled by the agents of a superior social class to attend school was a further reason why the London poor were so often hostile or apathetic towards elementary education.

Three main points of view may be traced among Board members and others involved with London elementary education. Their debates and discussions were so lively as to make School Boards and board schools a major topic in the late nineteenth-century press and Parliament. These points of view cannot be rigidly pinned down to political parties, but they do belong to quite specifically Conservative, Liberal and socialist attitudes.[33] Indeed, Marxist theories of the class basis of society and social policy might almost have been devised with the history of English education in mind.

Conservatives, using the term fairly loosely, were concerned above all with maintaining the existing order of society. The most astute modern historian of Conservatism in the period points out that in Conservative thinking in the 'sixties there remained 'a strong vein of suspicion of popular education, a fear that by enlarging the mental horizons of the working classes, laying them open to Radical influences, and stimulating them to entertain ideas above their station, it would prove subversive of the social order'.[34] Although Conservatives in the School Board period seldom opposed elementary education as such,[35] their actions, nationally and locally, revolved around the belief that the schools should contribute to the maintenance of social stability. They were, initially at least, opposed to compulsory education, to free elementary schools, and to advanced, or 'higher grade' elementary schools. That they contributed to the introduction of these reforms indicates that their tactics changed in response to pressure; the ends, however, remained constant.

The touchstones of Conservative policy in elementary education were the level of the School Board rate and the position of the voluntary Anglican schools. Battle lines on the London School Board did not take long to form, and the 'economical party' and the 'Church party' formed a close alliance. These combined forces believed that Church education would encourage both working-class docility and lower rates, and throughout the School Board period they attempted to foster the voluntary schools at the expense of the Board's own schools. The Church was always well represented on the Board; the height of its numerical power was reached in 1888, when there were no fewer than sixteen members of the Anglican clergy (not all of them supporters of the 'Church party') amongst the Board's fifty-five members.[36]

Fury at the level of School Board expenditure and the School Board rate led to the formation, probably early in 1884, of the Metropolitan Association for Limiting the Expenditure of the School Board for London. The Association received the enthusiastic support of a considerable number of Conservative Members of Parliament and was led by a Board member who later became a Conservative M.P., Edwin Hughes.[37] Although the Association seems not to have lasted long, the opinion for which it spoke did. Its adherents continually attacked the Board's 'extravagance', taking a strong line during the great piano debate of 1890–1. Pianos were to be used in schools with halls for singing lessons, gymnastics and drill. Their opponents regarded them as the very epitome of unnecessary expenditure and the issue was a hot one in the 1891 Board election. A typical attack came from a Conservative M.P., F.D. Dixon-Hartland, who alleged that money had been spent 'upon pianos, harps, and other things, quite beyond the children's station'.[38]

Higher grade or 'higher standard' schools were introduced during the Moderate (Conservative) control of the London School Board, initially in 1887 and with rather more vigour in 1891. However, most Conservatives, including the Board's chairman, the Rev. J.R. Diggle, long opposed them.[39] An extreme 'economist' on the Board, W.H. Bonnewell, asserted in 1882 that proposals for such schools were 'a monstrous injustice to the ratepayers' and destructive of an Englishman's 'rugged independence'.[40] A revealing comment on this issue, a good expression of basic Conservative philosophy, was made in 1891 by Lord George Hamilton, who had been in effect minister of education from 1878 to 1880 and who was to be the chairman of the London School Board briefly in the mid-1890s. A Conservative second-rank politician over a lengthy period, Hamilton declared:

> What was wanted was to give to the children of the working man a sound, a compact, and a thorough education in those subjects which children during the limited time they were at school could master; and that those children of exceptional ability or whose parents were prepared to make sacrifices for them should be transferred to some graded schools and taught by teachers of special ability and knowledge at the cost of the parent. . . .What ought to be resolutely fought was any attempt to grasp a secondary system of graded education and applying it to the education of the School Board. Such an education under such circumstances would be bad for the children, bad for the teachers, and worse for the ratepayers.[41]

Although Liberals usually came from similar social backgrounds to Conservatives, and although their social aims were usually similar, their education policy was quite different. This was notably true of the more radical Liberals who were strongly represented on the London School Board and who, with some socialists, composed the Board's 'Progressive' faction and controlled its policy in its last years. Their views stemmed largely from the belief in laissez-faire and individual self help which was so marked a feature of Liberal philosophy in the second half of the nineteenth century. Sometimes these views struggled with radical educational policies; for example, over abolition of school fees, where support among most Liberals for the 'manly spirit of independence' supposedly induced by school fees eventually gave way before increasingly strong Radical pressure for free schools.[42] If a working class well-educated by contemporary standards required higher rates, better-equipped schools and a more advanced system of education, Liberal educationists did not hesitate.

G.L. Bruce, one of the Board's prominent Progressive members, commented in 1896: 'I do not believe that the School Board's expenditure can be seriously reduced. It will rise and it ought to rise. I believe that our expenditure on education has been the wisest and most profitable expenditure that we have ever made.'[43]

Liberals believed that a well-educated working class was an aim desirable in itself. But additionally, it was also an important means of securing economic advance and social stability. E. Lyulph Stanley,[44] the ebullient figure who dominated London School Board Progressives over a long period, typified this view. In an article written in 1879 Stanley rejoiced in the habits of 'tidiness, punctuality, order, truthfulness' which board school children had learned in contrast with the pre-Board era. 'For the humanizing effect of schools in the last few years', he continued, 'we must be very thankful, and trust that fuller instruction will follow in the near future. But we can have no good instruction unless we are prepared to provide liberally for teachers [and for] well-equipped, well-lighted schools.'[45] Liberals like Stanley and Bruce strongly supported the development of higher grade schools on grounds both of economic efficiency and equality of opportunity.[46] Most Liberals believed in socializing the working classes, and opposed combining education with social reform no less than Conservatives. Stanley, for example, fell with all his colourful vigour upon 'wild and absurd' plans to supplement charitable feeding of necessitous children by Board action.[47] But they saw an expanding, generous system as more likely to achieve this end than the more rigid social controls favoured by Conservatives. This point of view was well put by Stanley in a comment made in 1899, when he was the Board's energetic vice-chairman:

> Really we want something more than the cheap, industrious clerks and the better application of science to industry. . . .We want our lower classes to be educated. . . .We want them in the schools and in the homes to learn the self-respect of citizens, to feel their responsibility as voters, to have the self-restraint, the thoughtfulness, the power of judging and weighing evidence, which should discipline them in the exercise of the great power they now wield by their industrial combinations and through their political action.[48]

From the start of the School Board's life the London trade unions and subsequently the socialist movement attempted to secure representation. Encouraged by the wide franchise and absence of property qualifications for members, nine working men stood for election to the first Board in 1870, though only Benjamin Lucraft, the Board's 'father' when he resigned in 1890, was successful.[49] Subsequent labour and socialist members included George Potter, Helen Taylor, Edward Aveling, Annie Besant, the Rev. Stewart Headlam, Mary Bridges-Adams and Graham Wallas. In general these members supported the Liberal programme, sometimes going beyond it, while wanting to avoid the opprobrium and the ideological problems involved in carrying out unpopular measures. This was particularly noticeable after 1888, when the first real socialist challenge was mounted and Mrs Besant and Headlam were elected to the Board.[50]

Three measures which they and other socialist candidates put forward in the 1888 election were abolition of school fees, provision of free school meals and the payment of trade union wage rates in Board contracts. Headlam in his address to his electors combined a classic socialist statement with classic Victorian consciousness of social gradations. It was a fundamental purpose of board school education, he said to make children

> Discontented with the evil circumstances which surround them. There are those who say that we are educating your children above their station. That is true; and if you return me I shall do my utmost to get them such knowledge and such discipline as will make them thoroughly discontented, not indeed with that state of life into which it shall please God to call them, but with that evil state into which anarchy and monopoly has [sic] forced them, that so by their own organized and disciplined effort they may live fuller lives than you have been able to live, in a more beautiful world than you have had to toil in.[51]

Although Headlam worked in steady coalition with the Liberals, this manifesto enunciated a fundamentally different philosophy from either Liberals or Conservatives.

The Board's Moderate majority was not dislodged in the 1888 election, but Mrs Besant and Headlam made much of the running in the ensuing period, initiating or supporting successful resolutions in favour of trade union wages, free schools, pianos in schools and enquiring into the problem of underfed children. In 1889 they helped to pass an historic statement made in reply to an angry ratepayer, who protested that children of wealthy tradesmen attended board schools while the children of the poor were excluded: 'All citizens have an equal right to send their children to schools built and supported by them, and. . .the Board are of opinion that there is considerable advantage in having children of all classes attending the same schools.'[52] It is not surprising that the jubilant Headlam wrote in May 1890 that Mrs Besant 'does pretty well what she likes with us' and that 'it is Mrs Besant, and not Mr Stanley, who is the real leader of the advanced party.'[53]

But when it came to enforcing compulsory attendance the socialists were more hesitant. It was no part of their doctrine to prosecute, fine or imprison poor parents who did not send their children to school. No sooner was Annie Besant elected to the Board than she noted in her column in the *National Reformer* the need in many families for their children's help, or sheer inability to send them to school. The parents, she wrote after one meeting, were 'gaunt, hunger-pinched men and women, all, but one, decent folk who did not want to keep their children ignorant, but sometimes there were no boots, sometimes there was a baby to mind, sometimes there was no food, sometimes there was sickness. . . .It is heartbreaking work'.[54] A little earlier she had reflected: 'One has to choose between leaving the child ignorant or having it starved, so that one must do harm, any way. . . .It make's one heart sick'.[55]

Both Mrs Besant and Headlam told themselves and their readers that they could not support sanctions in favour of compulsory attendance so long as school fees remained. But school fees were largely abolished after 1891, and the social problems remained. The socialist dilemma was then even more acute, as F.J. Gould, a teacher between 1879 and 1896 under the London School Board, noted in an article in 1902. He quoted a conversation with a mother in Leicester, where he was then a member of the School Board, who had kept her daughter at home to assist with the washing, and reflected on 'the painful complexity of interest involved – the mother's need of help; the child's need of education; society's claim that the child, as its ward, shall be trained to intelligent citizenship. The mother must yield; and the mother must suffer; but, alas! no commonwealth can truly gain by the sufferings of mothers.'[56]

When it came to prosecutions it was often the socialist journals who were most antagonistic towards the School Boards. Robert Blatchford, for example, the famous socialist editor of the *Clarion*, accused the Manchester School Board of persecuting the poor. Its prosecutions before the Police Court, he asserted, were 'an outrage upon the liberties and rights of the people'.[57] Journalists were fond of writing sensational articles which made the Boards seem tyrannous, both conservative papers which had doubts about compulsory attendance[58] and radical papers which supposedly supported it. In an address in 1892 William Hurden, President of the Metropolitan Board Teachers' Association, commented: 'The worst enemies. . .of regular attendance are the newspapers. . .and, strange to say, the Democratic newspapers are the worst offenders. The same newspapers that at times contain glowing articles on the advantages of education also contain one sided reports of School Board cases, that tend to make the working of the bye-laws an absolute impossibility.'[59]

It is not surprising that in prevailing social conditions those who believed most ardently in the value of educating working-class children should on occasion attempt to prevent its effective execution. But this meant that the Board's teachers and officials, already under severe pressure from the right, faced opposition too on their left, thus rendering their work even more difficult.

Attitudes towards elementary education for the working classes were clearly expressed in some of the thousands of cases which appeared annually before the London police magistrates. These cases arose only if other means of ending truancy had failed. The London School Board first issued a warning, called an 'A' notice, urging defaulting parents to send their children to school. If this was unsuccessful a 'B' notice followed, in which the parent was required to attend a meeting to explain the reason for absence. These could be hectoring, unpleasant occasions, in which a poor parent, frequently a mother, had to defend herself before middle-class Board members and officials. In the hands of a sympathetic Board member a 'B' meeting was not necessarily a terrifying experience, but the threat of prosecution always lay close to the surface.[60] In the year ending 25 March 1889 the Board's 268 visitors issued 96,450 'A' notices and 94,968 'B' notices. In the same year there were 12,831 summonses,[61] a figure which rose sharply towards the end of the century.

One of the Board's most persistent complaints lay in the behaviour of the magistrates. Not enough summonses were granted, School Board cases were subject to delays or adjournments, and fines were sometimes derisory. As the Board's Liberal chairman, Edward North Buxton, pointed out in 1882: 'To inflict a fine of 1*d*., without costs, on a parent who has been summoned sixteen times, is to encourage him

Plate XVII A 'B' meeting, 1883. Note the presence of the author, George R. Sims, and the illustrator, Frederick Barnard.

and his neighbours in defiance of the law, and obstinate indifference to the welfare of the children.'[62] In 1900 a case was cited by a Finsbury visitor in which a parent had been summoned 53 times, paying a fine every two or three months from the earnings of his child during the period.[63]

Why did the London magistrates behave in so unsympathetic a fashion towards the Board? For one thing, School Board cases bored them. One witness told the Departmental Committee on the Jurisdiction of the Metropolitan Police Magistrates and County Justices in 1899 that magistrates in the Lambeth Police Court spent only about two minutes on each case, hearing 50 or 60 in an afternoon before proceeding to other business.[64] A typical case might run like this:

> Visitor (reading from his notes): 'Adolphus, aged eleven, working in Standard II. has made 47 attendances out of 80.'
>
> The Magistrate: 'What have you to say, Mrs Jones?'
>
> Defendant: 'Please, sir, I ain't got no boots to put on 'is feet. My 'usband's been out of work this four months, and I've got six little ones at 'ome.'
>
> Superintendent: 'This is a bad case, sir. The boy has been constantly seen playing in the streets. There are two previous convictions.'
>
> Magistrate: 'You must send the boy to school, and if you want boots, you should apply to the missionary. Ten shillings or fourteen days.'[65]

Second, there was a considerable fear, especially in the Board's early years but lingering to the end, of violent protest against the novelty of attendance by-laws. One London magistrate commented in 1899 that if as many summonses had been granted in the 1870s as the Board had wished, 'we should have had an insurrection — we should have had an *émeute*'.[66] This was a fear not restricted to magistrates or even to Conservatives. John Reeves, a London School Board visitor for many years, remembered much later an experience which took place 'some years' after his appointment in 1872. He was visiting a family one morning when the Rev. J.A. Picton, a Nonconformist clergyman, a Board member (1870–9) and later a Liberal M.P., eavesdropped without being seen by the mother to whom Reeves was speaking. She 'came to the door', Reeves wrote,

> and began at once to abuse me in the most offensive manner, giving me no opportunity of saying a word in reply. When she had finished

I gave a few words of earnest warning as to the attendance at school of one of her children and then left. The rev. gentleman, in the most solemn manner, cautioned me not to say anything to excite the people.[67]

But most important and most significant, magistrates refused to co-operate with the School Board because they did not believe in the value of compulsory elementary education. Conservative in their politics, upper middle-class in their attitudes, they saw no reason to encourage the poor to rise above their station. This sort of attitude, a constant and major source of concern to the Board, declined in its last years, but it never disappeared.[68]

The magistrates were by no means always unsympathetic to the poor. Very often, indeed, they looked upon themselves as their friends, protecting them from unnecessary prosecutions and doing what they could to mitigate the effects of poverty. This could result in odd alliances; socialists and Conservatives, for example, joining together in charitable work; joining also in opposition to strict enforcement of compulsory school attendance. Who, one may well ask, were the real friends of the poor? Was it the School Board, which wanted to prosecute, fine and even imprison parents whose children played truant? Or was it the magistrates, who felt pity for the parents and children and who flouted the attendance laws and by-laws in their favour? Was it the Board, which wanted to give the London working class an education which might alter and enrich their lives? Or was it the magistrates, anxious to guard against social change? 'Did the Board', a Bath magistrate asked bleakly in 1884, 'wish to educate the children of the poor as gentlemen?'[69]

Space forbids a detailed treatment of London School Board cases in the magistrates' courts.[70] The example of Montagu Williams, while extreme, is typical of many magistrates who aroused the wrath of the Board. Williams, a successful criminal barrister and literary man about town, was appointed in December 1886 to a London police magistracy by Henry Matthews, the Conservative Home Secretary. Before his death in 1892 he sat at a number of magistrates' courts. He busily engaged in organizing blanket and clothing funds, and he was known among the poor, the *Dictionary of National Biography* commented, as 'the poor man's magistrate'. He supported school feeding, the creation of a Ministry of Health and a system of graduated taxation on incomes.[71] But his sympathy with the poor did not extend to their education.

Williams was probably more disliked by the London School Board and its staff than any other London magistrate of his day. Colourful and flamboyant, he did not hesitate to dismiss cases of the most flagrant breach of the by-laws. In one case in 1890 which became a *cause célèbre* to the Board, a woman applied to Williams at the North London Police Court for the remission of a fine of five shillings imposed upon her husband in that court for not sending their children to school. *The Times* reported:

> She had nine children . . . and her husband was out of work. Mr Montagu Williams – Why did not the children go to school? The applicant – Because they had no boots, and I could not send them out in that way. Mr Montagu Williams – Nine children! Husband out of work! No boots! Five shillings fine! (To the applicant) – I cannot remit your fine, but will give you 5s. out of the poor-box to pay it.[72]

The next year, at Worship Street Court, East London, Williams again showed his contempt for the Board and its by-laws. One of the large number of cases before him involved a girl of nearly fourteen, the minimum leaving age under the existing by-laws unless the child had passed the Sixth Standard of attainment in the three elementary subjects. Told by the superintendent of visitors about the attendance requirements, Williams replied: 'Then I don't know where we are getting to, or where we shall get to. And the rates go up.' He commented that 'if his information with regard to the 4th standard was correct, a child in the 6th standard must be a highly educated person'.[73] In a second case: 'Mr Montagu Williams said that in his opinion it was for the parents to say whether a child should go on attending after having passed the 4th Standard.' Both cases and others of a similar kind were adjourned for six weeks.[74]

Occasionally cases were appealed from the magistrates to the higher courts. This happened in 1884 in the case of *London School Board v. Duggan*. Here the case came to the Queen's Bench Division before the formidable Sir James Fitzjames Stephen. Stephen was a judge of a very different calibre from the impetuous Williams, though his opinion of compulsory education was similar. His many publications were not confined to the law, although he made important contributions in this field. His *Liberty, Equality, Fraternity* (1873) has been called by a leading authority 'the finest exposition of conservative thought in the latter half of the nineteenth century'.[75] In it Stephen attacked what he called 'an exaggerated estimate of the power of education. Society cannot make silk purses out of sows' ears, and there are plenty of ears in the world which no tanning can turn even into serviceable pigskin.'[76]

The *Duggan* case involved a girl aged twelve years seven months, the daughter of parents described to the Court as 'sober, hardworking, respectable people'. She was working as a nursery maid for a wage of three shillings a week. It was decided, first by the magistrate and then on appeal, that the girl's employment was a 'reasonable excuse' under Section 74 of the Education Act of 1870.[77] Stephen interjected during the trial: 'It would, indeed, be a sad thing if any statute is to be taken as denying the sacred duty of a child to help to support its parents.' In his opinion he said:

> She has been discharging the honourable duty of helping her parents, and, for my own part, before I held that these facts did not afford a reasonable excuse for her non-attendance at school I should require to see the very plainest words to the contrary in the Act. I may add that there is nothing I should read with greater reluctance in any Act of Parliament than that a child was bound to postpone the direst necessity of her family to the advantage of getting a little more elementary instruction for herself.[78]

The dominant influence on the Board, especially in its final years, was that of its Progressive members. Their aims were to provide a good basic education, to establish an 'educational ladder' whereby the able child could receive higher elementary education, and to 'civilize' or socialize the children of the working classes, thereby achieving a stable, contented society, in which industrial production would be advanced and individual well-being maximized. These aims can be further summarized as improvements in the schools and acceptance by the working classes. How far were they achieved?

On one level the board schools at the turn of the century still struggled with fearful problems. It remained an agonizing task to teach children whose hungry bodies and squalid homes dulled their minds. Horace Mann's analysis of 1854 remained pertinent; school must have seemed irrelevant to poverty-stricken children and the subject matter often incomprehensible. Classes remained large – 60, 70 or more in the London infant schools at the end of the Board's life, and not much smaller in other schools[79] – and in the mid-nineties much attention was devoted to classes of various ages in a number of schools which were alleged to contain as many as 100 and even more children.[80] Teaching methods were in many cases still mechanical and unimaginative. Writing in 1901 Edmund Helps, a London H.M.I., commented that history and geography were taught in too detailed and piecemeal a fashion, resulting in children learning no history or geography at all. He added:

> This method of teaching a subject, bit by bit, instead of broadly, and in correlation with other subjects, pervades our whole system of Elementary education. It is a legacy of past Codes when little parcels of information were made up during the year, labelled, and paid for at the end of the year.[81]

But this damning picture, with its reference to the payment by results system, was not the whole truth. In the late nineteenth century real educational progress was made, 'elementary' education took on a new meaning, and the London School Board was a leader in a number of respects. New school buildings were greatly superior to the early ones. Old buildings and their furniture were modernized, although problems of heating and lighting remained severe in almost all schools.[82] Kindergarten methods entered the infant schools. Cookery instruction was widespread. As we have seen, pianos had come to many schools. Physical education made steady progress. At the end of the Board's life it owned three swimming baths, and many schools used the baths which belonged to London borough councils; 48,535 pupils took swimming lessons in 1902-3. Football and cricket were popular, and in 1900 Thomas Chesterton, organizing teacher of boys' physical education, noted with pleasure

> the keen interest shown by a large number of teachers, especially of boys' departments, in the encouragement of outdoor games amongst their pupils. It is, indeed, remarkable in some schools to see with what ingenuity such games as football, rounders, cricket &c. are carried out, in spite of the fact that in many instances the playgrounds are of limited area, and the ground in every case asphalted. A visit to the parks, open spaces, and commons in and around London, on any Saturday morning throughout the year, will convince the most casual observer that every effort is made by the teachers to foster a love of healthy outdoor sports and athletic games amongst their pupils.[83]

Military drill was replaced or supplemented by the Swedish variety,

Plate XVIII *A board school cookery class*

more concerned with developing the body than with creating future soldiers. Pencils, pens and paper replaced slates; blackboards appeared. School libraries, no new venture but pitifully inadequate, were renewed and enlarged, and visual aids like maps, diagrams and pictures were in wide use. More sophisticated methods of elementary science teaching supplanted the simpler forms of 'object lesson'. Manual training centres for the teaching of woodwork and, less frequently, metalwork, were spreading and becoming less geared to the supposed needs of school discipline or industry than to those of education as such. The Board collaborated with a number of voluntary or semi-voluntary agencies to encourage the children's development out of school hours; the London Schools Swimming Association, the London Schools Football Association, the London Schools Dinner Association, the Children's Happy Evenings Association (which provided recreation in board school buildings), the Children's Country Holiday Fund, which during the summer of 1903 provided holidays for nearly 40,000 London children. Higher grade schools were belatedly (and inadequately) developed, and in the ordinary board schools more advanced subjects were taught. History and geography, following changes in the Board of Education's Code in 1900, were taught to all London School Board children, and in 1903, of the Board's 550,000 pupils of all ages nearly 50,000 learned French, 30,000 algebra and 10,000 botany. Various other scientific and mathematical subjects, including physics and chemistry, were also taught to small numbers of children. Pupil-teachers were given a longer school life and received improved training, and they no longer supplied the majority of the schools' teaching staff as in the Board's first years; in 1903 there were four adult teachers to every pupil teacher. With the break-up of payment by results in the 1890s, teaching became less rigid and mechanical. The result was that, as contemporaries noted, schools became happier places, and the children more interested and involved in their work.[84]

Improvement in the schools was a cause of their increased patronage by the middle classes. One of Charles Booth's assistants noted in 1891 that despite various defects the better board schools, with about 30 per cent of the pupils, were an 'inspiriting and satisfactory sight', and provided an education 'in quality, scope, and teaching power, distinctly in advance of what even middle-class parents, a few years ago, could secure for their children in the ordinary private school'.[85] The Cross Commission was conscious of the changing class composition of the London board schools, and the Board's chairman was anxiously asked whether it was true that some of their pupils arrived at school in carriages with servants to carry their books.[86] In 1893 the superintendent of visitors in the West Lambeth division reported that over 2,500 children from apparently middle-class homes attended board schools, including one case in the East Dulwich district in which 'a gentleman of ample means and his coachman each send their children to the same Board School'.[87] The Fleet Road Board School, Hampstead, was referred to by the journalist Charles Morley in 1894 as 'an Eton for nothing a week', partly because of the secondary school scholarships won, partly because the pupils came mainly from the homes of skilled workers (notably makers of pianos), clerks and small shopkeepers.[88] This increasing middle-class patronage, while doing little in itself to solve outstanding social problems, must have contributed to a willingness to provide amenities and spend money on the elementary schools.[89]

As time passed London board schools became increasingly accepted by the London poor and their children. Evidence to suggest this is abundant though scattered and difficult to quantify. The constantly increasing demand for clerks and other white collar workers[90] meant that many working-class children were entering occupations different from those of their parents. An early indication of how parents might react to this kind of change was imagined by George R. Sims in his ballad 'Polly',[91] in which a London coster was made to say:

There, he's off! the young varmint, he's needled;
    whenever I talks about work
He puts on his cap and he hooks it; he's a notion he'll
    go for a clerk.
The green-stuff ain't up to his 'ighness; he don't like
    to serve at the stall;
He fancies hisself in a orfice, a fillin' o' books
    with his scrawl.
It's the School Board what gives 'em these notions,
    a stuffin' boys' heads full of pride,
And makes 'em look down on their fathers – these
    School Boards I ne'er could abide.
When I was his age I was workin', a-wheelin' the
    barrer for dad,
And a-fetchin' the stuff from the markets, when
    hosses was not to be had.

With the passage of time parents must in some cases have become reconciled to or even proud of their children becoming clerks.

Many observers noted the changed behaviour of the London working class towards the end of the nineteenth century. There is no doubt that some part of the change was due to the work of the School Board, but it was not made easily. In the early years hostility and, on frequent occasion, violence were manifested towards the Board, its teachers and officials.[92] Assaults on London attendance officers were reported to the end of the Board's existence,[93] but they were far less common in the later years. The Annual Report of the London County Council's Education Officer for 1908-9 carried some interesting reminiscences on educational progress since 1870 by an inspector and six head teachers who had served the Board and Council since the 1870s. Most of the contributors noted the sharp decline in truancy and remarkable changes in attitude of both parents and children. A headmistress in Limehouse, who had served for 38 years, commented: 'The children of to-day come to school willingly, are more intelligent and amenable to discipline, with improved habits, being the children of those who realize, and know, by experience what "school" really is.' A similar comment came from a headmistress of a higher grade school in Bermondsey, also with 38 years' service, who wrote: 'The present parents have passed through the schools, and, realizing and appreciating the advantages of the training, show a sympathetic attitude to the teachers and their work. . . .The responsiveness of the children to-day, even those with the fewest home advantages, is in advance of the old days.'[94]

Similar sentiments were expressed by a number of other knowledgeable people. In 1893 the Rev. T.W. Sharpe, Senior Chief H.M.I., wrote: 'The Education Act was not passed a year too soon; London would have been filled with a savage population in the year 1893 if the 400 schools built by the board had not done their civilizing work.'[95] In 1897: 'Each succeeding year will tell a better tale, the parents will be better educated and take more interest in the education of their children. . . .The ratepayer. . .hardly realizes in how short a time the great work has been done; probably no municipal authority has ever carried out so quickly the magnificent provision that has been made by the School Board for London.'[96] In 1899 Sir John Bridge, Chief Metropolitan Magistrate and a London police magistrate since 1872, told a government committee that the early hostility towards the School Board had ended: 'There is no longer, I think, any

Plate XIX *A meeting of the London School Board*

feeling of this kind: "We hate the School Board; we do not wish our children to go to school." The feeling now of the parents, as well as of the children themselves, is this – the children say, as a rule, "We like school," and the parents say, "We wish them to go to school." The whole thing is changed from what it was first of all.'[97] In 1901 Sir Charles Elliott, chairman of the Board's Finance Committee, told another government committee that there had been 'a very remarkable change in the attitude of the parents', and he went on to speak of 'the current of public opinion which has now set in our favour'.[98] In 1903, commenting on an improved record of attendance, the Board's School Accommodation and Attendance Committee concluded that 'The people of London have at least been aroused to a fuller appreciation of the value of sending their children regularly to school'.[99] In the same year the London School Board inspectors, conscious of the Board's approaching end, wrote:

> London is now dotted all over with magnificent school buildings that are well staffed, well equipped, and in which, as a whole, splendid educational work has been done. . . .The results achieved by the Board have not been confined to the children. The influence of the schools has had a very wholesome and civilizing effect upon parents in the poorer quarters of London. We, who have had to visit the schools in the slums of London, have been greatly struck with the change that comes over a district when a Board School has been fairly established.[100]

This evidence, while plentiful and free from serious contradiction, comes from above. Moreover the witnesses, in order to be competent, had often to be interested parties. Quotations of this kind do not tell us what working people themselves, especially the poor, thought about school.[101] Did they accept it as desirable or merely resign themselves to the inevitable? The question cannot be satisfactorily answered, although the latter is more likely to have been the correct answer. Certainly the social background of an area was a factor which influenced, though it did not necessarily determine, the attitudes of both parents and children and the regularity of the children's attendance at school. For example, Stephen Street School, Lisson Grove, which drew on a very poor neighbourhood, had an average attendance in 1897–8 of only 67.5 per cent of its roll, while Dulwich Hamlet, a small school in a prosperous area, boasted 91.9. On the other hand, Johanna Street, Lambeth, a by-word for crippling poverty, had a rate of 76.1, and

Fleet Road, Hampstead, that 'Eton for nothing a week', reached no more than 83.5 per cent. (The average for all the Board's schools in that year was 81.4.)[102] Similar varying tendencies can be found from other schools and other years.

But the steady rise in numbers of children attending school and the remarkable, permanent improvement in attendance at the Board's schools, from 82.0 per cent in 1900 (80.2 as early as 1877) to 88.1 in 1904,[103] suggest that even the poor, while not enthusiastic, had become reconciled to their children's elementary education. Whether this had led to acceptance of the norms of their society or to ideas above their station is another question.

NOTES

[1] Some of the points discussed in this article are considered at greater length in my monograph *School Attendance in London, 1870–1904: A Social History* (Hull, 1969).

[2] p. 9.

[3] S. Webb, *London Education* (London, 1904), pp. 3, 5–6.

[4] P.P. 1861 XXI, iii, pp. 317–598.

[5] *School Attendance in London*, pp. 9–10, 21–7.

[6] *Final Report of the School Board for London, 1870–1904* (London 2nd ed. 1904), chart opposite p. 220. This volume is the most valuable single account of the Board's history.

[7] See E.G. West, *Education and the State* (London, 1965), chs. 9–11, for a defence of the quantity and quality of the pre-Board education system. West's arguments appear to me to be overwhelmingly contradicted by the available evidence.

[8] *School Attendance in London*, pp. 35–7.

[9] Ibid, pp. 42–53.

[10] Ibid, ch. IV.

[11] P.P. 1904 XXXII, pp. 20, 29, 31. Eichholz certainly recognized the problems which remained. He estimated, for example, that 90 per cent of the children at the Johanna Street Board School, Lambeth, were prevented from performing adequately in school by virtue of their physical condition (ibid., p. 20).

[12] B. Simon, *Studies in the History of Education, 1760–1870* (London, 1960), ch. VII.

[13] *Parl. Deb.*, 3rd ser., CCII, 8 July 1870, 1736. Though personally in favour of compulsion, Forster indicated that this split in working-class ranks was part of the reason why it was not incorporated into the Act.

[14] Quoted in A.W. Humphrey, *Robert Applegarth: Trade Unionist, Educationist, Reformer* (Manchester and London, n.d. 1913), p. 212.

[15] 'The composition of the working classes', *Contemporary Review*,

Vol. XVIII (November 1871), pp. 515–18; reprinted in *Our New Masters* (London, 1873), pp. 3–10.

[16] P.P. 1887 XXX, pp. 403–4.

[17] *School Attendance in London,* pp. 10–18. See the exhaustive treatment of casual labour in G. Stedman Jones, *Outcast London* (London, 1971), esp. Part I.

[18] C. Booth (ed.), *Labour and Life of the People, Volume II; London continued* (London, 1891), p. 21.

[19] *School Attendance in London,* pp. 64–70; School Board for London, Minutes of Proceedings, Vol. LIX, 12 November 1903, p. 1069; Vol. LX, 21 January 1904, pp. 303–4. The London School Board was one of the less important agencies to deprive the poor of their homes. Others included railways, streets and public buildings and other forms of 'urban improvement'.

[20] School Board for London, Report of the Bye-Laws Committee for the half-year ended Christmas 1878 (1879), p. 195.

[21] P.P. 1887 LXXXIX, p. 8; *School Attendance in London,* pp. 60–1.

[22] 'The industrial position of women', *Fortnightly Review,* Vol. LIV, N.S. (October 1893), p. 501.

[23] *School Attendance in London,* pp. 70–4.

[24] P.P. 1852–3 XC, xl–xli, lxxxix–xc.

[25] Report of the Committee of Council on Education, 1882–3 (P.P. 1883 XXV), p. 313.

[26] C. Booth (ed.), *Life and Labour, Volume I: East London* (London, 1889), p. 129. Booth noted: 'The clearance for the school-house has been made very often in the midst of the worst class of property' (p. 130).

[27] From 'The Adventure of the Naval Treaty', first published in the *Strand Magazine,* Vol. VI (October–November 1893); quoted in W.H.G. Armytage, *Four Hundred Years of English Education* (London, 1964), p. 147.

[28] H.B. Philpott, *London at School: The Story of the School Board, 1870–1904* (London, 1904), p. 40. Philpott was referring specifically to the first board schools.

[29] School Board for London, Report of the School Management Committee, 1898–9 (1899), Appendix, unpaginated.

[30] According to H. Jephson, *The Sanitary Evolution of London* (London, 1907), p. 313. The figures, with commentary, were published in the form of two long letters in *The Times,* on 22 February 1884, pp. 3–4, and 1 March 1884, p. 6.

[31] School Board for London, Minutes of Proceedings, Vol. XVIII, 8 March 1883, pp. 505–6. Williams went on to become a barrister, magistrate, writer and advocate of Welsh culture.

[32] 28 of the Board's 326 members were women, a much higher proportion than has ever sat in the House of Commons.

[33] For an expert unravelling of the political background to educational controversies in the period, see Gillian Sutherland, *Policy-Making in Elementary Education 1870–1895* (London, 1973). See also L. Ward,

An Investigation into the Educational Ideas and Contribution of the British Political Parties (1870–1918), London University Ph.D. thesis, 1970; and K.M. Hughes, 'A political party and education: reflections on the Liberal Party's educational policy, 1867–1902', *British Journal of Educational Studies*, Vol. VIII (May 1960), pp. 112–26.

[34] P. Smith, *Disraelian Conservatism and Social Reform* (London, 1967), p. 75.

[35] Seldom, but not without exception. The anonymous, well-informed 'D.C.L.' wrote in 1878 in an oddly punctuated passage: 'No one, at all conversant with human nature, can have failed to observe, that all who spring from a lower caste, almost without exception, if lucky enough to have passed merely 'in the lowest Standards', indignantly repudiate any offer of work, that an illiterate man, of mere thews and sinews, would only, too gladly accept.' (D.C.L., *The Education Craze and its Results; School Boards, their Extravagance and Inefficiency* (London, 1878), p. 155.) The author demonstrated his political allegiance by attacking the London School Board for having furnished their meeting room with a carpet costing £300, 'with the characteristic munificence of true Liberals when dealing with the money of other people' (ibid., p. 27).

[36] *School Attendance in London*, p. 28.

[37] See reports and comment in *The Times*, 26 February 1884, p. 4; 8 March 1884, pp. 11–12.

[38] Ibid., 12 November 1891, p. 10. See also T. Gautrey, *'Lux Mihi Laus': School Board Memories* (London, 1937), pp. 108–9.

[39] See J.D. Mellor, The Policy of the School Board for London in Relation to Education in and above Standard V, London University M.A. thesis, 1955, esp. chs. 5, 8 and 11.

[40] *School Board Chronicle*, Vol. XXVII, 25 February 1882, p. 182.

[41] *The Times*, 25 November 1891, p. 7.

[42] Ward, op.cit., pp. 97–121, 322–5; Sutherland, op.cit., pp. 265, 283–7.

[43] 'Is the London School Board rate too high?' *Contemporary Review*, Vol. LXIX (April 1896), p. 607.

[44] For Stanley, see the painstaking thesis by A.W. Jones, The Work for Education of the Hon. E. Lyulph Stanley, later Fourth Baron Stanley of Alderley, Fourth Baron Sheffield, Durham University M.Ed. thesis, 1968.

[45] 'National education and the London School Board', *Fortnightly Review*, Vol. XXVI N.S. (October 1879), pp. 535–6.

[46] See e.g. Bruce, op. cit., pp. 606–7, and Stanley, 'Higher Elementary Schools', *Contemporary Review*, Vol. LXXVIII (November 1900), pp. 650–1.

[47] 'If they fed the children it would soon follow that they should clothe and house them', he declared to the Board in 1899. 'The case of poverty, short of actual destitution, was best met by well-organised charity.' (*School Board Chronicle*, Vol. LXII, 25 November 1899, p. 559; see also Gautrey, op. cit., p. 93.

[48] E. Lyulph Stanley, *Our National Education* (London, 1899), pp. 139–40.

[49] Humphrey, op. cit., pp. 229–32; G.D.H. Cole, *British Working Class Politics, 1832–1914* (London, 1941), p. 54.

[50] See my article, 'Annie Besant and Stewart Headlam: the London School Board Election of 1888', *East London Papers*, Vol. 13 (Summer 1970), pp. 3–24.

[51] Quoted in ibid., pp. 10–11.

[52] School Board for London, Minutes of Proceedings, Vol. XXX, 14 February 1889, pp. 468–9; 21 February 1889, pp. 514–15; 14 March 1889, pp. 678, 693.

[53] *Church Reformer*, Vol. IX, May 1890, pp. 107, 109. See also *School Attendance in London*, pp. 31–2, 34, 81–2, 88, 95.

[54] *National Reformer*, Vol. LIII N.S., 20 January 1889, p. 42.

[55] Ibid., Vol. LII N.S., 30 December 1888, p. 428.

[56] *School Attendance Gazette*, Vol. III, June 1902, pp. 103–4; reprinted from the *Pioneer* (Leicester).

[57] R. Blatchford, *Dismal England* (London, 1899), pp. 170–84.

[58] A report in *The Times* on 9 February 1876 (p. 11) relating to the prosecution and brief imprisonment of a man for first not sending one of his children to school and then not paying a fine of 2s. 6d., resulted in his fine being paid for him and public donations of nearly £3 within a few days (*School Attendance in London*, p. 98).

[59] *The Board Teacher*, Vol. IX, 1 November 1892, p. 232.

[60] For authentic-sounding reconstructions of 'B' meetings see G.R. Sims, *How the Poor Live* (London, 1883), pp. 19–23, 26–7; J. Runciman, *School Board Idylls* (London, 1885), pp. 21–32; C. Morley, *Studies in Board Schools* (London, 1897), pp. 210–24. Perhaps in these meetings more than anywhere else, the suffering, the neglect and the cruelty which characterised the lives of the London poor were laid open to the observer.

[61] School Board for London, Annual Report, 1888–9 (1889), pp. 30–1.

[62] School Board for London, Chairman's Annual Statement, 1882, p. 3.

[63] *School Attendance Gazette*, Vol. II, January 1901, p. 164.

[64] P.P. 1900 XL, p. 45.

[65] Philpott, op. cit., p. 94. Philpott added: 'Some of the cases are briefer even than this; few are much longer' (p. 94). The limit of fines was raised from five to twenty shillings in 1900. Prison was a last resort, not used (especially in this later period) unless all attempts to raise money by fines or distress warrants for the seizure and sale of goods had failed.

[66] P.P. 1900 XL, p. 65.

[67] J. Reeves, *Recollections of a School Attendance Officer* (London, 1913), p. 14.

[68] See, e.g. Philpott, op. cit., p. 93; *School Attendance Gazette*, Vol. II, March 1901, pp. 198–9, 216; Vol. IV, July 1903, pp. 134–5; School Board for London, Minutes of the School Accommodation and

Attendance Committee, 1 October 1902, pp. 124–5; P.P. 1900 XL, p. 27.

[69] Quoted in P.F. Speed, The Elementary Schools of Bath, 1862–1902, Bristol M.A. thesis 1958, Vol. II, p. 325. The Board's case (or the case of those of its members who believed in the enforcement of its policies) was put for it definitively by one of its teachers, William Hurden, of the Metropolitan Board Teachers' Association, in a speech in 1892: 'Poverty, however abject it may be, cannot be accepted as an excuse for keeping children from school. But a moment's thought will show that to accept poverty as an excuse would perpetuate the very conditions that are a disgrace to our boasted civilisation. If the children are hungry and half-naked, the statesman and the philanthropist must feed and clothe them. To leave them without education would be to leave them hungry and half-naked all their lives.' (*The Board Teacher*, Vol. IX, 1 November 1892, p. 232.)

[70] For further discussion, see *School Attendance in London*, ch. V.

[71] M. Williams, *Later Leaves* (London, 1891), pp. 153–71, 258–9; M. Williams, *Round London: Down East and Up West* (London, 1892), preface and part I, ch. IV. See also his obituary in *The Times*, 24 December 1892, p. 7.

[72] *The Times*, 27 June 1890, p. 4.

[73] For details of the Education Department's Code of 1891, see the Report of the Committee of Council on Education, 1890–1; p.p. 1890–1 XXVII, pp. 115–83. The reading qualification for Standard IV was 'To read a passage from a reading book, or history of England.' For Standard VI the qualification was 'To read a passage from one of Shakespeare's historical plays, or from some other standard author, or from a history of England' (p. 145). 'Reading with intelligence will be required in all the Standards, and increased fluency and expression in successive years' (p. 144).

[74] *The Times*, 10 February 1891, p. 13. For attacks on Williams see Reeves, op. cit., pp. 15–16, and Stewart Headlam in the *Church Reformer*, Vol. IX, December 1890, p. 277 and Vol. X, April 1891, p. 85.

[75] E. Barker, *Political Thought in England from Herbert Spencer to the Present Day* (London, 1915), p. 172.

[76] *Liberty, Equality, Fraternity* (London, 1967 ed.), p. 142.

[77] Section 74 excused children from attendance in cases of 'efficient instruction in some other manner' than attendance at a public elementary school, 'sickness or any unavoidable cause', and the lack of a school within three miles (or less, as the by-laws might specify) of home. The judges in this case effectively created a new criterion of 'reasonable excuse'.

[78] 13 Q.B.D. 176 (27 May 1884); *The Times*, 28 May 1884, p. 3. Stephen's dictum calls to mind the slogan of Vichy France: *Travail, Famille, Patrie*.

[79] Philpott, op. cit., p. 81. Shortly before the end of the Board's life its regulation class sizes, not always observed, were not more than 60

in average attendance (*not* the number of names on the class roll) in Standards I, II and III (ages 6-10), 50 in Standards IV and V (10-12) and 40 in the higher Standards. These figures could be modified at the discretion of the School Management Committee. (School Board for London, School Management Committee, Code of Regulations & Instructions for the Guidance of Managers, Correspondents, and Teachers, 1902, article 13.)

[80] See, e.g., P.P. 1894 XXX-i, pp. 10-11; *The Times*, 5 February 1894, p. 7; 19 October 1894, p. 8; E. Lyulph Stanley, 'The present London School Board and the coming election', *New Review*, Vol. XI (November 1894), pp. 456-7; [J.W. Martin], *The Workers' School Board Program* (Fabian Society Tract No. 55, London 1894), pp. 5-6, 8-9; Progressive School Board Election Council, *The Case Against Diggleism* (London, 1894), ch. 3.

[81] P.P. 1902 XXV, p. 13.

[82] P.P. 1900 XX, pp. 16-17; P.P. 1902 XXV, p. 11; *Final Report of the School Board for London*, pp. 56-7. 'A London Board School on a dark winter's day', remarked the Senior Chief H.M.I., Thomas King, in 1899, 'is a dismal place. There is not light but darkness visible, and in the gloom dim forms of children may be descried poring hopelessly over their tasks in the heavy mephitic atmosphere.' (P.P. 1900 XX p. 16.)

[83] In T.A. Spalding and T.S.A. Canney, *The Work of the London School Board* (London, 1900), p. 241.

[84] This paragraph draws on the following sources: Philpott, op. cit., chs. IV-V, VIII, XI, XIX; G.A.N. Lowndes, *The Silent Social Revolution* (London, 2nd ed., 1969), ch. II; R.J.W. Selleck, *The New Education, 1870-1914* (London, 1968), *passim*; S. Maclure, *One Hundred Years of London Education, 1870-1970* (London, 1970), ch. 3; J. Lawson and H. Silver, *A Social History of Education in England* (London, 1973), ch. IX; *Final Report of the School Board for London*, pp. 34-57, 91-147, 158-60; Spalding and Canney, op. cit., Part III; and the very valuable reports of H.M.I.s., notably those for 1899 (P.P. 1900 XX, pp. 1-32) and for 1901 (P.P. 1902 XXV, pp. 5-54).

[85] Mary C. Tabor in C. Booth (ed.), *Labour and Life of the People, Volume II: London continued* (London, 1891), pp. 478-9, 507-8.

[86] P.P. 1887 XXIX, p. 537. For similar questions see ibid., p. 598; P.P. 1886 XXV, p. 97; P.P. 1887 XXX, pp. 657-8).

[87] *Church Reformer*, Vol. XII, March 1893, p. 54. See also Philpott, op. cit., pp. 52-3 and P.P. 1904 XXXII, p. 30.

[88] Morley, op. cit., pp. 85-107. See also Maclure, op. cit., p. 57, and F.M.L. Thompson, *Hampstead, Building a Borough, 1650-1964* (London, 1974), p. 416 and Plate 14.

[89] Yet prejudice against board schools continued to the end. Late in 1903 a protest was made in Putney against a proposed board school on the grounds that the school would 'spoil. . .a good residential part of Putney'. The area, the protestors felt, was not one which 'produced

scholars for the Board Schools'. (School Board for London, Minutes of Proceedings, Vol. LX, 17 December 1903, p. 211.)

[90] Between 1871 and 1901 numbers engaged in public administration and commercial occupations rose by 2.7 times (330,000 to 893,000), while the occupied population increased by just over a third (11.9 million to 16.3 million). (B. R. Mitchell and Phyllis Deane, *Abstract of British Historical Statistics* (London, 1962), p. 60. See also D.C. Marsh, *The Changing Social Structure of England and Wales 1871-1961* (London, rev. ed., 1965), ch. V.)

[91] First published in *The Referee*, no. 62, 20 October 1878, p. 2; afterwards frequently reprinted in *The Dagonet Ballads*.

[92] See e.g. G.A. Christian, *English Education from Within* (London, 1922), pp. 18–20; Gautrey, op. cit., pp. 35–6, 91; log book of the Nichol Street Boys' School, 18 March 1879, pp. 127–8; London County Council, Annual Report of the Education Officer for the Year 1908-9 (London, L.C.C., 1910), pp. 25, 34.

[93] *School Attendance Gazette*, Vol. II, March 1901, p. 215; Vol. III, December 1902, p. 240; Vol. IV, September 1903, p. 163.

[94] London County Council, op. cit., pp. 23–40. See also Charles Booth, *Life and Labour of the People in London, Third Series: Religious Influences*, Vol. 4 (London, 1902), pp. 202–3.

[95] P.P. 1894 XXX-i, p. 12.

[96] P.P. 1898 XXII, p. 262.

[97] P.P. 1900 XL, p. 51.

[98] P.P. 1902 XXV, pp. 3, 5.

[99] School Board for London, Report of the School Accommodation and Attendance Committee, 1902-3, School Attendance Report (1903), iv.

[100] School Board for London, Report of the School Management Committee, 1902-3 (1903), xii.

[101] One need not, perhaps, take too seriously Marie Lloyd's popular song, dating apparently from the 1890s:

'I hate the horrid School Board,
So does Brother Jack –
Nothing but a wacky, wacky, whack, whack, whack!'

(Quoted in E. Short, *Fifty Years of Vaudeville* (London, 1946), p. 231.) On the other hand, in 'The Coster Girl in Paris' (1912), she acknowledged: 'At the board school I went to, they taught me to parlez-vous. . . .' (*The Golden Age of the Music Hall,* London, President Records, RHA 6014, undated).

[102] School Board for London, Report of the School Management Committee, 1897-8 (1898), pp. 66, 84, 98, 102, 150. See also *School Attendance in London*, pp. 112–14.

[103] Attendance at voluntary schools rose in the same period from 79.4 per cent to 84.6 per cent. Between 1905 and 1914 attendance at all London elementary schools, council and voluntary, varied between 88.0 and 90.1 (*School Attendance in London*, pp. 112–14).

Notes on Contributors

SIMON FRITH ('Socialization and Rational Schooling: Elementary Education in Leeds before 1870') is Lecturer in Sociology at the University of Warwick. Born in Sussex, he was educated at Oxford University and has an M.A. in Sociology from the University of California, Berkeley. He has published in the *Italian Journal of Sociology* and his current research interests are the sociology of youth culture and rock music.

J. M. GOLDSTROM ('The Content of Education and the Socialization of the Working-Class Child 1830–1860') is Senior Lecturer in Economic and Social History, Queen's University, Belfast. After leaving school at fourteen he worked as a typewriter mechanic for nine years, became a schoolmaster and later took a Ph.D. at Birmingham University. He is the author of *The Social Content of Education, 1818–1870* (1972) and is currently working on an economic history of the British funeral industry in the nineteenth century.

J. S. HURT ('Drill, Discipline and the Elementary School Ethos') is Lecturer in the School of Education at Birmingham University. Educated at London University, he taught for several years in grammar schools and at the Polytechnic of Central London. The author of *Education in Evolution* (1971), he is at present engaged in a study of elementary education between 1870 and 1914. Dr Hurt is a Fellow of the Royal Historical Society.

DONALD K. JONES ('Socialization and Social Science: Manchester Model Secular School 1854–61') is Lecturer in the School of Education at the University of Leicester. Born in Lancashire, he was educated at Sheffield University and taught for several years in grammar schools, further education establishments and a college of education in Lancashire and the West Riding. He has published several articles on aspects of nineteenth-century educational history in academic journals, and his current research interests concern the educational activities of former members of the Anti-Corn Law League.

PHILLIP McCANN ('Popular Education, Socialization and Social Control: Spitalfields 1812–1824') is Professor of Education in the Department of Educational Foundations at Memorial University of Newfoundland. Born in Cheshire, he was educated at London University
and taught for several years in secondary modern schools in London.
After taking a Ph.D. at Manchester University he held posts at Keele
University and at Goldsmiths' College. His published works include
The Educational Innovators, 1750–1880 (1967), with W.A.C. Stewart,
and he is currently working on a study of Samuel Wilderspin and the
infant school movement and on the history of education in Newfoundland.

BERYL MADOC-JONES ('Patterns of Attendance and Their Social Significance: Mitcham National School 1830–1839') is Lecturer in Sociology at Roehampton Institute of Higher Education. Born in Wales, she
studied sociology at Exeter University and at the University of Toronto.
She has taught in secondary schools in England, at Toronto Teachers'
College and at Memorial University of Newfoundland. She is at present
working on a doctorate on the social aspects of elementary education
in the early nineteenth century.

W.E. MARSDEN ('Social Environment, School Attendance and Educational Achievement in a Merseyside Town 1870–1900'), is Senior
Lecturer in the School of Education at the University of Liverpool.
Born in Lancashire and a graduate of Sheffield University, he has degrees
in geography and education and has taught in secondary schools and at
a college of education. Publications include *North-West England* (2nd ed.
1975), *Changing Environments in Britain series* (1974), *Evaluating the
Geography Curriculum* (1976) and numerous articles in academic
journals on a variety of environmental, geographical and educational
topics. His current research interests include curriculum studies and
inter-disciplinary approaches to the history of education.

DAVID RUBINSTEIN ('Socialization and the London School Board
1870–1904: Aims, Methods and Public Opinion') is Lecturer in Social
History at the University of Hull. A former teacher in London comprehensive schools, in 1969 he published *School Attendance in London
1870–1904: A Social History*. He is also the co-author of *The Evolution
of the Comprehensive School 1926–1972* (2nd ed. 1973), the co-editor
of the Penguin Special *Education for Democracy* (2nd ed. 1972) and

the compiler of *Victorian Homes* (1974). David Rubinstein's current research interests are the labour movement, housing and recreation in the Victorian period.

HAROLD SILVER ('Ideology and the Factory Child: Attitudes to Half-Time Education') is Professor of Education (Social History) at Chelsea College, University of London. Born in Yorkshire, he is a graduate of Cambridge University and has worked as a translator and interpreter and taught in technical colleges. He is the author of *The Concept of Popular Education* (1965), *Robert Owen on Education* (1969), *Modern English Society* (1970) with Judith Ryder, *The History of British Universities* (1970) with S. John Teague, *Equal Opportunity in Education* (1973), *A Social History of Education in England* (1973) with John Lawson, *The Education of the Poor* (1974) with Pamela Silver and *English Education and the Radicals* (1975). He is at present working on aspects of English and American nineteenth century educational and social history.

Index

Spitalfields Benevolent Society,
13, 14, 16, 26, 27.
Spitalfields Mechanics' Institute,
29.
Spitalfields Outrages, 5-6.
Spitalfields, parish of Christ Church,
2, 6, 9, 11.
Spitalfields Soup Society, 12, 13,
14, 16, 26, 28.
Stanley, E. Lyulph, 242, 244.
Stephen, Sir James Fitzjames,
Liberty, Equality, Fraternity
(1873), 248.
Sunday Schools, 9.
    Leeds, 74, 82.
    Methodist, Leeds, 81.
    Spitalfields, 9-10.
    Wesleyan Methodist, Spitalfields,
    10-11.
    Zion, Leeds, 82-4.

Taylor, Helen, 185, 186, 243.
Templer, Benjamin, 119, 122, 123,
124, 127, 128, 130, 131, 132.
    socratic method of teaching,
    127, 134.
    teaching of political economy,
    130-1.
Templar, Benjamin, *Reading Less
Lessons in Social Economy*,
126.
Templar, Benjamin, *The Religious
Difficulty in National Edu-
cation* (1858), 135.
Thompson, E.P., 8, 61.
Trades Union Congress, 185.
Trimmer, Mrs. Sarah, *The Charity
Spelling Book* (1791), 94-5.

Unwin, W.J., *Training School
Reader* (Congregationalist)
(1851), 101.
Utilitarianism, 125, 184.
Utilitarians, 171.

Volunteer Crops, 180.
Volunteer Rifle Club Movement, 170, 178, 179.

Watts, Dr. John, 117.
Weavers:
    Leeds, 68.

Spitalfields, 3, 27, 28.
Webb, Sidney, 231.
West, E.G., 42.
Whately, Archbishop Richard, 102.
Whately, Archbishop Richard,
Easy Lessons in Money Matters
(1833), 112.
Wheler Chapel, Norton Folgate,
13, 14.
Wigram, Rev., 59, 60, 62.
Wilderspin, Samuel, 4, 5, 23, 27,
29, 30.
Wilks, Edward, 143, 145, 147, 148,
160.
Williams, T. Marchant, 237.
Wilson, Rev. Daniel, 1, 6, 23, 24.
Wilson, Joseph, 6, 23.
Wilson, Stephen, 6.
Women's Peace and Arbitration
Association, 186.
Women's Peace and Arbitration
Auxiliary, 185.
Working class, labouring poor:
    and education, Mitcham, early
        nineteenth century, 64-5.
    and education, Spitalfields, early
        nineteenth century, 29-30.
    skilled, and education, London,
        late nineteenth century,
        234-5.
    unskilled, and education,
    London, late nineteenth
        century, 235-7
    and political economy teach-
        ing, 136.
    and national education, Leeds,
        85-7.
    and religion, Spitalfields, early
        nineteenth century, 28.
    and religion, mid-nineteenth
        century, 106.
    and religious instruction, 135.
Workmen's Education Committee,
185.
Workmen's Peace Association, 184,
185, 186.
Wright, Thomas, ('The Journey-
man Engineer'), 234.
Wyse, Thomas, M.P., 113.

Yates, Rev. Richard, 6.